URBAN
ENVIRONMENTAL
EDUCATION
REVIEW

URBAN ENVIRONMENTAL EDUCATION REVIEW

Edited by Alex Russ and
Marianne E. Krasny

COMSTOCK PUBLISHING ASSOCIATES

AN IMPRINT OF

CORNELL UNIVERSITY PRESS

ITHACA AND LONDON

First published 2017 by Cornell University Press
First printing, Cornell Paperbacks, 2017

Printed in the United States of America

Library of Congress Cataloging-in-Publication Data

Names: Russ, Alex, editor. | Krasny, Marianne E., editor.
Title: Urban environmental education review / edited by Alex Russ and
    Marianne E. Krasny.
Description: Ithaca ; London : Comstock Publishing Associates, an imprint of
    Cornell University Press, 2017. | Includes bibliographical references and index.
Identifiers: LCCN 2016051662 (print) | LCCN 2016056978 (ebook) | ISBN
    9781501705823 (cloth : alk. paper) | ISBN 9781501707759 (pbk. : alk. paper) |
    ISBN 9781501712784 (epub/mobi) | ISBN 9781501712791 (pdf)
Subjects: LCSH: Urban ecology (Sociology)—Study and teaching. | Human
    ecology—Study and teaching.
Classification: LCC HT241 .U72437 (print) | LCC HT241 (ebook) |
    DDC 307.760071—dc23
LC record available at https://lccn.loc.gov/2016051662

Cornell University Press strives to use environmentally responsible suppliers and materials to the fullest extent possible in the publishing of its books. Such materials include vegetable-based, low-VOC inks and acid-free papers that are recycled, totally chlorine-free, or partly composed of nonwood fibers. For further information, visit our website at www.cornellpress.cornell.edu.

Contents

Foreword

Cities drive our societies and our cultures, and the proportion of the world's population living in urban environments continues to grow. At the same time, the wicked problems facing the world, such as climate change, food security, and poverty, present some of the greatest challenges facing cities and those who live in them. This volume, drawing on contributions from around the globe, is therefore both timely and important. Developed by a lineup of talented writers, researchers, and thinkers, it is filled with insights and ideas about how we can use the power of education to create vibrant urban communities and healthier urban environments.

Environmental educators have long sought to improve the quality of life and foster environmental efforts in urban settings. What is different today is the rapid rate of urbanization coupled with an ongoing push for land development, both of which have led to declining access to green spaces in cities and increasing fragmentation in nearby natural areas. These trends in urbanization and development have incurred serious consequences, from exacerbating the divide between the rich and poor, to increasing threats to ecosystems and species impacted by urban sprawl, to introducing threats to human health linked to environmental degradation. These threats are faced individually and collectively across the planet, and solutions seem out of reach for many.

While the situation is inarguably daunting, the environmental education community recognizes a unique moment of opportunity among such rapid and ongoing change. Urbanization is changing the cultural landscape in ways that bring together a diversity of ages, races, ethnicities, and newly arrived immigrants. It is bringing together new faces, voices, and perspectives. This volume provides an opportunity for a wide audience to benefit from the new wisdom that is being generated, as well as to learn from the mistakes of the past, so that we can work collectively to create a brighter future for all to embrace.

We are presented with an exciting opportunity to explore key questions about the role of education in helping to create more sustainable communities: How can we raise awareness about the importance of ecosystem services and their relationship to healthy cities? How can we work effectively in urban areas to connect more people to nature? What does it mean to use a collective impact model to build sustainable communities? How can we create civically engaged communities and build trust within them? How do we design education programs to create resilient communities capable of addressing the challenges of a changing climate? This volume shines the spotlight on how environmental educators can work effectively in urban communities around the world, and it emphasizes the importance of understanding our urban footprint and its impact on environmental quality.

We look forward to seeing the impact of this resource in spurring creative new ideas and partnerships to advance our work in urban communities. It will provide a treasure chest of ideas and inspiration while at the same time showcasing the issues and challenges facing an increasingly concerned urban population. The contributors to this volume have provided you with an astonishingly diverse and provocative resource, but its value is not intrinsic; it depends on what you and countless others do with it. If you are prepared to rise to the challenge, then turn the page.

Justin Dillon
Head of the Graduate School of Education,
University of Bristol, UK

Judy Braus
Executive Director, North American Association
for Environmental Education, USA

Kartikeya Sarabhai
Director, Centre for Environmental Education, India

Luiz Marcelo de Carvalho
Professor, São Paulo State University, Brazil

URBAN
ENVIRONMENTAL
EDUCATION
REVIEW

Alex Russ and Marianne E. Krasny

Highlights

- Urban environmental education fosters learning about place, participation, and partnerships in cities, and it contributes to urban sustainability.
- Similar to how cities are innovation hubs, urban environmental education generates novel educational approaches that contribute to the field of environmental education more broadly.
- This book integrates research and practice with the goal of helping aspiring and practicing environmental educators achieve educational, youth and community development, and environmental quality goals in cities.

Background

Environmental educators working in cities are faced with the challenges of environmental degradation, poverty, and social inequity. Yet they also have tremendous opportunities to leverage rich human and natural resources. Cities are places where people holding diverse perspectives, knowledge, and values bump shoulders on a daily basis; in fact, these exchanges are what make cities "innovation hubs." Cities are also places where people can visit nature in iconic urban parks and can work with neighbors to create new public green spaces like community gardens and pocket parks. How can urban environmental educators address the challenges and leverage the opportunities in cities to meet their own program goals, while also generating novel approaches to environmental education more broadly? Given that the majority of the Earth's inhabitants now live in cities, urban environmental education is critical to urban sustainability and may even generate the innovations that lead the field of environmental education into the future.

The history of environmental education in cities mirrors the history of environmental education. Around the turn of the twentieth century in the United States, the nature study movement emerged in response to concern that as children migrated with their families from farms to cities, they would lose opportunities for practical and experiential learning about natural history. In the 1970s, environmental educators saw how children living in cities experienced pollution and poverty, and they designed participatory action approaches to engage youths in addressing these issues. More recently, urban environmental educators have borrowed ideas from environmental art, ecological restoration, urban planning, adult education, youth and community development, and social-ecological systems resilience to design novel educational approaches.

We define urban environmental education as any practice that creates learning opportunities to foster individual and community well-being and environmental quality in cities. Urban environmental education practices have varying goals for the individual learner, including knowledge gain, self-efficacy, and opportunities to form social ties and engage in stewardship and policy action. Urban environmental education also creates opportunities for community members to come together around local environmental restoration, planning, policy, and other environmental actions. In these ways, urban environmental education contributes to urban sustainability and resilience.

Whereas sustainability has historically emphasized integrating natural resources conservation and social and economic development, resilience "shifts policies from those that aspire to control change in systems assumed to be stable, to managing the capacity of social-ecological systems to cope with, adapt to, and shape change" (Folke et al., 2002, p. 13). Coping with, adapting to, and shaping change is critically important in a world facing disruptions due to a warming climate. As cities experience flooding, heat waves, and other climate-related disasters, we see the concept of resilience gaining currency. Some sustainability scholars also have recognized the importance of change, stating, "Sustainability is not some fixed, perfect state but rather an evolving one that responds to changes in ecological processes as well as changes in human culture and institutions" (Newman and Jennings, 2008, p. 9). Thus sustainability and social-ecological systems resilience are related concepts and both are goals of urban environmental education. While recognizing the growing importance of resilience, authors in this volume more commonly use the term sustainability. In this book, urban sustainability refers to cities that provide opportunities for humans, communities, and ecosystems to thrive and develop, while continually responding to global and local social and environmental change by smaller adaptations and in some cases larger transformations.

An example of how urban environmental education might contribute to individual and sustainability outcomes comes from community gardening education programs, which are mentioned in multiple chapters. Through community gardening, participants build self-efficacy and connections with other gardeners, while transforming a vacant lot into a site that fosters neighborhood ties and provides food and wildlife habitat. In many cases, positive feedback loops lead from individual outcomes such as self-efficacy, to sustainability outcomes such as enhanced green space, which in turn creates opportunities for psychological well-being and other individual and community benefits. As more and more urban dwellers become involved in greening initiatives, they challenge the notion that people living in cities are solely concerned about social issues and that caring for one's fellow beings is incompatible with caring for our environment. In fact, community well-being is dependent on urban green spaces and other aspects of environmental quality. In short, urban environmental education can be for individuals, communities, and the environment.

This Volume

This book aims to deepen our understanding of the role of urban environmental education in fostering urban sustainability. It takes the view that environmental educators need not look to distant pristine nature to reach their goals, but rather can take advantage of urban nature right outside their doorstep. Building on research and practice, the chapters suggest novel approaches to educating about the urban environment and to participatory urban planning, stewardship, and governance.

To cover a range of urban environmental education topics, we assembled an international community of eighty-two scholars from environmental education and related fields. In the thirty chapters of this volume, these scholars share their fascination about cities as living laboratories for environmental and educational innovations. Each chapter briefly reviews relevant research and practice and proposes ideas to enhance urban environmental education. Chapters are organized in five sections: Urban Context, Theoretical Underpinnings, Educational Settings, Participants, and Educational Approaches.

Chapters in Urban Context review urbanization and characteristics of sustainable cities and describe urban environmental education in the context of green transition communities, rapidly growing cities, and cities in the developing world. The Theoretical Underpinnings chapters explore critical environmental education, environmental justice, sense of place, climate change education, community assets, trust, and environmental governance. Chapters under Educational Settings address urban environmental education embedded in nonformal institutions, urban communities, primary and secondary schools, and university campuses. Urban environmental education involves any urban resident, thus the chapters in the Participants section discuss educational activities with young children, youths, and adults and tackle questions related to intergenerational education, inclusive education, and educator professional development. Finally, chapters in Educational Approaches explore methods and tools used in urban environmental education: cities as classrooms, environmental arts, adventure education, urban agriculture, ecological restoration, green infrastructure, urban digital storytelling, and participatory urban planning; the final chapter reviews five urban environmental education trends.

Readers can explore chapters in any order and adapt the content for different cultural contexts. The book is useful for environmental educators working in cities in any organization and for future urban environmental educators studying at universities. It is also useful for current and aspiring environmental professionals who want to understand how they can best work with their education colleagues. Thus the book may interest planners and other decision makers who influence urban development and want to incorporate educational ideas into their programs.

Cross-Cutting Themes

The chapters in this book reveal the diversity and richness of environmental education programs in cities. At the same time, common, cross-cutting themes emerge. These themes are encapsulated by a description of nonformal urban environmental education as "relating environmental content to the everyday lives of urban learners, ensuring learner autonomy, and integrating the institutions of environmental education providers within the broader array of social institutions in the urban environment" (chapter 12). Relating content to the lives of learners entails a focus on urban *place*; ensuring learner autonomy reflects *participatory* approaches to environmental education; and integrating institutions suggests governance and other *partnerships*. In short, this statement reflects the cross-cutting themes we have distilled from the chapters: place, participation, and partnerships.

Place

Through the wealth of practices presented, this book demonstrates how environmental education is no longer only about taking children outside the city to experience pristine nature, but includes an impressive array of approaches *in* cities, ranging from nature play to green infrastructure creation, to art and political action. In addition, starting in chapter 1, authors redefine cities, which, rather than being blights on an otherwise pristine landscape, are places where nature can be found and ecosystem services are provided. Further, and important given increasingly urban demographics, cities are places where learners can readily observe how ecosystem and social processes are tightly intertwined. Chapter 12 reflects the significance of specific urban places in environmental education: "In urban settings, connecting content to locally relevant situations and drawing on community concerns may be particularly important to counteract traditional conceptualizations of canned nature programs."

In addition to calling for situating environmental learning in cities, chapters address how participants in planning and other environmental education programs actively reconstruct urban places. For example, chapter 6 (Environmental Justice) states, "Urban environmental education that integrates environmental justice can help participants construct, critique, and transform our cities in more just and sustainable ways." Summing up the place theme, chapter 7 (Sense of Place) describes how environmental education can help urban residents rediscover, reimagine, and recreate their urban neighborhoods and cities as legitimate social-ecological systems worthy of study, stewardship, and planning, and in so doing help residents develop an ecological place meaning in cities.

Participation

Nearly all authors describe participatory approaches to urban environmental education. Although this theme is prominent in nonformal education settings, it is also present in the chapters focused on schools and educational policy. For example, the Four Asian Tigers (chapter 3) includes descriptions of participatory whole-school approaches and inquiry-based learning.

Four types of participatory practices in environmental education—participation as encounters with nature, as action, as social learning, and as deliberative dialogue (Læssøe and Krasny, 2013)—can be found in this book. Early Childhood (chapter 16) describes children spending time in urban nature yet also taking action to address problems they perceive during their time outdoors. Focusing on participation as social learning, Critical Environmental Education (chapter 5) notes that "Addressing wicked sustainability issues like climate change calls for forms of education and governance that create new spaces for collaborative and social learning." Continuing the focus on wicked problems from the point of view of deliberative dialogue, chapter 10 claims that "while environmental education programs that are prescriptive or stress immediate technical fixes (e.g., recycling) may influence environmentally responsible behaviors, they are unlikely to help participants generate the innovative solutions needed to address [wicked] urban sustainability issues . . . participatory approaches to environmental education . . . are critical."

Participation, however, is not without its challenges. For example, Cities as Opportunities (chapter 4) talks about the challenges to participation in India, including illiteracy, socioeconomic disparity, and cultural biases. Further, in some situations such as when a city is immediately threatened by flooding, government regulations, social marketing, and other more government-directed approaches are called for. Moreover, participatory approaches are subject to critiques related to tokenism or to claims that youths are the principal decision makers when in fact adult guidance is needed and prominent behind the scenes (chapter 17). Recognizing legitimate concerns about participation and at the same time reinforcing notions of place, chapter 29 claims that "participatory efforts—from regional planning for sustainable transit systems, to community greenway planning, to the creation of safe places for children to play—perform vital roles in engaging people in the shared process of place making."

Partnerships

Authors speak of multiple types of partnerships or boundary crossings, some of which have not been widely discussed in the environmental education literature. These include partnerships across disciplines, across ethnic and cultural divides, and across organizations or governance actors, all three of which are needed to address wicked sustainability problems. Andrade and colleagues (chapter 4) sum up how critical partnerships are: "Over the past two decades, Brazil has come to the realization that the current state of the environment is too dire for environmental education to be carried out as individual initiatives." Chapter 12 refers to partnerships when it states that "environmental education includes public health, environmental justice, social equity, diversity, justice, and other concerns—many of which are intensified in the urban context."

Focusing on disciplinary partnerships, chapter 27 describes how the Urban Ecology Center in Milwaukee, Wisconsin, "showcases a green building, solar power station, public art, urban wasteland being transformed into a park, riparian habitats, classrooms, and a climbing wall. . . . Educational efforts such as these are rich in their ability to string together disciplines like civil engineering, landscape architecture, and building design to trace both ecological and human processes, all grounded in the learners' lived environment." Chapter 10 describes more broadly the importance of integrating across social and ecological disciplines to foster environmental literacy and address wicked problems in urban settings.

Turning to partnerships across social divides, chapter 26 argues that education situated in local restoration efforts involves "consciously forming partnerships; integrating local values, traditions, and socioeconomic alongside ecological considerations; and being sensitive to diverse cultures and issues of power.... Doing otherwise can lead to misinterpretations, failure, and even environmental injustices." Although as environmental educators we often talk about diversity, our goals are not always clear (e.g., diversity efforts that try to help marginalized peoples or seek to engage multiple perspectives in order to generate sustainability innovations). Chapter 13 argues for "equitable knowledge sharing," which "reveals a subtle change in perspective from expanding existing outreach programs to simply being more inclusive of nontraditional audiences" to "[r]ecognizing and honoring each actor's assets." In doing this work, perhaps the most important question we can ask ourselves is: Are we open to learning as much from our partners as we are to sharing our expertise with them?

Finally, whereas chapters 10 and 11 focus specifically on governance, many chapters indirectly touch on this concept by describing partnerships with government, university, business, and civil society actors. Such partnerships may start as more narrow efforts to bridge formal and nonformal educational institutions and then expand to actors not directly engaged in environmental education. One example comes from Singapore (chapter 3), which "has adopted a cross-sectoral "3-P" (People, Public, and Private) partnership strategy to promote urban environmental education. Its efforts to embed issues of recycling, energy, and water conservation into the formal curriculum are enhanced by building a network of environmental advisors from governmental and nongovernmental organizations and industries." Environmental educators can also "help form a bridge between the municipal leadership and residents" (chapter 2).

Place, Participation, and Partnerships: Applications for Practice

How can educators contribute to urban sustainability? The authors and editors of this volume do not offer a set of prescriptions. Rather, we encourage educators and aspiring educators to read the chapters, learn from the research and from fellow students and practitioners, and realize that education is in part a process of learning from mistakes and building on what worked well. Education is also a process of adapting our practices based on what we learn and observe, and in some cases more radically transforming what we do as new situations arise. In this spirit, we offer a set of principles that reflect our three cross-cutting themes: place, participation, and partnerships.

Start by designing your programs around local urban *place*. This means recognizing that cities are places to celebrate, including their natural and cultural elements. It means helping participants acquire ecological place meanings that encompass not only buildings but also wildlife, green infrastructure, and opportunities for outdoor recreation and environmental stewardship in cities. And importantly, it means reclaiming, restoring, and creating new urban places that contribute to urban sustainability. Through web-based technologies, participants in programs designed around local place can learn about and exchange ideas with similar efforts elsewhere, as well as learn about global sustainability issues. In this way, programs that begin with urban place can engage in regional and global social and environmental movements and policy efforts.

Design your programs to incorporate *participation* to the extent possible. This includes participation as encounters with nature, as action, as social learning, and as deliberative processes. But don't go overboard. In some instances, for example, when children and communities are faced with an immediate threat or when the program has an "instrumental" outcome (e.g., to train adults to prune trees, chapter 18), more directive approaches are called for. And knowing how to balance participants' ability to act on their own vs. their need for guidance is an important consideration (chapter 17).

Finally, strategically build *partnerships* both within your programs and between your organization and other governance actors. Bridging disciplinary, ethnic, cultural, and organizational divides is critical to addressing wicked environmental problems. Partnerships also can be designed more narrowly to realize a program's objectives; for example, what disciplines, individuals, and organizations will help incorporate storytelling into a program that aims to foster ecological place meaning? What is my organization's niche, and what other organizations do I partner with, to contribute to green space planning in my city?

Conclusion

Just as cities are hubs for technological and social innovations, the chapters in this book demonstrate how urban environmental education is generating educational innovations. In particular, urban environmental education offers opportunities for participants to reconstruct place and recreate the meaning of place in cities and thus play an active role in transforming the places where most of the world's population lives. Cities also offer opportunities for environmental education to experiment with and integrate multiple forms of participation in settings ranging from community gardens to daylighted rivers, from coastal shorelines to green buildings, and from art installations to city parks. Finally, dense networks of stewardship organizations in cities enable environmental educators to form strategic partnerships and become part of environmental governance networks. Focusing on the way we think and act related to place, participation, and partnerships may provide ideas, inspiration, and resources for the field of environmental education more broadly. It may also help us to generate the innovations needed to address climate change and future sustainability issues.

Acknowledgments

We would like to thank the many urban environmental educators from around the world who have inspired us to see what is possible in cities. We would also like to thank Richard Stedman, Tania Schusler, Thomas Elmqvist, and other scholars who have helped us to understand place, participation, and partnerships in cities. Finally, we extend our deepest gratitude to our families for supporting our efforts.

This publication was developed under Assistant Agreement No. NT-83497401 awarded by the U.S. Environmental Protection Agency (EPA). It has not been formally reviewed by EPA. The views expressed are solely those of the authors, and EPA does not endorse any products or commercial services mentioned.

References

Folke, C., Carpenter, S., Elmqvist, T., Gunderson, L., Holling, C. S., et al. (2002). *Resilience and sustainable development: Building adaptive capacity in a world of transformations.* Stockholm, Sweden: Environmental Advisory Council, Ministry of the Environment.

Læssøe, J., and Krasny, M. E. (2013). Participation in environmental education: Crossing boundaries within the big tent. In M. E. Krasny and J. Dillon (Eds.), *Trading zones in environmental education: Creating transdisciplinary dialogue* (pp. 11–44). New York: Peter Lang.

Newman, P., and Jennings, I. (2008). *Cities as sustainable ecosystems: Principles and practices.* Washington, D.C.: Island Press.

Part I
URBAN CONTEXT

1

ADVANCING URBANIZATION

David Maddox, Harini Nagendra,
Thomas Elmqvist, and Alex Russ

Highlights

- Cities are human habitat—integrated systems of people, infrastructure, and nature—and are key to human-nature relationships and global sustainability.
- We need cities that are resilient, sustainable, livable, and just.
- Urban environmental education can help debunk common assumptions: that cities are ecologically barren, nature is only in wilderness, and city people don't care for or need nature.
- Telling the story of "advancing urbanization"—both the global acceleration of urbanization and the promise offered by urbanization—is an essential role for urban environmental education.

Introduction

Cities—their design and how we live in them—will be key in our struggle for sustainability, indeed our future. As cities grow, as they are newly created, and as more and more people choose or require them as places to live, our decisions about urban design and city building will determine the outcomes of long-term challenges related to resilience, sustainability, livability, and justice. Rather than being the essential cause of the global environmental dangers we face, cities will be central to success in overcoming these dangers. Such success will be based on science and policy, but also on widespread public engagement with and understanding of both the challenges and the potential solutions found in building cities. Environmental education can play a critical role in fostering public engagement through clarifying and transmitting the challenges, values, actions, and methods for achieving sustainable, resilient, livable, and just cities.

What Is Urban?

At their core, urban spaces are human settlements of various sizes, densities, and physical arrangements. Major urban centers, cities, towns, and even organized collections of populated zones that make up metropolitan regions are "urban"; that is, "urban" comprises a diversity and continuum of types of spaces, not one form. The dense and compact European city surrounded by rural land is one form. Classic American cities and their sprawl is another model. Garden cities, clustered townships, and other urban forms all have characteristics in common.

What are the unifying features of these diverse urban forms? People—and their communities—is one. Buildings, streets, and other gray infrastructure is another. And nature is a third. By including nature as a key characteristic of cities we do not mean nature as an idealized or hoped-for feature. Nature is an attribute of every city, both within its borders and as a connection to the wider landscape, because while cities are social and infrastructural spaces, they are also ecological spaces. They are social-ecological spaces of functioning ecosystems of living and nonliving things. In this sense cities are essential human habitat.

Acknowledging that cities are themselves ecosystems that exist along gradients with surrounding periurban and rural areas has deep implications not only for the humanity and livability of the world's urban zones, but also for global sustainability more broadly. Urbanization is advancing throughout the world. Urbanization as a positive concept for the good of the Earth is also advancing around the world among thoughtful scholars and within progressive city leadership. It is also advancing in the hands of people on the streets who are building better cities, block by block, through community gardens, street tree plantings, parks, and embedded natural areas, and who are engaging in participatory decision making. Telling the story of this advancement—both the global acceleration of urbanization and the promise

offered by urbanization—is an essential role for an emerging urban environmental education.

The Growth of Cities

The world is increasingly urban, interconnected, and changing. With current
trends, by 2030 the global urban population is estimated to be 4.9 billion, nearly
double that of 2000. During this period the total urban area is expected to triple.
That is, urban land area is expanding faster than urban populations (Elmqvist
et al., 2013). This massive change in where humans live on the planet will have
inevitable local and global ecological consequences.

Indeed, more than 60 percent of the urban area of the 2030s has yet to be built
(Elmqvist et al., 2013). In three areas—Sub-Saharan Africa, China, and India—
the combined urban population is expected to grow by more than one billion
people. By 2030, nearly one-third of the world's urban inhabitants will live in
China or India (Seto, Güneralp, and Hutyra, 2012). Africa will urbanize faster
than any other continent; its urban population is expected to more than double,
from 300 million in 2000 to 750 million in 2030. Around 75 percent of Africa's
total population growth is expected to occur in cities of less than one million.
African cities are often settlements with weak governance structures, high levels
of poverty, and low capacity in environmental management and science. Currently, more than 43 percent of Africa's urban population lives below the poverty
line, more than in any other continent, making socioeconomic development a
priority. Generally weak state control, the presence of a feeble formal economic
sector, and the scarcity of local professional skills will constrain responses to the
complex environmental challenges posed by rapid urbanization. Even under
current conditions, urban areas all over the planet are facing severe challenges,
including shortages of natural resources, environmental degradation, climate
change, demographic and social changes such as increasing income inequality and poverty, and inconsistent management of sustainability transitions that
would reduce ecological impacts.

Climate change, increased migration of people, and ecological degradation
will severely test societies and urban regions. The urbanization process also presents opportunities, however. That 60 percent of the urban area of the cities of the
2030s is yet to be built is a chance to avoid repeating the city-building mistakes
of the past. The infrastructure we build in cities—where we put the roads and the
buildings, and how we organize resource use—tends to be with us a long time.

The immensity of new building now underway is a chance to get it right, both for people and for nature.

Values

What are the cities we want to create in the future, the cities in which we want to live, cities that work for both people and the Earth? What is their *nature*? A vision is needed for city building, one that is fundamentally built around goals and informed by values. Visions, goals, values, and actions, along with scientific data and experiential knowledge, are the essence of education, including environmental education.

Certainly the cities we need are *resilient*, so our cities will still exist after the next "one-hundred-year storm," now occurring with increasing frequency. Certainly they are *sustainable*, since we need our cities to balance consumption and resources so they can last into the future. As we build this vision we know that cities must also be *livable*, because cities are now the places where most of us live. And *justice* must also be key to our urban environments. We have struggled to build just cities for a long time; largely we have come up short.

These are the key characteristics of the cities of our dreams: resilient, sustainable, livable, and just. What are the values that are foundations for these goals? They are, at a minimum, inclusiveness, equity, respect for people and knowledge, innovation, and conservation.

The United Nation's Urban Sustainable Development Goals offer some guidance, a global consensus on what is important (United Nations, 2015). Among the seventeen Sustainable Development Goals approved in 2015 is one explicitly about cities, #11: "Make cities inclusive, safe, resilient and sustainable." This goal offers a road map to the operational values we should investigate, appropriate, share, and teach in the emerging urban world; the road map should include targets for open space, sustainable environmental management, and access to nature and its myriad benefits and services. At the center of the goal #11 and our general approach to cities, explicitly and implicitly, is nature, both as a literal feature of the cities we require for resilience, sustainability, livability, and justice, and as a metaphor for the kinds of cities we desire.

The Richness of the Urban Environment

Why should we care about the impacts of urbanization on ecosystems? In addition to the intrinsic value of nature, urban ecosystems are essential for human well-being and, ultimately, for urban resilience and sustainability. Because urban nature has explicit benefits, its availability to all people is a matter of justice. The environmental consequences of the rapid growth of cities—especially poorly designed and managed ones—is starkly apparent. Urban expansion has degraded and destroyed natural habitats in and around cities worldwide, transforming forests, coastal mangroves, lakes, and wetlands into vast expanses of concrete and polluted travesties of their former ecological vigor.

Yet cities are far from barren. In contrast, cities are often rich in biodiversity (Aronson et al., 2014). Cities can be key stopovers along migratory routes of birds. Some cities are biodiversity hotspots in their own right. They contain small but thriving pockets of biodiversity with native and nonnative (novel) species assemblages (Faeth, Bang, and Saari, 2014). Such assemblages of urban species and habitats provide a range of ecosystem services that are critical for the sustainability of cities, indeed for the *life* of cities. Wetlands clean water that has been contaminated with industrial pollutants and sewage; trees may clean the air of pollutants; and urban ecosystems provide important habitats for insects, birds, bats, and other pollinators and urban wildlife.

For humans, exposure to green spaces fosters physical well-being and psychological relief from stress. Urban green spaces include not only city parks, but also the wide array of macro- and micro-urban places, from wetlands and bioswales, to street trees, pocket parks, community gardens, and even biophilic workspaces. A diversity of people and communities work in and interact with nature in these spaces, including from civil society (e.g., civic groups, activists), government, and the corporate sector (Kazemi, Beecham, and Gibbs, 2011; Beninde, Veith, and Hochkirch, 2015). Parks, community gardens, sidewalks shaded by trees, and lakes and coastal beaches act as important nodes for people to congregate and strengthen social bonds among disparate urban residents.

Natural areas in cities also often hold an important place in the cultural landscape of residents and are sometimes considered sacred and worshipped in Asia, Africa, and elsewhere. In New York City, immigrants and other residents demonstrate care, stewardship, and spiritual practices in natural areas and parks (Svendsen, Campbell, and McMillen, 2016). Urban ecosystems also provide resources for foraging in cities, offering food and livelihood security for vulnerable communities through the provision of fish, herbs and vegetables, fodder, fuelwood, and other resources. Many urban ecosystems historically functioned as urban commons, providing collective resources for entire communities in times of scarcity and need.

In addition to enhancing individual and community well-being, urban natural areas provide a buffer against local and global environmental factors such as pollution and climate change. Similarly, through urban agriculture, urban green spaces buffer against economic and food insecurity of the urban poor. In short, green urban spaces are key to global sustainability and need to be recognized as positive forces in shaping human stewardship of the entire biosphere (Elmqvist et al., 2013).

That cities have dire environmental and biodiversity challenges is certainly true. That they are ecologically dead, or are the causes of all the world's environmental problems, is false. Yet many cities are experiencing a crisis of green and open space, especially in the Global South. The lack of accessible green and open space contributes to desperately poor conditions for both people and nature (Wolch, Byrne, and Newell, 2014). Thus, having sufficient access to good quality urban green space is an issue of ecological and social concern that impacts quality of life and social justice. We must be vigilant to maintain such access for *all* citizens as cities restore their green spaces and build new green infrastructure; such urban sustainability initiatives often attract younger and higher-income residents, leading to exclusion of longer-term residents who can no longer afford housing, or so-called "environmental gentrification."

Role for Education

In a world of advancing urbanization, urban environmental education can play a key role. The story of cities as ecological spaces needs to be told—both in cities and outside them—to adults and to the many young people who increasingly populate the world's growing cities; to our leaders in government, business, and civil society making decisions about the built and natural environment; and to each other in our daily lives. Such stories will have a critical impact on the willingness of the inhabitants of the cities of the future to protect and care for—and create—their urban environments.

Thought leaders and educators can communicate the connection between the urban environment and human and global environmental health. They also can communicate that merely recording the presence of species in urban environments does not necessarily indicate their health; that actions such as the thoughtless use of pesticides and planting invasive species may deprive native fauna of feeding and nesting habitats; that the persistence of many species in urban environments, such as macaques, langurs, and birds of prey in Indian cities, can be attributed to cultural traditions of good will toward life; that local food production with diverse methods is central to local health; that all people, not just the rich, deserve access to ecosystem services; and that consumption and transportation choices are key to global sustainability. Finally, educators can communicate that there is a connection between green urban design and resilience, sustainability, livability, and justice.

Urban environmental education can play a pivotal role in telling these stories by teaching about urban biodiversity, ecosystem services, and nature and about the myriad connections between the built and natural world in cities. Urban environmental education that is sensitive to its local cultural context and incorporates scientific insights from urban social-ecological systems thinking can make a significant difference, encouraging residents to care about their environment and giving them the knowledge on which to act. Urban environmental education also can engage people directly in action, where lessons are learned through hands-on and collective stewardship practices like community gardening rather than through directed teaching. What is learned through such active participation in and reflecting on stewardship practices may lead to more informed engagement in environmental practices and policy-related decision making in the future.

The dire challenges of urban environmental pollution and degradation—and their relevance to resilience, sustainability, livability, and justice—can quickly lead to the trap of purely dismal narratives. This does not have to be the case. In addition to a narrative of ecological loss and the consequences for human well-being, we can develop and communicate positive messages of real change that simultaneously convey facts, challenges, and potential solutions. We must emphasize the importance of ecological, social, and technical solutions while also addressing the challenges of equity, conflict, and exclusion.

Thus, while focusing on the "what" questions of the intended human, social, and environmental outcomes, the field of urban environmental education can equally focus on the "how" questions of process. This entails helping people to understand—often through hands-on engagement in stewardship and related practices—the ways in which social and environmental change can be initiated and inclusively scaled up in their own cities and social-ecological contexts. In this regard, urban environmental education can play the key influential role that only it can fill: helping to creatively reconceptualize, redesign, and redevelop existing and emerging cities by helping people learn about and create green infrastructure, influence urban planning and design, change individual behaviors, and undertake collective environmental actions.

Conclusion

Urban environmental education in an emerging urban world faces multiple challenges. Is there a uniquely urban version of environmental education? To a large extent, that is a subject for this book. We know that some established environmental assumptions must be adjusted in a modern urban context: that nature can only be found in the wilderness, that cities are the enemy of sustainability, that cities are ecologically barren, and that city people don't engage with nature. All are largely false or misleading.

How can we advance an urban vision that serves people and our planet, a vision that is fundamentally imbued with values? Tell the story, far and wide, that cities are essential hot spots of nature that serve people and the Earth. Nature exists in cities, and it needs to be seeded, grown, and nurtured as a commons. And importantly, urban residents all over the globe are creating innovative approaches that simultaneously address social and environmental injustice. These are stories that must be told to students, to teachers, to leaders, to community members, and to ourselves. This is the key and essential role—advancing progressive urban environmental ideas in a global context—for an emerging urban environmental education. Telling this critical story is the challenge to which environmental education is called in the urban twenty-first century.

References

Aronson, M. F. J., La Sorte, F. A., Nilon, C. H., et al. (2014). A global analysis of the impacts of urbanization on bird and plant diversity reveals key anthropogenic drivers. *Proceedings of the Royal Society B, 281.*

Beninde, J., Veith, M., and Hochkirch, A. (2015). Biodiversity in cities needs space: A meta analysis of factors determining intra urban biodiversity variation. *Ecology Letters, 18*(6), 581–592.

Elmqvist, T., Fragkias, M., Goodness, J., Güneralp, B., et al. (2013). Stewardship of the biosphere in the urban era. In T. Elmqvist, M. Fragkias, J. Goodness, B. Güneralp, et al. (Eds). *Urbanization, biodiversity and ecosystem services: Challenges and opportunities: A global assessment* (pp. 719–746). Dordrecht: Springer.

Faeth, S. H., Bang, C., and Saari, S. (2014). Urban biodiversity: Patterns and mechanisms. *Annals of the New York Academy of Sciences, 1223*: 69–81.

Kazemi, F., Beecham, S., and Gibbs, J. (2011). Streetscape biodiversity and the role of bioretention swales in an Australian urban environment. *Landscape and Urban Planning, 101*(2), 139–148.

Seto, K., Güneralp, B., and Hutyra, L. R. (2012). Global forecasts of urban expansion to 2030 and direct impacts on biodiversity and carbon pools. *Proceedings of the National Academy of Science, 109*(40), 16093–16088.

Svendsen, E. S., Campbell, L. K., and McMillen, H. (2016, in press). Stories, shrines, and symbols: Recognizing psycho-social-spiritual benefits of urban parks and natural areas. *Journal of Ethnobiology.*

United Nations. (2015). Sustainable Development Goals. Retrieved from http://www. un.org/sustainabledevelopment/sustainable-development-goals.

Wolch, J. R., Byrne, J., and Newell, J. P. (2014). Urban green space, public health, and environmental justice: The challenge of making cities 'just green enough.' *Landscape and Urban Planning, 125*, 234–244.

2

SUSTAINABLE CITIES

Martha C. Monroe, Arjen E. J. Wals,
Hiromi Kobori, and Johanna Ekne

Highlights

- Multiple perspectives about the same place can generate conflict as well as creative approaches to foster urban sustainability.
- In cities around the world, small-scale sustainability innovations are emerging, which can serve as models for other cities.
- Monitoring the outcomes of such innovations, including through citizen science and other forms of citizen data collection, can contribute to their effectiveness.
- Environmental educators can work with government and other sectors to help attract, broker, and support coalitions that energize citizen engagement in greening urban areas.

Introduction

Urban areas around the world are creating unique approaches to address social and environmental challenges and to move toward sustainability. With forethought and vision, urban residents are taking opportunities to learn about which strategies can improve their communities while using fewer resources and generating less waste. These innovations rarely encompass an entire city, but are important because they signal new ways of engaging residents in meaningful decisions and actions. This chapter highlights urban sustainability innovations from Sweden, Japan, and the Netherlands, explores common principles that may help explain their success, and illustrates the role of education and learning in these efforts.

The common factor across these examples is that they engage municipal nonprofit and government agency leaders with residents in multiple ways. Leaders and residents learn about sustainability as they build skills for participatory decision making. They offer ideas and realize that their contributions matter. They collect data that help others address problems more effectively.

Our cases demonstrate a variety of interactions between residents and expert leaders in fostering sustainability innovations in cities. The cases have outlived their inception phase and continue to grow and improve their outcomes despite setbacks, changing circumstances, and even opposition. As a result, these cases are a useful microcosm of the possible.

Sweden: Sustainability-Inspired Innovation in Malmö

The third largest city in Sweden, Malmö (population approximately 300,000) has taken significant steps over the past decade to engage its residents in sustainability. Several efforts, led by a headstrong and progressive mayor with professional training in urban planning, have resulted in international attention. Municipal staff members head up many of the sustainability strategies, but local residents also have opportunities to engage in actions to improve community and environmental well-being.

Augustenborg, a public housing community of three thousand people, demonstrates challenges and opportunities in engaging residents in exploring ways to address sustainability issues related to storm water runoff. When community meetings initially did not generate much involvement, the city hired a community involvement specialist to engage with residents; he coordinated efforts to knock on doors, chat at coffee shops, and visit playgrounds. The specialist asked what people would like to see in their community, how it could be more attractive, how they could contribute to these efforts, and what kinds of interests and skills they could bring. As the project got under way, it was clear that the staff members were listening to and using residents' ideas, thus empowering them to become more engaged. Residents originated the design of storm water drains and a community rabbit hutch, and they created opportunities for planting flowerbeds.

At the same time, city employees worked to reduce the amount of water that flowed into the combined storm water and sewage system. They converted a municipal building roof to a green roof and experimented with the minimal depth of soil needed to grow sedum and moss. An eco-friendly competition resulted in the redesign of a laundry facility to reduce wastewater. The winning entry uses automatic soap dispensers to ensure quantity and quality and allows wastewater to flow into a small digester and pond before moving to the stream. After reducing its storm water runoff by 80 percent and generating many other sustainability innovations, the formerly run-down, crime-ridden community rebounded into a desirable village that is attracting new residents.

Malmö found that problems are easiest to address if the city owns the building (such as city office buildings or public housing) or is responsible for energy and other policies (such as requiring energy use limitations through contracts). By treating environmental and social problems as opportunities for experimentation and learning, Malmö used forms of urban environmental education, such as community discussions and competitions, to generate and select new ideas. This approach, combining collaborative adaptive management (Berkes, 2009; Monroe, 2015) and social learning, enables people to move toward new ideas, building support along the way.

In the storm water case, the city purposefully engaged residents in designing new infrastructure, and the infrastructure directly addressed the problem of storm water runoff. In another case, the city designed new infrastructure to encourage behavior change, but then realized additional measures were needed to change the intended behaviors. To increase the number of bicycle riders in the compact and flat city of Malmö, the municipality began by improving cyclist safety. They created an extensive network of about 500 km of bicycle paths and lanes that separated cyclists from cars, enforced vehicle speed limits of 40 km/hr, gave the right of way to cyclists in crosswalks and intersections, and made a practice of clearing bike lanes of snow before clearing the streets (Figure 2.1). These policy and infrastructure changes were essential to improve safety, but they alone did not increase cycling behavior.

The city developed a program that encourages residents to leave their cars at home through three-month contracts where people agree to ride for the duration, receive small rewards such as a rain poncho or helmet, are recognized in the agency newsletter as being part of the biking community, and are given before and after health exams to track personal changes. Residents keep a journal of their experiences and meet with peers to discuss their struggles and successes, strengthening their feeling of being part of a new social norm. This combination of information, incentives, peer support, and feedback integrates several social marketing strategies to reconfigure the landscape of habits (McKenzie-Mohr, 2011).

FIGURE 2.1. Dedicated cycle paths make it easy to travel by bicycle in Malmö, Sweden. Credit: Martha C. Monroe.

Organizers believe that the act of trying something new increases people's receptiveness to information about the behavior and willingness to provide timely positive feedback about the value of the action. Many new cyclists continued to bike long after the contract period.

Japan: Citizen Science to Foster Urban Sustainability

Yokohama is the second largest city in Japan with a population of 3.7 million. As the first Japanese city to open its port to the rest of the world in 1859, Yokohama has a long tradition of innovation. Currently, the city is promoting a global model of sustainable management through partnerships with citizens and other sectors.

Here citizen science is viewed as a mechanism for addressing urban sustainability challenges. Citizen science engages the public in collecting reliable data for scientists and policy makers (Bonney et al., 2014). The rapid development of information technology and its use in everyday life has made it possible for greater numbers of lay people to become involved in citizen science, thus accelerating its potential to address global environmental issues such as climate change, loss of biodiversity, and ecosystem management and conservation, and to involve citizens in decision making regarding urban sustainability. Three examples of citizen science projects in Yokohama, however, rely less on the cyber community yet still engage stakeholders in hands-on action-research while communicating face to face.

Monitoring Sewage Treatment Plants

The first project aimed to make visible the role of sewage treatment in the Sakai River basin. Many Japanese environmental organizations and residents are concerned about the quality of water in rivers and participate in water quality monitoring. Most citizens, however, do not understand the role of sewage treatment and reclaimed water, even though almost half the water volume in major urban rivers is from treated sewage effluent.

In 2014, a collaboration involving citizens, a local environmental organization, a university, and federal and local government agencies launched a citizen science project to compare the sewage treatment processes used on three different rivers. The participants collected water samples at the discharge outlet of each sewage treatment plant as well as upstream and downstream on each river, and measured ammonium and nitrate concentrations using a simple commercial assay tool (Figure 2.2). University researchers and students measured biological

FIGURE 2.2.   Members of a nongovernmental organization and students monitor water quality above and below sewage treatment plants. Credit: Keisuke Tsukagawa.

oxygen demand (an indicator of organic pollution). The project demonstrated that the nutrient loads were higher at the sewage treatment plant that used standard activated sludge treatment compared to those using additional aeration or regulation of ammonium.

Creating Dragonfly Habitats in an Industrial Bay

A second example shows the value of citizens monitoring dragonfly biodiversity around artificial ponds in the heavily industrialized Yokohama Bay. The dragonfly is an important symbol in Japanese culture and a popular charismatic species. In 2003, the "How far can dragonflies fly?" project was launched, and ten local companies created dragonfly ponds on their properties. Citizens monitored the *Anisoptera* dragonfly for a week in August every year for ten consecutive years. Each captured dragonfly was identified, marked, and recorded before its release.

Species richness has held constant in recent years. The research also revealed the movement of dragonflies between ponds. An endangered species that was originally found at only one site is now widespread in six ponds. These results demonstrate that restored ponds serve as an ecological stepping-stone, part of an ecological network in the city. The project also demonstrates the conservation importance of citizen science that enables citizens, business, local government researchers, and university students to collaborate.

Community-Based Urban Greening

An urban greening community project in Ushikubo-nishi (1,600 households) in the northern part of Yokohama works with community groups and a university to increase biodiversity in residential areas (Kobori, Sakurai, and Kitamura, 2014). The project was funded by a special tax to the Yokohama municipal government to stimulate sustainability initiatives in the community. It was designed by the local community through discussions with various sectors for one year before being launched in 2013.

Few studies have assessed the biodiversity of private gardens in Japan. Participants in this citizen science project collected data to determine the initial environmental characteristics of private gardens in the community. They used both a web-based monitoring system and direct observation of gardens. University professors and students in conservation and environmental education helped residents monitor biodiversity. Data revealed that twenty-four species of birds and twenty-two species of butterflies existed in the community in 2012 (Kobori, Sakurai, and Kitamura, 2014). The project also helped

determine the social factors necessary for enhancing conservation, restoration, and management of the private gardens and for increasing community
solidarity. A survey of the residents' association (810 respondents) revealed
that citizens had high expectations of the greening activity and acknowledged
the importance of communication (Sakurai et al., 2015). This project suggests a strategy for integrating ecological and social factors in sustainable
systems management.

The Netherlands: Creating a Sustainable Neighborhood through Social Learning

The Eva-Lanxmeer Foundation was created in the 1990s by a group of Dutch
citizens who, despite their different backgrounds (e.g., age, gender, expertise,
income), all shared an aspiration to live more sustainably (Wals and Noorduyn, 2010). The participants came from different parts of the Netherlands
and met in a series of workshops that focused on creating a sustainable urban
neighborhood from scratch. They used principles of sustainable living self-
determined by community members (e.g., all members owning, designing,
and maintaining the community garden; adhering to the principles of permaculture), the government (e.g., using a double water system separating
gray and black water streams, solar energy, triple-pane glass), and the private
sector (e.g., using eco-friendly architecture and design). During the initial
workshops a joint vision of a new urban community emerged that combined
active citizen participation with ecological construction, organic design, and
architecture. The municipality of Culemborg gave the group "seed money"
to organize themselves and to hire an outside facilitator with experience in
multistakeholder innovation processes.

The group began planning and developing an area of twenty-four hectares
for two hundred residences and a number of businesses and offices. The plan
called for a socioeconomically integrated neighborhood consisting of a mix of
social or public housing (30 percent), middle-income rental and private property
(20 percent), and upper middle- and higher-income private homes (50 percent).
Their plans also included an ecological city farm to connect the community to
food production, local food systems, and local employment. The community
was created near the Culemborg railway station to reduce the need for cars; the
heart of the community is now completely car-free. Today, the community also
runs its own local energy plant, and all wastewater is treated on location using
gravel beds, sand filters and helophytes, and separate black and gray wastewater
streams (Figure 2.3).

FIGURE 2.3. The green commons is car-free, child-friendly, and maintained by the inhabitants. Credit: Huub van Beurden.

The process of reaching agreement about what a sustainable neighborhood actually means as well as designing and implementing the plans required significant interaction and mutual learning among the various stakeholders. In a study involving the key stakeholders, the making of a sustainable neighborhood was reconstructed as a social learning process of civic engagement (Wals and Noorduyn, 2010). Data collection involved interviews with key informants, focus group discussions with inhabitants, and the analysis of secondary documents (e.g., meeting minutes, newsletters, and e-mail correspondence). The study focused on the interactions when the first residents collaboratively designed the community garden that forms the heart of the neighborhood.

A question that can be distilled from the Eva-Lanxmeer experience and research is: How can environmental educators assist organizations and communities to become "learning systems" that work toward sustainability? This case suggests that a learning system requires that people learn from and with one another and collectively gain the ability to withstand setbacks and deal with insecurity, complexity, and risks. The pioneers in Culemborg not only had to accept one another's differences, but also had be able to put these differences to use in generating simple and creative solutions to problems ranging from how to resolve the tension between birds in neighborhood gardens and allowing cats to roam outdoors, to how to deal with the differences among residents' willingness and abilities to actively contribute to the social, psychological, and physical well-being of the place. The Culemborg example supports the notion that learning for the social-ecological well-being of a community requires synergy among multiple actors. Creating this synergy implies the blurring of formal and informal learning, which is an important lesson for urban environmental education seeking to discover its role in the myriad of sustainability innovations emerging in cities across the globe. Opportunities for this type of learning expand with increased permeability between disciplines, generations, cultures, institutions, and sectors (Wals and Schwarzin, 2012). Through this complementarity and synergy, new spaces open up for learning-based transitions toward sustainability.

Conclusion

The three country cases represent multistakeholder learning where members of the local community work with their municipality and other sectors to jointly design, implement, monitor, and evaluate a "place" that is seeking to become more sustainable. In all three communities, residents are changing behaviors because they have reconceptualized their role or lifestyle and had opportunities to try out new practices. Educators, communicators, and facilitators are helping urban areas move toward sustainability by creating a supportive environment for residents and experts to share ideas, to contribute data to build knowledge about the impacts of existing management practices and new sustainability innovations, and to try out new behaviors. Educators can help form a bridge between the municipal leadership and residents, recognizing that government support is essential to encourage residents to experiment and change.

The communities in Swedish, Japanese, and Dutch cities are creating environments that integrate the social, the ecological, and the environmental. At the same time, they need to become competent in monitoring progress both in terms of the participants' learning and capacity building to become more effective in their work and in assessing the social-ecological impact of their change. The resulting feedback is essential in lifelong continuous learning toward sustainability.

References

Berkes, F. (2009). Evolution of co-management: Role of knowledge generation, bridging organizations and social learning. *Journal of Environmental Management, 90*(5), 1692–1702.

Bonney, R., Shirk, J. L., Phillips, T. B., Wiggins, A., Ballard, H. L., Miller-Rushing, A. J., and Parrish, J. K. (2014). Next steps for citizen science. *Science, 343*(6178), 1436–1437.

Kobori H., Sakurai, R., and Kitamura, W. (2014). Designing community embracing greenery in private area: Attempts for developing green community utilizing Yokohama Green Tax through collaboration among government, district, and university. *Environment and Information Science 43*, 34–39 (in Japanese).

McKenzie-Mohr, D. (2011). *Fostering sustainable behavior: An introduction to community-based social marketing*. Gabriola Island, British Columbia: New Society Publishers.

Monroe, M. C. (2015). Working toward resolutions in resource management. In R. Kaplan and A. Basu (Eds.) *Fostering reasonableness: Supportive environments for bringing out our best* (pp. 239–259). Ann Arbor: Michigan Publishing.

Sakurai R., Kobori, H., Nakamura, M, and Kikuchi, T. (2015). Factors influencing public participation in conservation activities in urban areas: A case study in Yokohama, Japan. *Biological Conservation, 184*, 424–430.

Wals, A. E. J., and Noorduyn, L. (2010). Social learning in action: A reconstruction of an urban community moving towards sustainability. In R. Stevenson and J. Dillon (Eds). *Engaging environmental education: Learning, culture and agency* (pp. 59–76). Rotterdam: Sense Publishers.

Wals, A. E. J., and Schwarzin, L. (2012). Fostering organizational sustainability through dialogical interaction. *The Learning Organization, 19*(1), 11–27.

3

FOUR ASIAN TIGERS

Geok Chin Ivy Tan, John Chi-Kin Lee,
Tzuchau Chang, and Chankook Kim

Highlights

- Highly urbanized cities can leverage technological advancements and cross-sector collaborations to support urban environmental education.
- Four Asian cities—Singapore, Hong Kong, Taipei, and Seoul—demonstrate similarities and differences in their approaches to urban environmental education.
- Asian governments recognize urban environmental education as an important vehicle to foster environmental sensibility and responsibility in students and have implemented strong environmental educational policies.
- Schools play an important role in urban environmental education by initiating projects within the school (green roofs) and outside school compounds (green forests) and by adopting a whole-school approach (green schools).

Introduction

Rapid urbanization creates challenges as well as opportunities for urban environmental education. From the perspective of environmental education or education for sustainable development, it is important for students not only to appreciate natural beauty, but also to understand and participate in efforts to resolve local and global environmental problems as citizens and to adopt environmentally friendly lifestyles. This chapter examines innovative approaches, both within schools and across multiple sectors, to urban environmental education in the highly urbanized environments of Singapore, Hong Kong, Taipei, and Seoul.

The twentieth century marked the rise of four emerging Asian economies—Singapore, Hong Kong, Taiwan, and South Korea—the so-called "Four Asian Tigers." The four economies pursued aggressive industrialization to boost economic growth, resulting in rapid urbanization. Today their cities are faced with acute urban problems. Singapore faces a lack of natural resources as well as air pollution and a need for water conservation. Hong Kong is beset with housing shortages, high population density, and air pollution. Taipei encounters water pollution and land use conflict. Seoul experiences air pollution and problems related to municipal solid-waste management. Despite such environmental problems, all four cities strive to become greener cities. Seoul, Hong Kong, and Singapore are the only three cities in Asia, ranked 7, 8 and 10 respectively, in the 2015 top sustainable cities globally (Batten and Edward, 2015). Seoul, for example, aspires to become a city where technology is ubiquitous and facilitates residents accessing information and adopting an eco-friendly lifestyle. Hong Kong relies on technology such as smart cards as well as laws and regulations to shape citizens' behaviors. Singapore also uses technology and laws to effect positive environmental changes.

As each of these highly urbanized cities faces the complex challenges that come with development, they look to urban environmental education to foster environmental awareness and environmentally responsible behaviors. For example, all four cities have policies that mandate the inclusion of environmental education in the school curriculum, including projects that engage students in learning about the environment within the highly built-up urbanized setting. In this chapter, we present urban environmental education approaches using case examples from the Four Asian Tigers.

Approaches to Urban Environmental Education

The Four Asian Tigers use a variety of approaches to environmental education in cities. In addition to integrating environmental education into the school curriculum, these include inquiry-based field trips, technology, partnerships, and urban environmental centers. We explore each of these strategies below.

Infusing Urban Environmental Education in the School Curriculum

In Hong Kong, environmental studies/science is not a formal or independent subject in the primary and secondary school curriculum (Tsang and Lee, 2014). While some content related to sustainable development and environmental studies can be found in liberal studies, geography, and biology, the status of environmental education in the formal school curriculum remains peripheral. Despite that, schools assume an important role as sites of learning and knowledge about and for the environment. Green roofs have become a popular vehicle for school-based environmental education. A local school, for example, installed a green roof, which facilitated students learning about plants and involved student environmental ambassadors in cultivating plants (Environmental Campaign Committee, 2008). Hui (2006) suggested that green roofs have the green education potential of linking with the topics of biodiversity, building and roof construction, energy conservation, urban heat island effect, gardening, and horticulture, thus providing a bridge between theory and real life, which in turn strengthens student learning.

In Singapore, environmental education is likewise not a separate subject but rather is taught through infusion into existing subjects including geography and science (Tan, 2013). Some schools have gone further to develop specific environmental education projects or to adopt a whole-school approach. Several schools have adopted nearby green spaces (such as wetland reserves, reservoirs, and parks) and used them as outdoor classrooms and to conduct fieldwork. Other schools offer after-school activities or opportunities to work with local communities through environmental or green clubs. Being exposed to real-life situations along with mentoring by their teachers enables students to delve deeply into environmental issues and problem solving. For example, some schools embarked on the Green Audit program to promote students' awareness of resource conservation in their schools. Students calculate the schools' water and electricity usage as well as the amount of waste generated. They use their findings to suggest ways to cut down on unnecessary usage or to recycle waste (Ministry of Environment, 2002).

Taiwan passed a national Environmental Education Act in 2010, which requires school students and public servants, including the president of Taiwan, to take a minimum of four hours of environmental education courses every year. In addition, the act requires Taiwan's Environmental Protection Agency to allocate a specific fund for implementing environmental education. The quality of environmental education personnel, institutes, facilities, and centers of learning has been systematically improved in tandem with the passing of the act. It does not come as a surprise then, given the weight and importance allocated to environmental education by the government, that environmental education has been infused into Taiwan's national curriculum framework.

Similar to Hong Kong and Singapore, Taiwan encourages a whole-school approach and the development of green schools (Lee and Efird, 2014). The Green School Partnership was initiated in 1998 to encourage schools to take a whole-school approach, including implementing school-wide environmental policies, environmental management of buildings and facilities, teaching environmental topics, and attempts to instill environmental awareness in the daily lives of teachers and students. The Sustainable Campus Project, implemented in 2003, helps schools transform their campuses into models of sustainability through promoting energy efficiency, water conservation, materials recycling, and the cultivation of an ecologically healthy environment. More recently, these programs have emphasized climate change and disaster education in response to growing local and global concern.

In South Korea, the National Environmental Education Act was enacted in 2008. The importance of "Low Carbon and Green Growth" has been widely promoted to the public and in schools. This has spawned initiatives such as the implementation of "Creative Activity" as a cocurricular environmental activity in primary schools and the launch of the elective "Environment and Green Growth" in high schools (Chu and Son, 2014, p. 145). Similar to the other three countries, South Korea promotes the whole-school approach. For example, the School Forest project expands green spaces by transforming barren school grounds into environmentally friendly forests or garden areas. With more than seven hundred schools participating as model schools since 1999, this project has given students the opportunity for hands-on contact with nature in their everyday environment.

Advancing Inquiry through Field Trips

In Hong Kong, Cheng (2009) suggested that a study of environmental issues could help students explore strategies for resolving environmental problems. Cheng and Lee (2015) analyzed four types of outdoor/environmental learning activities including inquiry-based and structured learning experiences in the field, authentic outdoor learning experiences, and virtual fieldwork. They investigated the use of virtual field trips and using GIS and remote sensing complemented by field trips or field inquiry in environmental learning.

In Singapore, inquiry and investigation are also used to excite students about environmental learning. For example, the recently revised geography curriculum and assessment require students to investigate their environment and develop critical thinking skills through geographical inquiry during field trips organized by geography teachers (Tan, 2013). The geographical inquiry process requires students to formulate questions, gather data, and use reasoning to explain patterns in data collected from the field. Such inquiry skills enhance students' understanding of the dynamics of interaction between people and the environment.

Encouraging the Use of Technology in Environmental Education

Students are encouraged to use the powers of technology in their learning and to come up with creative and useful tools for the wider community. For example, in Korea, a group of high school students developed information boards about plants in a small urban park. The information boards are equipped with quick response codes or near-field communication tags; thus visitors can readily access information about the park and its plants using their smart phones. This is but one example in Korea, where the well-developed information technology sector and high-speed Internet found in cities are used to educate and promote awareness, as well as make urban areas more desirable and greener for the general public.

Promoting Cross-Sectoral Partnerships

Singapore has adopted a cross-sectoral "3-P" (People, Public, and Private) partnership strategy to promote urban environmental education. Its efforts to embed issues of recycling, energy, and water conservation into the formal curriculum are enhanced by building a network of environmental advisors from governmental and nongovernmental organizations and industries (Ministry of Environment, 2002). Other programs have been initiated to increase the public's understanding of the environment and to instill a lifelong commitment to caring for the environment. For example, the Nature Society nongovernmental organization conducts nature appreciation activities, environmental conservation projects, and surveys in partnership with schools and the public.

The Hong Kong Education Bureau also works with multiple sectors, including with the Environmental Protection Department and the Environmental Campaign Committee to run the Green School Award Scheme. Another Education Bureau partnership with the Environmental Campaign Committee operates the school Waste Separation and Recycling Scheme. Nongovernmental organizations in Hong Kong also have contributed to enhancing the public's environmental awareness through advocacy, community participation, and education (Lee, Wang, and Yang, 2013). In addition to partnerships with nongovernmental organizations, the Hong Kong Education Bureau works across school and out-of-school settings. It produced a handbook on "Education for Sustainable

Development for Primary Teachers," implements Outdoor Education Camp Schemes such as "Climatology, Geography and Ecology Study Camps" and "Science and Ecology Trips" (Education Bureau, 2013), and is launching the Student Environmental Protection Ambassador Scheme.

Establishing Environmental Education Centers and Sites

The importance of green spaces for the well-being of the individual and the collective citizenry, as well as the role of green space in environment sustainability, cannot be overestimated. This is particularly so in a modern urban city, where the quality of life is dependent on the amount and proximity to green spaces available to the populace (Ministry of Environment, 2002). Singapore is continuously seeking a pragmatic balance between development and conserving the natural environment. Hence, it has made a conscious effort to conserve existing nature preserves like the Central Catchment Nature Reserve and the Sungei Buloh Wetland Reserve. Nature preserves, parks, and park connectors, including the blue and green spaces in the Gardens by the Bay, serve as sites for environmental education activities such as exploring and investigating environmental issues (Figure 3.1).

FIGURE 3.1. In the Gardens by the Bay, Singapore, artificial supertrees act as vertical gardens and showcase sustainable urban practices related to creative design, climate regulation, water conservation, and energy generation. Credit: Alex Russ.

Similarly, government agencies and nongovernmental organizations in Taiwan and Hong Kong have built environmental education centers and programs, at places like the Hong Kong Wetland Park and Mai Po Marshes, to promote environmental learning, outdoor activities, and eco-tours for students and the general public. The Wetland Park conducts workshops to train kindergarten teachers to conduct environmental education for their students in the park. Another world-class attraction is the Hong Kong Geopark, a UNESCO-designated site, which features distinct rock formations, diverse ecological resources, and Chinese cultural villages, all of which serve as venues for environmental education activities during school field trips and for public visitors.

Conclusion

The Four Asian Tigers have all adopted measures to solidify the presence of urban environmental education in an attempt to increase environmental awareness and responsibility among their citizenry. Environmental education in Taiwan is firmly entrenched in the school curriculum as a result of strong and systematic support from the government. Schools in Hong Kong, Taiwan, and Singapore have increasingly adopted a whole-school approach to environmental education, focusing not just on facilities but also on fieldwork and other opportunities to interact with nature within and outside of school. In all four countries, schools serve as important sites of environmental education by providing opportunities for students to interact with the environment through systematic and structured programs under the guidance of their teachers.

But the isolated efforts of individual schools and teachers are not enough. What these Four Asian Tigers have shown is that the successful integration of environmental education into the national curriculum depends on a multi-pronged approach involving joint and sustained efforts by the government ministries, public and private organizations, and schools, at local, regional, and national levels. Leveraging cross-sector partnerships, technological advancements, and human capital within the city, multiple resourceful approaches to environmental education are emerging in Asian cities, which help to tackle the challenges of city life and of the highly urbanized landscape.

References

Batten, J., and Edward, C. (2015). *Sustainable cities index 2015: Balancing the economic, social and environmental needs of the world's leading cities*. Arcadis Design and Consultancy.

Cheng, M. M. H. (2009). Environmental education in context: A Hong Kong scenario. In N. Taylor, M. Littledyke, C. Eames, and R. K. Coll (Eds.), *Environmental education in context: An international perspective on the development of environmental education* (pp. 229–241). Rotterdam: Sense Publishers.

Cheng, I. N. Y., and Lee, J. C. K. (2015). Environmental and outdoor learning in Hong Kong: Theoretical and practical perspectives. In M. Robertson, G. Heath, and R. Lawrence (Eds.), *Experiencing the outdoors: Enhancing strategies for wellbeing* (pp. 135–146). Rotterdam: Sense Publishers.

Chu, H-E, and Son, Y-A. (2014). The development of environmental education policy and programs in Korea: Promoting sustainable development in school environmental education. In J. C. K. Lee and R. Efird (Eds.), *Schooling and education for sustainable development (ESD) across the Pacific* (pp. 141–157). Dordrecht: Springer.

Education Bureau, Hong Kong. (2013). *Environmental report 2013*. Hong Kong: Education Bureau.

Environmental Campaign Committee, Hong Kong. (2008). *Approved case of environmental education and community action projects 2008–2009 (Minor Works Projects)*. Hong Kong: Environmental Campaign Committee.

Hui, S. C. M. (2006). Benefits and potential applications of green roof systems in Hong Kong. In Proceedings of the 2nd Megacities International Conference 2006, December 1–2, pp. 351–360.

Lee, J. C. K., and Efird, R. (2014). Introduction: Schooling and education for sustainable development (ESD) across the Pacific. In J. C. K. Lee and R. Efird (Eds.), *Schooling and education for sustainable development (ESD) across the Pacific* (pp. 3–36). Dordrecht: Springer.

Lee, J. C. K., Wang, S. M., and Yang, G. (2013). EE policies in three Chinese communities: Challenges and prospects for future development. In R. B. Stevenson, M. Brody, J. Dillon, and A. E. J. Wals (Eds.), *International handbook of research on environmental education* (pp. 178–188). New York: Routledge/AERA.

Ministry of Environment, Singapore. (2002). *The Singapore Green Plan 2012: Beyond clean and green, towards environmental sustainability*. Singapore: Ministry of Environment.

Tan, G. C. I. (2013). Changing perspectives of geographical education in Singapore: Staying responsive and relevant. *Journal of Geographical Research, 59*, 63–74.

Tsang, P. K., and Lee, J. C. K. (2014). ESD projects, initiatives and research in Hong Kong and Mainland China. In J. C. K. Lee and R. Efird (Eds.), *Schooling and education for sustainable development (ESD) across the Pacific* (pp. 203–221). Dordrecht: Springer.

4

CITIES AS OPPORTUNITIES

Daniel Fonseca de Andrade, Soul Shava,
and Sanskriti Menon

Highlights

- Whereas multidimensional social and environmental problems have similarities around the world, different countries and cities afford different conditions and opportunities to address them.
- Cities in the Global South integrate into environmental narratives aspects of their colonial histories and decolonizing viewpoints, which are reflected in educational practices.
- Environmental education in cities of the Global South reflects how people construct perspectives and narratives to frame and address social and environmental issues, and it provides models for other countries seeking to simultaneously address environmental and social justice.

Introduction

People in cities are immersed in multidimensional environments where social, political, and economic issues cannot be separated from issues such as pollution and waste. Moreover, city inhabitants directly experience small changes in their environment. As a consequence, cities are perfect arenas for people to perceive the complexity of environmental problems and to put into practice and reflect upon local innovations to address those problems. Cities are also places where "tribes" meet. The diversity of cultures, religions, ethnicities, classes, and other "indicators of difference" pose opportunities and challenges related to understanding historical and current environmental conditions and what needs to be done to improve environments and communities.

Cities vary widely around the globe in terms of size, infrastructure, and complexity. Although a common set of environmental problems define modern global cities (e.g., air and water pollution, waste accumulation, car-centrism, limited green space), residents of different cities hold different values about such issues and have different ways to address them. Thus, defining environmental priorities and the "right" ways to tackle them differs among cities.

Now is a moment to broaden our concept of what kinds of lives can be lived in cities. The Global South provides opportunities to do just that. In particular, cities in the Global South offer an opportunity to address the question: What contributions can non-Western cultures offer in terms of wisdom and technical solutions to urban planning to foster individual, social, and environmental health? This chapter addresses the notion of "cities as opportunities." It is not written based on any specific city. Rather, it draws on urban experiences lived in the broader geopolitical context of the Global South.

The Global South

Cities of the Global South bring to the environmental equation issues specifically related to our colonial experiences and to our decolonial standpoint, that is, to our "roles" in the globalized world. When the "global" environmental movement erupted in the 1960s as opposition to industrialization and its negative environmental effects, it was met and mixed with other struggles pertinent to different realities in the Global South: struggles against colonial dictatorial governments, against social injustice, and against the creation and maintenance of poverty. So while some fought for the rights of trees, others contested changing regulations on rights to access, control, and use nature (Sethi, 1993). While some demanded the right to breathe purer air, others focused their attention on the underlying crisis of development and democracy (Wignaraja, 1993). As a result, environmental education in the Global South has tended to be politically laden, and themes such as colonialism, racism, environmental rights, poverty, and social injustice are necessarily implicated in our environmental education practices.

Santos (2002) argues that the Western project of civilization is totalitarian, that is, it does not allow exceptions in possibilities for ways of life. So anything that is not Euro-centered is seen as worse or wrong and should "evolve," "modernize," or "progress." As a result, a skewed and incomplete process of homogenization is underway.

In contrast, environmental education in cities of the Global South reflects local people's perspectives on environmental issues and how they construct narratives to frame and address these issues. This construction demands a deconstruction of the hegemonic Western epistemological biases on which our colonial educational and social systems are built. The colonialist role played by modern science (and modern rationality) in the legitimation of Western domination over other peoples and nature has been acknowledged by scholars (Shiva, 1998; Leff, 2006). There is a need to transcend this colonial and colonizing hegemony by posing challenging epistemological questions such as: What kind of knowledge is legitimate? How is it constructed, owned, and shared?

Ecology of Knowledge in Cities of the Global South

The overlap of biophysical, social, economic, political, and ethical issues and the diversity of social and ethnic backgrounds allow cities in the Global South to address complex questions like those above. People in the Global South have opportunities to define what kinds of cities we want to have and to rely on our cultural diversity to deliberate, develop, and implement solutions. Basically, we are in the advantageous position to learn from Western historical paths and their negative environmental consequences and to create our own alternative development pathways. By fostering an "ecology of knowledge" (Santos, 2002, p. 250), we can provide opportunities not only to creatively assess cities' problems and possible solutions, but also to bring into the process an underlying culture of respect for diversity and democracy. Generating an ecology of knowledge entails the legitimization of nonmainstream cultures' worldviews and narratives, and also the creation of conditions so that diversity can build overarching respect. This means valuing the knowledge of "the other" for its worth. Moreover, it entails the acknowledgment of one's partial view of reality.

For environmental education this presents an enormous opportunity. Promoting and mediating processes of dialogue around social-environmental issues, and recognizing the power of framing such issues through diverse lenses, put learners face-to-face with the complexity of urban environmental issues and the inadequacy of quick fixes and standardized, one-sided, imposed narratives. This can give rise to collective innovative outlooks, meanings, and ideas.

One approach found in the Global South is linking environmental education to other social movements. Are there, for example, connections between environmental education in cities and the housing movement? How might women's movements and environmental education converge? Are our perceptions changed when we see the issues around sustainability through the eyes of ethnic minority rights movements. A hybrid approach between environmental education and other urban social movements can transform educational discourses and practices and bring contextual relevance and legitimacy. It can also enable environmental education to expand its scale and reach.

This perspective also brings to environmental education an emancipatory element. By looking at where people live and how they view their problems, educators can help audiences reorganize priorities set out in general educational guidelines and acknowledge that one cannot formulate priorities by decree. It enables us to realize that a locality can create its own perceptions and narratives as well as strategies to address them. This is the heart of the idea of "sociology of absences" and "ecology of knowledge"; that is, localities create their own epistemologies and validate their own knowledge. This is being done in many cities in the Global South; we present examples from three countries—South Africa, Brazil, and India—below.

Urban Environmental Education in Southern Africa

Environmental crises in southern Africa are driving the integration of environmental issues into primary and secondary school and university curricula. In South Africa, emerging national programs such as Fundisa for Change support the teaching of contextualized environmental content through in-service training of teacher educators and teachers and through curriculum development. At a recent Fundisa for Change symposium, environmental education researchers and practitioners explored questions such as: How does environmental knowledge get repackaged as it moves from scientists to official documents, to government officials in the Department of Basic Education, to teacher training and textbooks, and finally to students in classrooms? Where does indigenous knowledge fit in a system where curriculum disciplines have been masquerading as neutral, unlocated, disembodied, and universal?

Efforts also are ongoing in the informal and nonformal education sectors. For example, to promote conservation of southern Africa's high numbers of endemic species, urban zoos and botanical gardens include environmental education centers that provide educational tours and learning materials focused on biodiversity and its conservation, including in the city (Figure 4.1). One such effort is Gold Fields Environmental Education Centre at the Kirstenbosch National Botanical

FIGURE 4.1. Gold Fields Environmental Education Centre at the Kirstenbosch National Botanical Gardens in Cape Town, South Africa, provides educational programs on biodiversity, global warming, biomes, and other topics. Credit: Alex Russ.

Gardens in Cape Town, which provides educational programs on biodiversity, global warming, biomes, and related topics, with an emphasis on the endemic Cape Town floristic kingdom.

Other organizations support the establishment of food gardens in urban schools and communities by providing plants and necessary expertise. The transformation of school grounds into thriving food and herb gardens provides an opportunity not only for learning but also for providing fresh foods to food-insecure students and their families. Implementation of sustainability practices across entire schools creates additional opportunities for teaching and learning. Whole-school initiatives include such activities as water-wise indigenous gardening, recycling, and energy and water saving.

In southern Africa, urban community gardening, recycling, and similar projects support livelihood subsistence within high-density residential areas while simultaneously developing a culture of environmental citizenry in the face of inadequate waste disposal, pollution, and disused land. Numerous waste recycling and reuse entrepreneurship opportunities are emerging, for example, the recycling of organic materials and used oil from fast-food restaurants. Several organizations are exploring green office buildings characterized by solar energy, plants integrated into the office, and paperless and travelless meetings. Such green design infrastructure provides learning opportunities for the commercial and industrial sectors. Finally, national and municipal governments, universities, nongovernmental organizations, and industry in southern African cities are forming networks that collectively address local governance and management challenges. Some have even become ongoing communities of practice formalized under the United Nations Regional Centres of Expertise (Westin et al., 2012/2013).

Urban Environmental Education in Brazil

Over the past two decades, Brazil has come to the realization that the current state of the environment is too dire for environmental education to be carried out as individual initiatives. As a consequence, national and city governments are converging their efforts to incorporate environmental education into government policy. Environmental education public policies increase the chances of the universality, permanence, and implementation of these educational programs, and thus that they will successfully address social-environmental problems (Andrade et al., 2014).

The innovative character of such efforts lies in how such policies are created. With the aim to design strategies that are socially and environmentally relevant to a locality and legitimate for educators, this process involves ongoing dialogue among policy makers and educators. Cities have created Environmental Education Inter-institutional Commissions composed of diverse actors to design local laws and plans for environmental education. What is interesting is that the very process of designing the policy becomes a formative exercise; it incorporates the principles and methods that will be put forth by the policy, such as dialogue, participation, democracy, and political involvement. This opens up institutional rituals to new actors, values, and realities. Social-environmental themes, problems, and narratives "absent" (cf. Santos, 2002) in hegemonic meta-narratives emerge and are acknowledged as legitimate, replacing traditional one-size-fits-all environmental educational "kits" that circulate worldwide.

The process of participating in such commissions is extremely challenging within an authoritarian, elitist, normative, and unjust culture such as that which prevails in Brazilian cities (Figure 4.2). Yet this in itself provides educational opportunities. The exercise of being with the "other" and acknowledging their narratives and mindsets is critical anywhere where populations are culturally and socially diverse. In Brazil, this process is generating new variables to be incorporated into the "normal" social-environmental discourse. Emissions, waste, and disasters are words that are slowly mixing with rights, (in)justice, racism, and sexism, shifting perceptions of the roots of social-environmental problems and related educational approaches. Approaches to integrating these and other "non-traditional" environmental education variables is an enormous opportunity that cities in the Global South offer to educators and to environmental education

FIGURE 4.2. In Rio de Janeiro, people living in richer parts of the city experience drastically different social and ecological conditions and environmental justice issues compared with people in favelas. Credit: Alex Russ.

practices more broadly. This is particularly important as Western cities themselves grow more diverse and residents face increasing poverty and exclusion.

Urban Environmental Education in India

In India, the complexity of civic issues and the struggles of marginalized groups are recognized as part of the context for urban environmental education. One environmental education strand has focused on strengthening inclusive participatory democratic governance while grappling with challenges to participation such as illiteracy, socioeconomic disparity, structural divisions, and cultural biases. For example, since 2006 in the city of Pune, Maharashtra, citizens can submit suggestions for development works as part of a participatory budgeting process (Menon, Madhale, and Amarnath, 2013). Education supporting this process has focused on advocating for the benefits of participatory approaches to decision making, training community facilitators, and developing methods for conducting fair participatory processes.

Urban environmental education in India also recognizes the challenge of choosing systems and technologies that are just and locally relevant and do not perpetuate urban planning models now recognized as unsustainable, such as sprawl caused by car-oriented transportation. Fortunately, imagining such a lifestyle is a powerful attraction and within reach for a growing middle class. An example of this approach is the school outreach program that accompanied the development of the Rainbow Bus Rapid Transit in Pune. The program helped students understand not only the impacts of private-vehicle-oriented urban transportation, but also the rights of hawkers, pedestrians, and cyclists, and that creating quality transportation infrastructure for everyone is the better choice.

Pune has also seen social movements, including for women's education, caste equality, and workers' rights. Drawing on this history, in the early 1990s Shreemati Nathibai Damodar Thackersey Women's University initiated a process of organizing the urban poor, primarily women, engaged in waste picking (Chikarmane, 2012). The waste pickers were retrieving recyclable materials and wastes from neighborhood waste receptacles in physically hazardous conditions and experienced harassment by the police and prejudices of caste and class. Further, the municipal waste system was ineffective, as it transported mixed waste to a dumpsite outside the city. The university intervened to form a waste pickers' union, called the Kagad Kach Patra Kashtakari Panchayat. The union has worked with the city government, local environmental organizations, and citizens' groups to evolve a waste-management strategy focused on collection of source-segregated waste materials (which are cleaner and safer for the waste collectors to handle), composting, and biogas plants. With support from the city government, a waste collectors' cooperative was formed to provide services for doorstep collection of household waste. Everyone benefits, as the city is cleaner with an improved waste-collection service, materials are recycled, decentralized recycling and waste processing incurs lower environmental and economic costs, and the workers have better work conditions.

The environmental education work undertaken by the union, the university, and associated organizations has been predicated on the rights of the waste picker women as well as a comprehensive understanding of solid waste management and the materials recycling economy. The educational effort has occurred at multiple levels: deliberations with citizens to help them understand source segregation of waste and accept waste picker women as formal waste collectors, with the municipal government to develop appropriate waste-management systems, and with the waste picker women to organize and negotiate for their right to work in dignity and safety.

Conclusion

Cities in the Global South incorporate perspectives and practices that reflect biophysical, social, economic, political, and ethical aspects of their colonial histories. Their responses to environmental issues reflect their decolonial roles as well as the diversity of cultures and ethnicities that bring different outlooks, values, and interests in addressing environmental problems. Thus an important role for urban environmental educators in the Global South is to integrate this colonial history and diversity in the framing, understanding, and dealing with contextual environmental issues.

In this chapter, we have described three initiatives that carry out this integration. Southern African cities are infusing questions about types of knowledge in environmental education in formal, nonformal, and informal education settings. In Brazil, urban environmental injustice is being tackled through the formation of municipal participatory commissions, where educators and other actors actively influence public policies. And in Pune, India, improving waste pickers' lives and work conditions creates opportunities for environmental learning. What these initiatives imply is that environmental problems are not "neutral" but rather are historical legacies, and are not only objective but also subjective and intersubjective. The intensity of colonial legacies and environmental problems in cities in the Global South is staggering, but it also makes them "cities as opportunities" for environmental education and urban sustainability.

References

Andrade, D. F., Luca, A. Q., Castellano, M., Güntzel-Rissato, C., and Sorrentino, M. (2014). Da pedagogia à política e da política à pedagogia: Uma abordagem sobre a construção de políticas públicas em educação ambiental no Brasil. *Ciência & Educação, 20*(4), 817–832.

Chikarmane, P. (2012). *Integrating waste pickers into municipal solid waste management in Pune, India*, Series: WIEGO Policy Brief (Urban Policies), No 8.

Leff, E. (2006). *Racionalidade ambiental: A reapropriação social da natureza*. Rio de Janeiro: Civilização Brasileira.

Menon, S., Madhale, A., and Amarnath. (2013). *Participatory budgeting in Pune: A critical review*. Pune, India: Centre for Environment Education.

Santos, B. S. (2002). Para uma sociologia das ausências e uma sociologia das emergências. *Revista Crítica de Ciências Sociais, 63*, 237–280.

Sethi, H. (1993). Survival and democracy: Ecological struggles in India. In P. Wignaraja (Ed). *New social movements in the South: Empowering the people* (pp. 122–148). London: Zed Books.

Shiva, V. (1998). Western science and its destruction of local knowledge. In M. Rahnema and V. Bawtree (Eds). *The post-development reader* (pp. 161–167). London: Zed Books.

Westin, M., Hellquist, A., Kronlid, D. O., and Colvin, J. (2012/2013). Towards urban sustainability: Learning from the design of a programme for multi-stakeholder collaboration. *Southern African Journal of Environmental Education, 29*, 39–57.

Wignaraja, P. (1993). Rethinking development and democracy. In P. Wignaraja (Ed.). *New social movements in the South: Empowering the people* (pp. 4–35). London: Zed Books.

Part II
THEORETICAL UNDERPINNINGS

5

CRITICAL ENVIRONMENTAL EDUCATION

Robert B. Stevenson, Arjen E. J. Wals,
Joe E. Heimlich, and Ellen Field

Highlights

- Over time, environmental education has evolved from a focus on nature conservation and ecological literacy to changing environmental behavior, and most recently, toward bringing multiple groups in society together around wicked sustainability issues.
- Increasing people's environmental knowledge, understanding, and awareness does not necessarily lead to them changing their environmental behavior.
- Contemporary urban environmental education engages different sectors of society in sustainability issues of food, water, energy, biodiversity, and health, and it creates spaces for meaningful interaction and learning that require the integration of different disciplines, perspectives, interests, and values.
- Ecologies of learning call for blending formal, nonformal, and informal learning, as well as utilizing multimedia information, communications technologies, and place-based forms of education.

Introduction

This chapter first outlines the historical development of environmental education, from developing awareness and understanding of the natural environment and its management, through communicating information about and solving environmental problems, to critical thinking about issues of quality of life and human-nature interrelationships, and finally developing capacity for integrating environmentally, socially, and economically sustainable development. These theoretical positions are reflected in different approaches to urban environmental issues. Traditional approaches taken by city councils assume that providing information to urban citizens through public service announcements, educational brochures, and websites will increase environmental knowledge and thereby result in the adoption of pro-environmental attitudes and, in turn, changes in individual behaviors (Zint and Wolske, 2014). An alternative socially critical perspective on environmental education, which is the focus of this chapter, emphasizes the influence of cultural norms and structural features of society on people's environmental actions and the need for participatory approaches that engage citizens in creating and determining appropriate actions to realize their own vision of a sustainable urban environment. Emerging learning spaces, or so-called "ecologies of learning," are described that engage urban citizens, young and old, in participatory collaborative activities such as community gardening, critical place-based education in urban schools, and social media environmental interest networks.

A Brief History of Environmental Education

The origins or roots of environmental education can be traced back more than a century to nature and outdoor study, the primary goal of which was to develop an understanding and appreciation of the natural environment through first-hand observations in the field. Conservation education followed with a focus on the preservation and management of natural resources, including native flora, fauna, and their habitats. An outdoor education movement emerged after World War II in Europe and North America, especially in the more urban areas as a reaction to urbanization and increasing loss of immediate access to natural areas, which led to the creation of the outdoor school or land lab. The field of environmental education came into its own alongside the 1960s and early 1970s environmental movement, which brought attention not only to the depletion of natural resources, but also to the problems of population growth and the degradation of air, land, and water (Gough, 2013). The environmental movement, however, was criticized for ignoring the problems of the urban environment in which many people lived. Education of children and adults about these problems was seen as vital for creating an enlightened citizenry, but generally with an emphasis limited to knowledge of the biophysical environment and environmental policies.

An acknowledgment of the need for urban environmental education emerged from UNESCO-sponsored intergovernmental conferences and workshops beginning in the late 1970s, which produced a series of influential policy statements that broadened the concept of environment beyond the natural to encompass the urban and built environment, and beyond biophysical factors to include social, cultural, economic, and political dimensions. These policies also emphasized that environmental education should engage students in critical thinking, problem solving, and decision making in relation to quality-of-life issues and in actively working toward the resolution of environmental problems. In the late 1980s, a new language and discourse—or slogan according to some—of sustainable development emerged in international policy circles suggesting the need for a "triple bottom line" integrating or balancing environmental, sociocultural, and economic considerations in future development. Despite concerns about the fuzziness of this foundational concept, it gave rise to education for sustainable development; in many countries the preferred terms later became education for sustainability, sustainability education, and, more recently, environmental and sustainability education.

Conceptual Thinking

Theory, research, and practice up until the mid-1980s all focused on the perceived ultimate goal of environmental education, especially in the United States, as being the development of responsible environmental behavior. Much of this early research and much current education and communication practice assumed a linear relationship, that is, that developing appropriate environmental awareness, knowledge, and attitudes would directly lead to changing individual behaviors. City councils adopted this approach for changing urban citizens' behaviors. In time, however, researchers recognized that changing behaviors was not a simple linear process.

Further, the arbitrary separation of cognition from affect and emotion in learning is challenged when we add intention and motivation for attempting, practicing, or ending a behavior. Learning, especially outside the formal schooling system, blurs distinctions among thought, ideas, facts, values, passions, and beliefs, and it entails understanding how an individual makes meaning from all his or her sources of information and emotion. The ancient Greek concept of conation already suggested that behaviors are guided by the blend of an individual's unique framing of what they know, feel, and then, as a result, intend to do.

Recent theory and research centered on the goal of fostering pro-environmental behaviors and actions have gone beyond an individual focus to acknowledge the importance of collective action (Gough, 2013) in transitioning to sustainable cities. Collective action is considered to be necessary when two conditions occur: (1) the negative effects of the issue are widespread and (2) extreme adverse outcomes could be reduced if many participants at a variety of levels take action (Ostrom, 2010). Collective action via the Internet is also important in considering how individuals can inspire the collective (Postmes and Brunsting, 2002) and in exploring the role of social movements in addressing environmental issues (Rydin and Pennington, 2010).

From the late 1980s, a group of mainly Australian scholars argued not only that institutional arrangements and wider social structures influence individual behavioral choices, but also that education systems continue to reproduce and maintain rather than question and transform current social conditions (e.g., passive consumerism), and they do little to foster a critical consciousness of social-ecological issues. An alternative socially critical approach to environmental education advocated engaging students in issue- or problem-based inquiries, including inquiries into the influence of cultural and structural features of society (e.g., prioritizing of economic concerns) on people's positions and actions related to human-environment relationships (Fien, 1993; Robottom, 1987). These inquiries were intended first to develop students' critical and analytical thinking about the values, interests, and ideologies involved in particular positions on a local or global social-ecological issue. Further, this approach emphasizes building decision-making and action capacity through deep engagement, reflection, and working individually and collectively toward (re)solutions of local issues. Within cities, this means that the urban governing structures should model and reflect multiple perspectives and provide avenues for residents to become engaged in addressing local problems. Related action inquiry approaches emerged in the United States, South Africa, Canada, and, most notably, in Denmark in the form of action competence (Jensen and Schnack, 1997), while similar critical and conscientization (the process of developing a critical awareness of one's social reality through reflection and action) orientations to environmental education stemming from the work of Paulo Freire took hold in Mexico (e.g., the work of Edgar González-Gaudiano) and Brazil (e.g., the work of Moacir Gadotti). (See chapter 18.)

The socially critical perspective calling for participation is particularly relevant when trying to engage citizens in sustainability challenges. Science and society increasingly recognize that we now need to better address urgent and wicked sustainability issues such as climate change, species extinction, rising inequity, and increased toxicity of water, soil, air, and living bodies. Urban populations in low-elevation coastal zones are vulnerable to sea-level rise, stronger storms, and other coastal hazards induced by climate change (130 countries have their largest urban populations in low-elevation coastal zones) (McGranahan, Balk, and Anderson, 2007). These issues can be seen as manifestations of "global systemic dysfunction" that cannot be dealt with from a single perspective. Their complexity requires the engagement of multiple stakeholders holding different perspectives and understandings of what it means and takes to become sustainable. Addressing wicked sustainability issues like climate change calls for forms of education and governance that create new spaces for collaborative and social learning; at times these spaces will need to be "disruptive" to break away from unsustainable routines and vested powers and interests that are not serving the well-being of people and planet (e.g., Hopkins, 2013).

New Spaces and Partnerships for Environmental Learning in Urban Communities

Given that moving toward sustainable cities demands creative engagement in emergent change, new learning approaches and ways of organizing learning that might contribute to the transformation of unsustainable urban systems, values, and routines are needed. One way to begin is to take locally relevant urban sustainability issues as a starting point for education and learning, advancing integrative ways of thinking, and engaging learners in change and transformation. Doing so calls for a different way of designing spaces for learning, or ecologies of learning arenas, that allow not only for boundary crossing between different disciplines, perspectives, interests, and values, but also blending formal, nonformal, and informal forms of learning, both virtual and real.

We see plenty of examples where such new ways of learning embedded within socially critical participatory approaches are being supported and developed. In recent decades, opportunities for intergenerational environmental learning through the creation of local partnerships have expanded with the considerable growth in popularity of community gardens in urban areas, especially in North America, where abandoned vacant lots have been used as sites for multigenerational, cultural, and science learning and action (Krasny et al., 2013). Further, school gardens that produce fresh locally grown food have been shown to have a range of educational, environmental, health, and social benefits for children, citizens, and communities (Bell and Dyment, 2008). Often such initiatives represent forms of resistance to limited availability of affordable fresh and healthy food in neighborhoods. Besides contributing to a sense of community, improving participants' health through increased vegetable consumption and exercise, and reducing reliance on fossil fuels for transporting food from rural farms, urban gardeners learn about the source of their food as well as engage in intergenerational sharing of knowledge of food production. In Edible School Gardens and similar projects, schoolchildren grow their own food in an educational garden they have designed with the support of local government, businesses, and community organizations, while simultaneously inquiring into and learning about food production, different foods, and nutrition.

Much of this type of learning can be considered place-based. Place-based education, which involves grounding at least part of citizens' learning in the local, offers a particularly useful approach to urban environmental education. What aspects of the local and place are important for engaging learners? Although the "local" is now interconnected with the regional and the global, the local community is the scale at which people's well-being is often determined. The biogeographical and sociocultural boundaries of place need to be considered as teaching and learning is defined and practiced within a place-based approach. Such education can help increase students' engagement in and understanding of their local community as well as potentially "have some direct bearing on the well-being of the social and ecological places people actually inhabit" (Gruenewald, 2003, p. 7).

Expeditionary Learning, a school reform and curriculum framework based on the educational values and beliefs of Outward Bound, is one place-based approach in U.S. cities that is compatible with socially critical issue- and inquiry-based environmental education. The focus is on project- or problem-based learning expeditions into the community, where students engage in interdisciplinary, in-depth group investigations of real-world urban issues. Students pose questions such as what is the nature, extent, and cause of poverty in their neighborhood, collect and analyze data, debate ideas about how the well-being and environment of groups living in poverty might be improved, propose plans or design experiments to improve the social and environmental conditions of local disadvantaged citizens, and create artifacts to communicate their ideas and findings to others (Blumenfeld, et al., 1991). Learning occurs through discovery, inquiry, critical thinking, problem solving, and collaboration.

Social media is another participatory space that has been identified as having capacity-building potential for environmental learning and activism. Popular social networking sites like Facebook and Twitter are used by youths to find others who share similar interests and concerns about environmental sustainability issues, especially when environmental extracurricular groups are not offered in their local school context or when their peers do not share their environmental ethic. In part, social networking sites facilitate meeting like-minded others due to the ease with which identity is constructed and shared through creating a profile, curating photos and information, and posting updates, which allow individuals to share their ideas and values. Facebook allows individuals to create and join interest groups focused on a specific issue or for a specific neighborhood in an urban context. These groups can create new relationships among residents, inform individuals about locally relevant issues, and provide avenues for organizing or taking action around the specific issue. A Facebook group called "Make A Change!" has engaged residents in the city of Port Moresby, Papua New Guinea, in discussions about plastic bag bans, ways to improve waste management, and hands-on beach cleanups. While the group is administered by a young woman under twenty-five years of age, members of multiple generations engage in critical online dialogue about their points of views and ideas on addressing these local issues. Due to the ease of access, ability to meet like-minded others, create focused interest groups, and critically exchange perspectives and ideas, social media sites are important spaces for individuals to build capacity for and direct their own environmental sustainability learning and action. Finally, information and communications-technologies-supported citizen science can also play a critical role in urban environmental and sustainability education, by building citizens' capacity to monitor and share their own data about the quality of their local environment and to use their own science to bring about social-ecological improvements (Wals et al., 2014).

Conclusion

To facilitate urban environmental education able to address wicked sustainability challenges, governments need to stimulate and support "learning ecologies" that blur the boundaries between science and society. Such learning ecologies require that education, research, civil society, the local government, and the private sector find ways to work together on common urban sustainability challenges. In order to create more sustainable urban communities, a blended approach is needed that creates synergy between teaching and learning, thinking and doing, the virtual and the real, improvements and transitions, and school and community, and that facilitates deep learning that not only expands people's knowledge and understanding about wicked sustainability issues but also touches their values, sense of place, and feelings of responsibility. Urban environmental educators can play a role in brokering these collaborations and designing spaces for joint learning.

References

Bell, A., and Dyment, J. (2008). Grounds for health: The intersection of green school grounds and health-promoting schools. *Environmental Education Research, 14*(1), 77–90.

Blumenfeld , P. C., Soloway, E., Marx , R. W., Krajcik, J. S., Guzdial, M., and Palincsar, A. (1991). Motivating project-based learning: Sustaining the doing, supporting the learning. *Educational Psychologist, 26*(3–4), 369–398.

Fien, J. (1993). *Education for the environment: Critical curriculum theorizing and environmental education.* Geelong, Vic., Australia: Deakin University Press.

Gough, A. (2013). The emergence of environmental education research: A "history" of the field. In R. B. Stevenson, M. Brody, J. Dillon, and A. E. J. Wals (Eds.), *International handbook of research on environmental education* (pp. 13–22). New York: Routledge/AERA.

Gruenewald, D. A. (2003). The best of both worlds: A critical pedagogy of place. *Educational Researcher, 32*(4), 3–12.

Hopkins, R. (2013). *The power of just doing stuff: How local action can change the world.* Cambridge: Transition Books.

Jensen, B., and Schnack, K. (1997). The action competence approach in environmental education. *Environmental Education Research, 3*(2), 163–178.

Krasny, M. E., Lundholm, C., Shava, S., Lee, E., and Kobori, H. (2013). Urban landscapes as learning arenas for biodiversity and ecosystem services management. In T. Elmqvist, M. Fragkias, J. Goodness, et al. (Eds.), *Urbanization, biodiversity and ecosystem services: Challenges and opportunities: A global assessment* (pp. 629–664). Dordrecht: Springer.

McGranahan, G., Balk, D., and Anderson, B. (2007). The rising tide: Assessing the risks of climate change and human settlements in low elevation coastal zones. *Environment and Urbanization, 19*, 17–37.

Ostrom, E. (2010). Polycentric systems for coping with collective action and global environmental change. *Global Environmental Change, 20*(4), 550–557.

Postmes, T., and Brunsting, S. (2002). Collective action in the age of the internet: Mass communication and online mobilization. *Social Science Computer Review, 20*(3), 290–301.

Robottom, I. (Ed.). (1987). *Environmental education: Practice and possibility.* Geelong, Vic., Australia: Deakin University Press.

Rydin, Y., and Pennington, M. (2010). Public participation and local environmental planning: The collective action problem and the potential of social capital. *Local Environment, 5*(2), 153–169.

Wals, A. E. J., Brody, M., Dillon, J., and Stevenson, R. B. (2014). Convergence between science and environmental education. *Science, 344*(6184), 583–584.

Zint, M., and Wolske, K. S. (2014). From information provision to participatory deliberation: Engaging residents in the transition toward sustainable cities. In D. Mazmanian and H. Blanco (Eds.), *Elgar companion to sustainable cities: Strategies, methods and outlook* (pp. 188–209). Northampton, Mass.: Edward Elgar Publishing.

6

ENVIRONMENTAL JUSTICE

Marcia McKenzie, Jada Renee Koushik,
Randolph Haluza-DeLay,
Belinda Chin, and Jason Corwin

Highlights

- Education programs focusing on environmental justice address how individuals and communities experience unequal privileges and repercussions in relation to the environment.
- Urban environmental education explicitly engages with environmental justice through topics such as disparities in access to nature and ecosystem services and in exposure to industrial pollution and other environmental risks, as well as impacts of gentrification.
- Approaches to address injustice include food sovereignty, political mobilization, and climate justice.
- Urban environmental education that integrates environmental justice can help participants construct, critique, and transform our cities in more just and sustainable ways.

Introduction

This chapter outlines the importance of environmental justice and issues of equity within urban environmental education. Environmental justice refers to mobilization in response to the fact that environmental hazards disproportionately affect some groups more than others, with environmental benefits also being disproportionately collected (Bullard, 1993; Haluza-DeLay, 2013). It is concerned with how environmental issues and benefits are related to social class, ability, gender, sexuality, race, ethnicity, colonization, globalization, and anthropocentrism. This chapter outlines a brief history of the environmental justice movement, considers its importance and uptake in urban environmental education, and closes with three case studies illustrating educational responses to environmental injustice in cities.

Environmental Justice: A Brief History

In the early 1970s, a number of high-profile incidents led to a growing understanding that environmentally hazardous sites were disproportionately located in or affecting communities of color and low-income communities in the United States, including African American, Latino, and Indigenous communities (Brulle and Pellow, 2006). The environmental justice movement was ignited by the siting of a toxic waste dump in the primarily African American city of Afton in Warren County, North Carolina, in 1978 (Gosine and Teelucksingh, 2008). Soil contaminated with polychlorinated biphenyls as a result of illegal roadside discharge was being transported across the state to be buried in Warren County, the poorest county in the state. Working with activists and church officials, the residents of Warren County petitioned for media coverage, organized protests, and lobbied politicians and members of the Congressional Black Caucus to oppose the siting of the toxic waste dump in their community (Gosine and Teelucksingh, 2008). Another early incident that gained media attention was "Love Canal," where toxic chemicals entered groundwater in a working-class community in Niagara Falls, New York, causing birth defects, miscarriages, and other health issues and resulting in legal action.

As federal environmental regulations became more stringent in the late 1980s and early 1990s, corporations began targeting Indigenous lands, with their quasi-sovereign status, for dumping of garbage and hazardous waste (Bullard, 1993). Many companies also were able to bypass stricter federal regulations and gain approval for dumping at the state level, illuminating how environmental inequality is enabled by political processes (Brulle and Pellow, 2006). Similar historical trends of poor communities being targeted for dumping are found in other countries around the world, as well as practices where wealthier nations transport their wastes to dump in poorer countries.

As work in environmental justice has expanded to examine additional forms of social inequity, a number of new approaches have been introduced, including ecofeminism, ecojustice, and just sustainabilities (Agyeman, 2003). Recent work considers who is welcomed and feels safe on the land based on gender, sexuality, race, ability, or other social categories. Related scholarship, such as settler colonial studies, has drawn attention to how Indigenous land in North America and other parts of the globe has been taken through European settlement and colonization (Coulthard, 2014). Turning Indigenous land into property for settlement and the associated displacement and genocide of Indigenous peoples is ongoing in North America and elsewhere, including through resource-extraction policies and practices. Current examples of environmental injustices include the significant negative health impacts of tar sands development on Indigenous communities in Alberta and Saskatchewan in Canada (Thomas-Muller, 2008), the effects of climate change on coastal communities, and how those living in poverty and poor nations are most vulnerable to associated rising sea levels and extreme weather events. Further, poor farmers in Africa and elsewhere are negatively impacted by extensive "land grabs" by international corporations and national governments. The linking of social inequities and environmental issues is tightly connected to place, including who has safe access or who is being displaced or marginalized in relation to land.

Environmental Justice and Environmental Education

Increasingly, environmental education is explicitly engaging with environmental justice issues via approaches that acknowledge and address how individuals and communities have unequal privileges and repercussions in relation to the environment. For example, Indigenous scholars and allies have engaged with questions of Indigeneity, colonialism, and racism in relation to environmental education (Tuck, McKenzie, and McCoy, 2014), including in cities (Corwin, 2016). Environmental education scholars have also focused on anthropocentrism and animal studies or have examined various aspects of power relations between humans and other species and to a lesser extent race, gender, ability, and sexuality (e.g., Agyeman, 2003; Newberry, 2003; Russell, Sarick, and Kennelly, 2002). Some approaches emphasize how multiple social and environmental inequities intersect and are interwoven with each other (Maina, Koushik, and Wilson, in press).

An assessment of popular environmental education curricula, such as those of Project Wild and the World Wildlife Fund, revealed little focus on environmental justice in the 224 lesson plans reviewed (Kushmerick, Young, and Stein, 2007). The researchers suggested, however, that many lessons in these curricula could be easily adapted to include an environmental justice focus. Particularly relevant were lessons about environmental health, which could include a focus on how health in marginalized communities is disproportionately affected by environmental issues (Brulle and Pellow, 2006). Additional examples for possible inclusion of an environmental justice focus included lessons on sustainable futures (intergenerational equity) and energy production from wastes (sociodemographic and spatial distributional inequity).

Indigenous and decolonizing approaches to education also offer promising directions for urban environmental education that engages with environmental justice issues. Indigenous theories and practice understand the land as encompassing all of the Earth, including the urban (Tuck, McKenzie, and McCoy, 2014). Colonial settler narratives of land as property and as involving unjust treatment of Indigenous communities can be questioned and disrupted by connecting students and educators to the land. Educators and students can utilize opportunities afforded by land education to question educational practices and theories that normalize settler occupation of land and pathologize Indigenous communities (Bang et al., 2014). Indigenous educators are increasingly engaging urban land-based education in supporting Indigenous identity. Three case studies described below illustrate how urban environmental education can incorporate these issues.

Urban Environmental Justice and Digital Media Education

Corwin (2016) conducted participatory research on environmental education programs for Indigenous and other youth of color in the small city of Ithaca, New York. In 2006, Corwin launched Green Guerrillas Youth Media Tech Collective, a job-training and youth-empowerment project that guided adolescents in making videos and other multimedia about social justice and sustainability. Calling themselves "sustainable storytellers who challenge the status quo," the group produced several feature-length "blockumentaries" and numerous short films, along with graphic design, Internet, and audio productions, over a period of five years. The participants presented their work and engaged in public speaking and outreach at K-12 schools, colleges, universities, conferences, community events, public hearings, and film festivals. Through their multimedia production and outreach, the Green Guerrillas sought to "make the connection between pollution and prisons" and advocated for a broad conception of sustainability, stressing that green technologies and approaches to agriculture need to be tied to social justice. The group also tried to connect environmental issues facing Indigenous people living in nonurban homelands with those facing Indigenous peoples living in cities (where the majority of Indigenous people in the United States now reside). In short, the group's activities fused a deep appreciation for promoting renewable energy, green building, local organic agriculture, and community gardening with advocacy on issues pertaining to incarceration, racial injustice, and police brutality. They shared their insights as they traveled to conferences in a vegetable-oil-powered van, whose solar-powered media lab allowed them to power outdoor showings of their videos.

In addition to video and related technologies and justice, two additional components informed the Green Guerrillas activities: Indigenous ways of knowing and opportunities for hands-on experiences with nature. Jason Corwin, co-coordinator of Green Guerrillas Youth Media Tech Collective, is a citizen of the Seneca Nation and facilitated the participants' exposure to a wide variety of Indigenous perspectives and issues facing Indigenous people. Some of the videos also featured environmental justice issues facing Native communities in North America, from the local Cayuga Nation in New York State to the Athabascan Dene in Alaska and the Secwepmec in British Columbia. The group also spent time making short videos about field trips they took to nature preserves and parks, which highlighted the aesthetic aspects of nature; these same videos were used at public forums to engage the local community in promoting racial equity in schools and in opposing hydraulic fracturing (aka "fracking") for natural gas in the surrounding region. By taking a holistic and comprehensive view of the environment and the concept of sustainability, the participants were able to connect the dots between the issues they were facing in their lives and historical trends of Indigenous land dispossession, slavery, discrimination, and environmental injustice.

An Equity and Environment Initiative

Since 2002, the city of Seattle, Washington, has prioritized its Race and Social Justice Initiative, which seeks to change the underlying systems perpetuating institutionalized racism and disparities. The city acknowledged the need to expose and expunge discriminatory municipal policies, procedures, and practices to be a truly democratic society. Seattle Parks and Recreation engaged with the initiative by expanding its environmental education programs to include low-income neighborhoods and communities of color, thus making programs more accessible to youth and other residents of diverse backgrounds.

Set within this context, early in 2014 residents of a racially and ethnically diverse Seattle neighborhood applied and received a grant from the city's Department of Neighborhoods to fund the construction of a mountain bike trail intended for use by local youths in a public green space within a residential area. Concerns were raised, however, about the lack of community youth voice in planning the bike trail, particularly given the Race and Social Justice Initiative and Seattle Parks and Recreation's use of environmental education as a tool for equity. The situation raised questions about the role of environmental education in relation to environmental justice for youth in this urban setting.

For Seattle Parks and Recreation youth program staff members, the bike trail controversy made real the historic deep-rootedness of white power and privilege related to land-use issues. They realized that placing environmental education programs in low-income or ethnically diverse neighborhoods does not automatically engage local youths. The city of Seattle also recognized the ongoing lack of integrating environmental justice into practice. In 2015, it issued the Equity and Environment Initiative—a partnership of the city, its communities, and local and national private foundations—which seeks to deepen Seattle's commitment to race and social justice in environmental work. This initiative created an Environmental Action Agenda centered on equity.

Environmental Justice Education in the Bronx, New York City

Youth Ministries for Peace and Justice, a community-based organization in the South Bronx, New York City, "trains young people to become community organizers" (http://www.ympj.org). This organization runs community activism and after-school education programs in the South Bronx, one of the poorest congressional districts in the United States, where most residents are Latino and African American. Compared to more affluent communities in New York City, local residents often struggle with lack of green space, limited access to health care and fresh produce, elevated rates of asthma, drug dealers, and noisy expressways running through their communities. At the same time, the only freshwater river in New York City, the Bronx River, runs through this area. For most of the twentieth century, this aquatic treasure was neglected—its banks were abandoned and industrialized, and its waters are still polluted by storm water and raw sewage due to combined sewer overflows.

Youth Ministries for Peace and Justice engages residents of the South Bronx, including youths and their families, in examining environmental justice issues. Educators and organizers at Youth Ministries for Peace and Justice—along with those from other local nonprofit organizations, community residents, environmental leaders, and elected officials—played a key role in raising public support for and awareness about the Bronx River. They succeeded in converting a former industrial site on the banks of the Bronx River into Concrete Plant

FIGURE 6.1. By stewarding the green roof on top of St. Joan of Arc Church in the South Bronx, students from Youth Ministries for Peace and Justice learn about how pervious landscapes mitigate storm water runoff. Credit: Alex Russ.

Park, which provides much-needed open space for recreation and learning. Currently, educators continue to help students and other residents realize that their community merits a better environment. Educational approaches include canoe trips on the Bronx River, creating environmental art installations, training students to inform community members about environmental and related social issues, running community campaigns against industrial and traffic pollution, and hands-on stewardship of green spaces (Figure 6.1). These programs are often combined with counseling youths, developing students' social skills, helping students with school homework, and other positive youth development activities (see chapter 17; Russ, 2016).

Conclusion

Examples such as the Green Guerrillas, the Equity and Environment Initiative, and Youth Ministries for Peace and Justice illustrate the ways in which race, colonization, poverty, and other social issues overlap with access, understandings, benefits, and related considerations of urban place, as well as how urban environmental education is addressing these intersections. Engaging in these considerations enables urban environmental education to avoid perpetuating historic oppressive relationships based on race, income, gender, or ability (see chapter 20). We suggest that social contexts and injustices should be central in approaches to and pedagogies of environmental education, rather than being on the margins. Specific approaches and issues incorporated into urban environmental education will depend on each city's or neighborhood's cultural and community settings in order to be appropriate for the historical and current contexts of the urban land on which environmental education is taking place. In all cases, a focus on resisting and disrupting environmental injustices is crucial for the practice of more just approaches to urban environmental education.

References

Agyeman, J. (2003). *Just sustainabilities: Development in an unequal world.* Cambridge, Mass.: MIT Press.

Bang, M., Curley, L., Kessel, A., Marin, A., Suzukovich III, E. S., and Strack, G. (2014). Muskrat theories, tobacco in the streets, and living Chicago as Indigenous land. *Environmental Education Research, 20*(1), 37–55.

Brulle, R. J., and Pellow, D. N. (2006). Environmental justice: Human health and environmental inequalities. *Annual Review of Public Health, 27*, 103–124.

Bullard, R. D. (1993). Anatomy of environmental racism. In R. Hofrichter (Ed.), *Toxic struggles: The theory and practice of environmental justice* (pp. 25–35), Gabriola Island, B.C.: New Society Publishers.

Corwin, J. (2016). *Indigenous ways of knowing, digital storytelling, and environmental learning: The confluence of old traditions and new technology.* Ithaca, N.Y.: Cornell University Press.

Coulthard, G. (2014). *Red skin white masks: Rejecting the colonial politics of recognition.* Minneapolis: University of Minnesota Press.

Gosine, A., and Teelucksingh, C. (2008). *Environmental justice and racism in Canada: An introduction.* Toronto: Emond Montgomery Publications.

Haluza-DeLay, R. (2013). Educating for environmental justice. In R. B. Stevenson, M. Brody, J. Dillon, and A. E. J. Wals (Eds.), *International handbook of research on environmental education* (pp. 394–403). New York: Routledge/AERA.

Kushmerick, A., Young, L., and Stein, S. E. (2007). Environmental justice content in mainstream US, 6–12 environmental education guides. *Environmental Education Research, 13*(3), 385–408.

Maina, N., Koushik, J., and Wilson, A. (in press). The intersections of gender and sustainability in Canadian higher education. *Journal of Environmental Education.*

Newberry, L. (2003). Will any/body carry that canoe? A geography of the body, ability, and gender. *Canadian Journal of Environmental Education, 8*(1), 204–216.

Russ, A. (2016). *Urban environmental education narratives.* Washington, D.C., and Ithaca, N.Y.: NAAEE and Cornell University.

Russell, C., Sarick, T., and Kennelly, J. (2002). Queering environmental education. *Canadian Journal of Environmental Education, 7*(1), 54–66.

Thomas-Müller, C. (2008). Tar sands: Environmental justice, treaty rights and Indigenous Peoples. *Canadian Dimension, 42*(2), 11–14.

Tuck, E., McKenzie, M., and McCoy, K. (2014). Land education: Indigenous, postcolonial, and decolonizing perspectives on place and environmental education research. *Environmental Education Research, 20*(1), 1–23.

7

SENSE OF PLACE

Jennifer D. Adams, David A. Greenwood,
Mitchell Thomashow, and Alex Russ

Highlights

- Sense of place—including place attachment and place meanings—can help people appreciate ecological aspects of cities.
- Sense of place is determined by personal experiences, social interactions, and identities.
- In cities, factors such as rapid development and gentrification, mobility, migration, and blurred boundaries between the natural and built environment complicate sense of place.
- Urban environmental education can leverage people's sense of place and foster ecological place meaning through direct experiences of places, social interactions in environmental programs, and nurturing residents' ecological identity.

Introduction

Different people perceive the same city or neighborhood in different ways. While one person may appreciate ecological and social aspects of a neighborhood, another may experience environmental and racialized injustice. A place may also conjure contradicting emotions, the warmth of community and home juxtaposed with the stress of dense urban living. Sense of place—the way we perceive places such as streets, communities, cities, or ecoregions—influences our well-being, how we describe and interact with a place, what we value in a place, our respect for ecosystems and other species, how we perceive the affordances of a place, our desire to build more sustainable and just urban communities, and how we choose to improve cities. Our sense of place also reflects our historical and experiential knowledge of a place and helps us imagine its more sustainable future. In this chapter, we review scholarship about sense of place, including in cities. Then we explore how urban environmental education can help residents to strengthen their attachment to urban communities or entire cities and to view urban places as ecologically valuable.

Sense of Place

In general, sense of place describes our relationship with places, expressed in different dimensions of human life: emotions, biographies, imagination, stories, and personal experiences (Basso, 1996). In environmental psychology, sense of place—how we perceive a place—includes place attachment and place meaning (Kudryavtsev, Stedman, and Krasny, 2012). *Place attachment* reflects a bond between people and places, and *place meaning* reflects symbolic meanings people ascribe to places. In short, "sense of place is the lens through which people experience and make meaning of their experiences in and with place" (Adams, 2013, p. 47). Sense of place varies among people, in history, and over the course of one's lifetime. People may attribute various meanings to the same place in relation to its ecological, social, economic, cultural, aesthetic, historical, or other aspects. Sense of place evolves through personal experiences and defines how people view, interpret, and interact with their world (Russ et al., 2015). In cities, sense of place echoes the intersections of culture, environment, history, politics, and economics and is impacted by global mobility, migration, and blurred boundaries between the natural and built environment.

Research and scholarship around the relationship between "place" and learning reflects diverse perspectives, many of which are relevant to urban environmental education. Education scholars point to the need for people to develop specific "practices of place" that reflect embodied (perceptual and conceptual) relationships with local landscapes (natural, built, and human). Further, some scholars and researchers have used a lens of mobility—the globalized and networked flow of ideas, materials, and people—to build awareness of the relationship between the local and global in the construction of place in urban centers (Stedman and Ardoin, 2013). This suggests that understanding sense of place in the city generates an added set of situations and challenges, including dynamic demographics, migration narratives, and complex infrastructure networks, as well as contested definitions of natural environments (Heynen, Kaika and Swyn-gedouw, 2006). One critical question is how we think about sense of place in cities when places and people are constantly on the move. Given rural-urban migration, sense of place today includes where a person came from as much as where he or she now finds herself. In one study in a large urban center in the United States, Adams (2013) found that notions of "home" and identity for Caribbean-identified youth were largely constructed in the northeastern urban context in which they found themselves either through birth or immigration. Such dimensions of place relationships are vital for thinking about meaningful and relevant urban environmental education.

Understanding sense of place in the urban context would be incomplete without a critical consideration of cities as socially constructed places both inherited and created by those who live there. Critical geographers such as Edward Soja, David Harvey, and Doreen Massey draw on a Marxist analysis to describe cities as the material consequence of particular political and ideological arrangements under global capitalism. Critical educators (e.g., Gruenewald, 2003; Haymes, 1995) have drawn upon critical geography to demonstrate how cities are social constructions imbued with contested race, class, and gender social relationships that make possible vastly different senses of place among their residents. For example, Stephen Haymes (1995) argued that against the historical backdrop of race relations in Western countries, "in the context of the inner city, a peda-gogy of place must be linked to black urban struggle" (p. 129). Although Haymes wrote this a while ago, his claim that place-responsive urban education must be linked to racial politics resonates today with the Black Lives Matter move-ment in the United States and ongoing need for environmental educators to be in tune with the political realities that so deeply inform a given individual's sense of place. This also resonates with the notion that different people may ascribe different meanings to the same place. The complexity of meaning surrounding urban places and our understandings of such contested meanings make a power-ful context for personal inquiry and collective learning.

In the United States, Tzou and Bell (2012) used ethnographic approaches to examine the construction of place among urban young people of color. Their results suggest implications for equity and social justice in environmental edu-cation, such as the damage that prevailing environmental education narratives could do to communities of color in terms of power and positioning. Further, Gruenewald (2005) suggests that traditional modes of assessment, such as stan-dardized tests, are problematic in place-based education; instead, we need to redefine education and research as forms of inquiry that are identifiably place-responsive and afford a multiplicity of approaches to define and describe people's relationships to the environment.

Sense of Place and Urban Environmental Education

Although not always explicitly stated, sense of place is inherent to many environmental learning initiatives (Thomashow, 2002). A goal of such programs is nurturing *ecological place meaning*, defined as "viewing nature-related phenomena, including ecosystems and associated activities, as symbols" of a place (Kudryavtsev, Krasny, and Stedman, 2012). This approach is prevalent in bioregionalism, the "no child left inside" movement, community gardening, sustainable agriculture, as well as in natural history, place-based, and other environmental education approaches. Place-based education has goals important to urban life, including raising awareness of place, of our relationship to place, and of how we may contribute positively to this constantly evolving relationship, as well as inspiring local actors to develop place-responsive transformational learning experiences that contribute to community well-being.

Nurturing a Sense of Place

With the global population increasingly residing in cities, ecological urbanism requires new approaches to understanding place. How does sense of place contribute to human flourishing, ecological justice, and biological and cultural diversity? Using a theoretical basis from literature described above, we offer examples of activities to help readers construct field explorations that evoke, leverage, or influence sense of place. (Also see a relevant diagram in Russ et al., 2015, p. 86.) In practice, urban environmental education programs would combine different approaches to nurture sense of place, perhaps most prominently place-based approaches (Smith and Sobel, 2010), which teach respect for the local environment, including its other-than-human inhabitants, in any setting including cities.

Experiences of the Urban Environment

Making students more consciously aware of their taken-for-granted places is an important aspect of influencing sense of place. Focusing on places students frequent, educators can ask questions like: "What kind of place is this? What does this place mean to you? What does this place enable you to do?" Hands-on activities that allow students to experience, recreate in, and steward more natural ecosystems in cities could be one approach to nurture ecological place meaning. Another activity could use conceptual mapping to highlight places and networks that are important to students, for example related to commuting and transportation, the Internet, food and energy sources, or recreation. Maps and drawings also might focus on sensory perceptions—sights, sounds, and smells—or locate centers of urban sustainability. Such maps can help students learn about specific neighborhoods, investigate the relationship among neighborhoods, or create linkages between all the places they or their relatives have lived. Further, mapping activities may help students recognize how their own activities connect to the larger network of activities that create a city and allow them to reflect on issues of power, access, and equity in relation to environmental concerns such as waste, air pollution, and access to green space.

Other observational and experiential activities to instill sense of place might include: (1) exploring boundaries or borders, for example, space under highways, transition zones between communities, fences and walls; (2) finding centers or gathering places and asking questions about where people congregate and why; (3) following the movements of pedestrians and comparing them to the movements of urban animals; (4) tracing the migratory flows of birds, insects, and humans; (5) shadowing city workers who are engaged in garbage removal or other public services as they move around the city; (6) observing color and light at different times of the day; (7) observing patterns of construction and demolition; and (8) working with street artists to create murals. All these activities could serve to develop new meanings and attachments to places that may or may not be familiar to people. These activities build on seminal works related to urban design, including Christopher Alexander's "Pattern Language," Randolph T. Hexter's "Design for Ecological Democracy," Jane Jacobs's "The Death and Life of Great American Cities," Jan Gehl and Birgitte Svarre's "How to Study Public Life," and the rich material coming from *New Geographies*, the journal published by the Harvard University Graduate School of Design.

Social Construction of Place Meanings

Activities that allow people to explore and interpret places together could contribute to developing a collective sense of place and corresponding place meanings. Participatory action research and other participatory approaches raise young people's critical consciousness, influence how they see themselves in relation to places, and build collective understandings about what it means to be young in a rapidly changing city. For example, photo-voice and mental mapping used during a participatory urban environment course allowed students to experience a shift from viewing a community as a fixed geographic place to a dynamic, socially constructed space and to describe how they experience and understand urban phenomena such as decay, gentrification, and access to green spaces (Bellino and Adams, 2014). These activities enabled students to expand their notions of what it means to be urban citizens and to transform their ecological identities in ways that prompted them to take steps toward imagining environmentally, economically, and culturally sustainable futures.

Further, ecological place meaning can be constructed through storytelling, communication with environmental professionals, interpretation, learning from community members, and sharing students' own stories (Russ et al., 2015), as well as through representation of places through narratives, charts, music, poetry, photographs, or other forms that encourage dialogue and reflection about what places are and how they can be cared for (Wattchow and Brown, 2011). Other social activities, such as collective art making, restoring local natural areas, or planting a community garden, could contribute to a collective sense of place that values green space and ecological aspects of place. New socially constructed place meanings can in turn help to promote community engagement in preserving, transforming, or creating places with unique ecological characteristics (e.g., fighting to keep a community garden safe from developers) and help to create opportunities to maintain these ecological characteristics (e.g., group-purchasing solar power). Environmental educators who are able to engage with a community over time can watch these initiatives take root and grow and can observe individual and collective changes in sense of place.

Developing an Ecological Identity

In addition to paying attention to social construction of place, environmental educators can nurture ecological identity, which fosters appreciation of the ecological aspects of cities. Humans have multiple identities, including ecological identity, which reflects the ecological perspectives or ecological lens through which they see the world. Ecological identity focuses one's attention on environmental activities, green infrastructure, ecosystems, and biodiversity, including in urban places. Ecological identity in cities can be manifested in realizing one's personal responsibility for urban sustainability and in feeling oneself empowered and competent to improve local places (Russ et al., 2015). Urban environmental education programs can influence ecological identity, for example, by involving students in long-term environmental restoration projects where they serve as experts on environmental topics, by valuing young people's contribution to environmental planning, respecting their viewpoint about future urban development, and recognizing young people's efforts as ambassadors of the local environment and environmental organizations (e.g., through work/volunteer titles, labels on T-shirts, or workshop certificates). Even involving students in projects that allow them to become more familiar with their community from an ecological perspective goes a long way toward adding an ecological layer to their identity and perception of their city (Bellino and Adams, 2014).

Conclusion

The environmental education challenge presented in this chapter is how to embed deeper meanings of place and identity in dynamic urban environments. Because urban settings tend to be diverse across multiple elements, ranging from types of green space and infrastructure to global migration, there are countless ways to proceed. In addition, while environmental educators can design and facilitate experiences to access and influence people's sense of place, it is also important for educators to have a strong notion of their own sense of place. This is especially critical for environmental educators who may not have spent their formative years in a city. Such persons may have a sense of place informed more by frequent and ready access to natural areas and less by access to urban diversity and the density and diversity of people found in an urban environment. It is important for all urban environmental educators to engage in reflective activities that allow them to learn about their personal sense of place, including what they value about the natural, human, and built environment. Demonstrating one's own continued learning, and learning challenges, will greatly aid in the process of facilitating other learners developing a sense of place in diverse urban settings. Through sharing our own experiences with places, all learners can deepen our awareness of and sensitivity to our environment and to each other. Such awareness and receptivity to place can positively influence collective and individual actions that help create sustainable cities.

References

Adams, J. D. (2013). Theorizing a sense of place in transnational community. *Children, Youth and Environments, 23*(3), 43–65.

Basso, K. H. (1996). Wisdom sits in places: Notes on a Western Apache landscape. In S. Feld and K. H. Basso (Eds.), *Senses of place* (pp. 53–90). Santa Fe, N.M.: School of American Research Press.

Bellino, M., and Adams, J. D. (2014). Reimagining environmental education: Urban youths' perceptions and investigations of their communities. *Revista Brasileira de Pesquisa em Educação de Ciências, 14*(2), 27–38.

Gruenewald, D. A. (2003). Foundations of place: A multidisciplinary framework for place-conscious education. *American Educational Research Journal, 40*(3), 619–654.

Gruenewald, D. A. (2005). Accountability and collaboration: Institutional barriers and strategic pathways for place-based education. *Ethics, Place and Environment, 8*(3), 261–283.

Haymes, S. N. (1995). *Race, culture, and the city: A pedagogy for Black urban struggle.* Albany: State University of New York Press.

Heynen, N., Kaika, M., and Swyngedouw, E. (2006). *In the nature of cities: Urban political ecology and the politics of urban metabolism.* New York: Routledge.

Kudryavtsev, A., Krasny, M. E., and Stedman, R. C. (2012). The impact of environmental education on sense of place among urban youth. *Ecosphere, 3*(4), 29.

Kudryavtsev, A., Stedman, R. C., and Krasny, M. E. (2012). Sense of place in environmental education. *Environmental Education Research, 18*(2), 229–250.

Russ, A., Peters, S. J., Krasny, M. E., and Stedman, R. C. (2015). Development of ecological place meaning in New York City. *Journal of Environmental Education, 46*(2), 73–93.

Smith, G. A., and Sobel, D. (2010). *Place- and community-based education in schools.* New York: Routledge.

Stedman, R., and Ardoin, N. (2013). Mobility, power and scale in place-based environmental education. In M. E. Krasny and J. Dillon (Eds.), *Trading zones in environmental education: Creating transdisciplinary dialogue* (pp. 231–251). New York: Peter Lang.

Thomashow, M. (2002). *Bringing the biosphere home: Learning to perceive global environmental change.* Cambridge, Mass.: MIT Press.

Tzou, C. T., and Bell, P. (2012). The role of borders in environmental education: Positioning, power and marginality. *Ethnography and Education, 7*(2), 265–282.

Wattchow, B., and Brown, M. (2011). *A pedagogy of place: Outdoor education for a changing world.* Monash, Australia: Monash University Publishing.

8

CLIMATE CHANGE EDUCATION

Marianne E. Krasny, Chew-Hung Chang,
Marna Hauk, and Bryce B. DuBois

Highlights

- Climate change education addresses immediate safety and risk reduction as well as longer-term actions to enhance environmental quality.
- Education that focuses exclusively on reducing our carbon footprint, or mitigation, is no longer realistic given that changes in climate are already occurring and threatening livelihoods, communities, ecosystems, and biodiversity.
- Education for adaptation and transformation can foster healthy ecosystem and community processes, consistent with reducing carbon footprint.
- The "reclamation, resilience, and regeneration" climate education framework encompasses learning about mitigation, adaptation, and transformation.

Introduction

In October 2012, Hurricane Sandy slammed into the New York and New Jersey shoreline with winds of 145 kilometers per hour and a storm surge 4.3 meters above mean low water. The superstorm flooded the city's subways, destroyed thousands of homes, washed away beaches and boardwalks, and caused at least fifty-three deaths and more than $18 billion in economic losses. On the other side of the world, between 2006 and 2014, Singapore experienced multiple 150-year record rainfalls and droughts. How can cities experiencing climate-related flooding and other disturbances protect their citizens now and into the future?

Environmental education—including school and public programs developed by universities and government agencies as well as initiatives that emerge from the efforts of grassroots organizations—can play a role in responding to and preparing for climate change and related disasters. But in so doing, environmental educators face a dilemma: How can we hold true to our foundational values of enhancing the environment, including efforts to mitigate climate change, while addressing the reality that climate change has already irreversibly changed our environment and that we need to adapt and transform? We address this question using examples of formal school curricula, engineered infrastructure development, and public outreach in Singapore and through an exploratory "three Rs" approach to climate-responsive environmental and sustainability education in the United States.

Formal Curriculum and Infrastructure Approach

Singapore has responded to climate change through a combination of building infrastructure to ensure safety, implementing climate change requirements in the school curriculum, and public education (Figure 8.1). An example of infrastructure is engineering efficient drainage systems. Reflecting government directives, climate change has been incorporated into the grade 8 and 9 syllabus with a focus on "variable weather and changing climate" (Chang, 2014). Climate change education in Singapore seeks to help learners develop knowledge, skills, values, and action to engage with and learn about the causes, impacts, and management of climate change. Students are expected to be proficient in climate change science, make informed judgments about climate change issues, convince others of their beliefs about the causes of climate change, and take personal action to reduce their carbon footprint. Complementing these infrastructure and school efforts is public education on floods, which is focused on public preparedness. For example, Singapore's Public Utilities Board communicates flood updates on the radio, Facebook, Twitter, and other websites. The public is actively engaged through crowd-sourced reporting of flood locations. In response to droughts, public education has focused on information dissemination and on providing an advisory to households to voluntarily manage water demand.

Whereas Singapore's multipronged efforts are impressive, Chang and Irvine (2014) recognize the need for a more integrated approach to prepare the public. For instance, they suggest developing a program to help the public prepare for

FIGURE 8.1. Like many coastal cities, most of Singapore is no more than a few meters above sea level; thus efficient drainage systems and education for public preparedness for floods are essential. Credit: Alex Russ.

precipitation extremes by identifying vulnerabilities and risks, creating an understanding of the notion of adaptive capacity (e.g., through improving drainage systems), and monitoring precipitation. They also promote a relief action program that describes what can be done for postevent recovery. In short, Singapore, which like many coastal cities around the world is highly vulnerable to sea level rise, has embarked on a comprehensive approach to protect and educate its citizens and can be expected to take on even greater efforts in the future.

Climate-Responsive Environmental and Sustainability Education: Reclamation, Resilience, and Regeneration (Three Rs)

In addition to efforts like those in Singapore that help residents prepare for and respond to the immediate threat of disasters, Hauk (2016) has called for more fundamental rethinking about how we address ongoing climate instability. She had proposed the three Rs approach to climate-responsive environmental and sustainability education. The Rs include *reclamation*, a form of mitigation or reducing our impact on and improving the environment; *resilience*, which incorporates notions of adaptation and adaptive capacity; and *regeneration*, which is most closely aligned with transformation or envisioning new social-ecological processes and systems. We suggest how environmental education can support each of these processes below.

Reclamation

Reclamation involves designing systems to reclaim lost ecological and social capacity. It can include ark-like preservation or conservation via sanctuaries, weather-proof libraries, seed banks, and reserves that maintain cultural lifeways. Whereas we often think of reclaiming in terms of mine reclamation, here we refer to reclaiming more complete sustainable living systems such as those incorporating indigenous ecological knowledge. Innovative technologies, including those informed by deep biomimicry (Mathews, 2011), can contribute to reclamation. Because reclamation is driven by an ethic of caring and by political and social structures that allow for the expression of that caring, it depends on a culture's commitment to sustainability. Further, because it invites reconsideration of marginalized ecosystems and lifeways, reclamation also depends on the cultural commons and the continuity and honoring of elder cultures that provide an alternative to practices with a high-carbon footprint (Bowers, 2013). While this seemingly excludes the possibility of reclamation for many cities, remnants of social and ecological memories are often retained, for example, by farmers who have immigrated or migrated to urban centers and grow vegetables and herbs in community gardens. Cuba's permaculture and organic farming revolution and use of appropriate technologies following the loss of Soviet support in the 1990s provides an example of reclamation. Such urban agriculture, as well as smaller-scale urban allotment and community gardens, bring together multiple generations and people with different skills and thus create opportunities for environmental learning.

Resilience

A person, a community, an ecosystem, or a social-ecology system can be resilient. Thus psychology, sociology, and ecology have developed definitions of resilience, all of which have in common notions of hardship, disturbance, recovery, adaptation, and, in cases where an individual, community, or system experiences "tipping point" changes, transformation (Table 8.1).

TABLE 8.1   Resilience definitions

TYPE OF RESILIENCE	DEFINITION
Community	Ability of communities to cope with and recover from external stressors resulting from social, political, and environmental change (CARRI, 2013)
Ecological	Magnitude of disturbance that a system can experience before it moves into a different state with different controls on structure and function (Holling, 1973)
Psychological	Processes of, capacity for, or patterns of positive adaptation during or following exposure to adverse experiences that have the potential to disrupt or destroy the successful functioning or development of the person (Masten and Obradovic, 2008)
Social-ecological systems	Capacity of a social-ecological system to adapt or transform so as to maintain ongoing processes in response to gradual and small-scale change, or transform in the face of devastating change (Berkes, Colding, and Folke, 2003)

Krasny, Lundholm, and Plummer (2010) suggest four ways in which environmental education programs can contribute to social-ecological and other forms of resilience:

- Environmental education can foster attributes of resilient social-ecological systems such as biological diversity, ecosystem services, and social capital (cf. Walker and Salt, 2006).
- Through collaboration with government agencies and nonprofit and community organizations, environmental education organizations can become part of polycentric governance systems, which offer options for adapting to and bouncing back from small disturbance and major disasters (cf. Ostrom, 2010, cited in Krasny, Lundholm, and Plummer, 2010).
- Resilience can help bridge the controversy over whether environmental education is an instrument to promote behavior change or a means to foster critical thinking and emancipation, by showing that environmental education can foster social-ecological systems (instrumental) and psychological (emancipatory) resilience simultaneously.
- Parallels among concepts from learning theory and social-ecological resilience may contribute to badly needed cross-disciplinary approaches to address linked social and environmental problems. For example, learning theory suggests that discrepant or unexpected events foster transformational learning, and social-ecological systems resilience suggests that major disturbances spur new approaches to environmental management and environmental education.

A study of environmental educators who experienced Hurricane Sandy in New York City revealed that educators commonly used the term resilience to describe their programs. They drew on their environmental education practice to create working definitions of resilience, which roughly mirrored the academic definitions of psychological, community, and social-ecological resilience. A program emphasizing psychological resilience sought to equip participants with the skills to respond to future disturbances; programs designed to support community participation in planning reflected community resilience; and those that fostered engagement in civic ecology practices, such as oyster and dune restoration, reflected social-ecological resilience (DuBois and Krasny, 2016).

Although educators in the New York City study commonly did not make a distinction between resilience and adaptation, they spoke about resilience more often. Possible explanations include being influenced by resilience-focused funding and resilience-related city government reports. But an intriguing possibility is that the notion of resilience as a pathway forward in the face of personal hardship as well as larger systems disturbance made this term resonate with educators. Or, as one educator put it, "Adaptation—sometimes there is a, I don't want to use the word helplessness—but less of a proactive feeling than resiliency. Resiliency says it's a pathway and process—the words adaptation and mitigation—not a lot of love in there."

Regeneration

Regeneration involves creating more fundamental, transformational change, recognizing that climate change is altering ongoing social-ecological processes and that systems may lose the ability to adapt (Hauk, 2016). Such transformations are consistent with the reorganization phase following tipping point disruptions in the adaptive cycle and with the emergence of entirely new processes at multiple scales (Gunderson and Holling, 2002; Krasny, Lundholm, and Plummer, 2010). Similar to resilient systems, regenerative systems are characterized by multiple and multiscale feedback mechanisms, including feedbacks among social capital, empowerment, urban food production, justice, and knowledge-sharing networks. For example, students engaged in community gardens may build social capital, which in turn may foster willingness to engage in further action for the common good, including actions that require creating new systems for managing collective resources such as urban open space. Urban environmental education can play a role in regeneration not only by helping young people engage in activities such as creating and monitoring artificial algal systems designed to filter contaminants or produce energy, but also by reflecting on the human, community, and ecosystem processes that enable such systems to thrive. We can think of regeneration as "re-weaving living systems." Williams and Brown (2012, pp. 44–45) argue that these more radically transformative approaches "redesign the mindscape" while restructuring environmental and sustainability education through "the development of a regenerative metaphorical language to inform sustainability teaching and learning." The learning is characterized by cooperation, mutual reciprocity, and vibrancy, and catalyzes transformations in the structure and pedagogy of learning contexts.

Summing Up

All three Rs—reclamation, resilience, and regeneration—can occur simultaneously. In fact, we may envision them as embedded processes, with reclamation occupying the more limited vision, followed by resilience and finally regeneration. Further, all three processes may depend on horizontal networks of nongovernmental organizations, scientists, government, and community groups that mobilize actions and on vertical integration of community action with larger political structures so as to effect larger changes (Soltesova et al., 2014).

Environmental education can incorporate reclamation, resilience, and regeneration. Environmental education for reclamation occurs when students become involved in preservation, conservation, and the establishment of sanctuaries of exemplar systems, including in small urban parks or gardens. Environmental education for social-ecological resilience focuses on building adaptive capacity, including through creating social networks to support collaboration and learning, which are in turn applied to an ongoing process of collaborative and adaptive management or so-called "learning by experience." Similar to environmental education for resilience, environmental education for regeneration incorporates an emphasis on feedback processes and nurtures participation in stewardship activities; it adds a focus, however, on learning through creating entirely new systems, like algal energy production, and on reflecting on how new types of complex systems operate.

Conclusion

Returning to our original question about the challenges environmental education faces in an age of climate change, we contend that environmental education can integrate mitigation and adaptation in cases where adaptation is grounded in processes that occur in healthy ecosystems and communities (Krasny and DuBois, 2016). Examples of so-called "ecosystem-based adaptation" include restoring populations of oysters that provide filtering and other ecosystem services and restoring dunes to serve as natural barriers for storm surges. Environmental education also can address adaptation in a manner consistent with its social values, including participation and equity, by incorporating "community-based adaptation" options. These include efforts to engage youths and adults in collaborative, hands-on stewardship and monitoring. Although many such initiatives may not sound like environmental education per se, we propose a definition of urban environmental education that, in addition to structured lessons, encompasses the learning that occurs through engagement in hands-on reclamation, restoration, and creating or monitoring regenerative systems. In some cases, this will mean that engagement in restoration and other forms of stewardship, normally considered a goal of environmental education, occurs prior to and creates a context for learning.

How might we integrate environmental education alongside mitigation, adaptation, transformation, and the three Rs of climate-responsive education? We can start by drawing on a long-term tradition of environmental education that has focused on mitigation. When efforts to foster pro-environmental behaviors address conservation, environmental education is consistent with the first R, reclamation. Climate-responsive environmental education expands to encompass ecosystem- and community-based adaptation, which is consistent with the second R, resilience. Finally, climate-responsive environmental education encompasses transformation or regeneration, the third R (Table 8.2). Although we refer here to social-ecological resilience and transforming social-ecological systems, environmental education also fosters psychological resilience and transforms individual lives. Both individual and social-ecological systems resilience and transformation are critical to addressing climate change.

In this chapter, we present two paradigms for climate change education in cities. The first is based on the real-life experience of Singapore, a small, coastal city-state in constant risk of flooding, whose options are limited by its size and

TABLE 8.2 Correspondence between three Rs and mitigation, adaptation, and transformation

CLIMATE RESPONSE CATEGORIES	THREE RS	EXAMPLES
Mitigation	Reclamation	Preserves that which incorporates indigenous knowledge, seed banks
Adaptation	Resilience	Ecosystem- and community-based adaptation (e.g., dune restoration)
Transformation	Regeneration	"Reweaving" new systems (e.g., algal energy production system)

location. Here, a more government-directed approach to ensure the safety of individuals and their water supply has been successful in saving lives.

The three Rs strives to move beyond existing ways of thinking and political structures that reinforce social and economic injustices and environmental degradation. It also suggests moving beyond top-down control strategies for emergency preparedness, even though such strategies may be desperately needed to save lives and infrastructure in the short run. Finding the balance between real-time responsiveness to ensure safety and save human lives, stewardship action coupled with reflection and integrated understandings of social-ecological systems, and long-term capacity building to create transformed energy and social systems is a critical challenge facing environmental education as we address social and ecological changes brought about by a warming and more erratic climate.

References

Berkes, F., Colding, J., and Folke, C. (2003). *Navigating social-ecological systems: Building resilience for complexity and change.* Cambridge: Cambridge University Press.

Bowers, C. A. (2013). The role of environmental education in resisting the global forces undermining what remains of indigenous traditions of self-sufficiency and mutual support. In A. Kulnieks, D. R. Longboat, and K. Young (Eds.), *Contemporary studies in environmental and indigenous pedagogies: A curricula of stories and place* (pp. 225–240). Rotterdam: Sense Publishers.

CARRI. (2013). Definitions of community resilience: An analysis (pp. 14). Community and Regional Resilience Institute.

Chang, C. H. (2014). Is Singapore's school geography becoming too responsive to the changing needs of society? *International Research in Geographical and Environmental Education, 23*(1), 25–39.

Chang, C. H., and Irvine, K. N. (2014). Climate change resilience and public education in response to hydrologic extremes in Singapore. *British Journal of Environment and Climate Change, 4*(3), 328–354.

DuBois, B., and Krasny, M. E. (2016). Educating with resilience in mind: Addressing climate change in post-Sandy New York City. *Journal of Environmental Education, 47*(4), 255–270.

Gunderson, L. H., and Holling, C. S. (Eds.). (2002). *Panarchy: Understanding transformations in human and natural systems.* Washington D.C.: Island Press.

Hauk, M. (2016). The new "three Rs" in an age of climate change: Reclamation, resilience, and regeneration as possible approaches for climate-responsive environmental and sustainability education. *Journal of Sustainability Education, 7*(2).

Holling, C. S. (1973). Resilience and stability of ecological systems. *Annual Review of Ecology, Evolution, and Systematics, 4*, 1–23.

Krasny, M. E., and DuBois, B. (2016). Climate adaptation education: Embracing reality or abandoning environmental values? *Environmental Education Research.* http://www.tandfonline.com/doi/abs/10.1080/13504622.2016.1196345.

Krasny, M. E., Lundholm, C., and Plummer, R. (2010). Resilience, learning and environmental education. *Environmental Education Research (special issue), 15*(5–6), 463–672.

Masten, A. S., and Obradovic, J. (2008). Disaster preparation and recovery: Lessons from research on resilience in human development. *Ecology and Society, 13*(1), 9.

Mathews, F. (2011). Towards a deeper philosophy of biomimicry. *Organization & Environment, 24*(4), 364–387.

Soltesova, K., Brown, A., Dayal, A., and Dodman, D. (2014). Community participation in urban adaptation to climate change: Potentials and limits for community-based adaptation approaches. In E. L. F. Schipper et al. (Eds.), *Community-based adaptation to climate change: Scaling it up* (pp. 214–225). New York: Routledge.

Walker, B. H., and Salt, D. (2006). *Resilience thinking: Sustaining ecosystems and people in a changing world.* Washington, D.C.: Island Press.

Williams, D., and Brown, J. (2012). *Learning gardens and sustainability education: Bringing life to schools and schools to life.* New York: Routledge.

9

COMMUNITY ASSETS

Marianne E. Krasny, Simon Beames,
and Shorna B. Allred

Highlights

- Social capital combines social connections, trust, shared social norms, and civic engagement.
- Sense of community is a feeling of belonging, of having influence, and that one's needs will be met through being part of a group.
- Collective efficacy refers to social cohesion, trust, and the willingness to take action for the betterment of one's community.
- Urban environmental education activities that engage people in working together toward a common goal may build social capital and sense of community and may demonstrate collective efficacy; in this way they contribute to urban sustainability.

Introduction

Urban environmental education activities at community centers and in public spaces often integrate community well-being alongside environmental goals. For example, the Abraham House community center in New York City has engaged young people in community gardening. Although the young people learned about and enhanced their local environment through gardening, the community center's actual goal is to "strengthen families and the larger community."

How can urban environmental education strengthen communities and enhance environmental quality in cities? In this chapter, we focus on three community assets—social capital, sense of community, and collective efficacy—that have been used to understand why some communities fare better than others and why people sometimes act not in their narrow self-interest, but for the common good. We connect social capital, sense of community, and collective efficacy to urban environmental education in order to better understand pathways toward urban sustainability that highlight collective action rather than changing individual behaviors.

Social Capital

Whereas social capital has multiple definitions, one can think of it as a combination of social connections, trust, shared social norms, and civic engagement. Social capital is important to urban environmental education because it is both an indicator of a community's well-being and a precursor of collective action to manage natural resources for the public good (Krasny et al., 2013). In this section, we review the research of two influential scholars: Robert Putnam, who focuses on how social capital contributes to the health of a community, and Elinor Ostrom, who explains how social capital fosters collective action.

Harvard political scientist Robert Putnam has written widely about social capital as contributing to community well-being and as part of the very foundations of participatory democracy. In fact, research has shown that social capital can result in reduced levels of adolescent pregnancy, delinquency, school failure, and child maltreatment, as well as enhanced levels of happiness and health, high-quality relationships with adults, and civil society skills such as the ability to convene productive meetings (for a review, see Krasny et al., 2013). Foundational to Putnam's definition of social capital is volunteering and other forms of participation in the civic life of the community. Putnam claims that as people have migrated to cities and as a result of television and other social changes, engagement in traditional forms of civic life, like Rotary Clubs or even bowling, is declining, and that this decline bodes ill for our society (Putnam, 2000). But other political scientists like Carmen Sirianni note that traditional forms of public engagement are being replaced by new forms, such as water quality monitoring and community gardening, or more broadly environmental stewardship (Sirianni and Friedland, 2005). This is good news for environmental education because environmental stewardship, while perhaps not environmental education per se, offers ample opportunities for youths and adults to learn about the environment. At the same time, environmental education programs situated in stewardship activities can contribute to social capital and thus help strengthen our communities.

But social capital not only fosters community well-being. Social capital is important for another reason: it contributes to sustainable resource conservation, which is central to the field of environmental education. Nobel Laureate Elinor Ostrom defined social capital as "a set of prescriptions, values, and relationships created by individuals in the past that can be drawn on in the present and future to facilitate overcoming social dilemmas" (Ahn and Ostrom, 2008, p. 73). Managing our natural resources for the collective good is one social dilemma that concerns political scientists and environmental educators. Communities with higher levels of social capital are more likely to manage natural resources for the collective good and to have the capacity to learn and adapt to environmental change.

Ostrom's work on the conditions under which people collectively manage resources for the public good provides an alternative to Garrett Hardin's tragedy of the commons, which assumes that in the absence of external controls, individuals always act in their own self-interest by exploiting commonly held resources and that these individual actions inevitably lead to environmental destruction. The question thus arises: How might environmental education help build social capital, which is critical to avoiding the tragedy of the commons?

Although the research is in its infancy, evidence is accumulating that environmental education programs can contribute to multiple aspects of social capital. For example, intergenerational environmental education programs can build social networks, and through working together toward a common goal—such as conquering a cliff in a rock-climbing Outward Bound program—environmental education participants can build trust (McKenzie, 2003). Urban environmental education also often involves participation in community gardening, shoreline cleanups, and other stewardship and problem-solving activities. Such civic engagement is one component of Putnam's definition of social capital, and research suggests that participation in civic activities fosters environmental citizenship behaviors (Chawla and Cushing, 2007). In short, research suggests that environmental education that engages participants in working together toward a common goal and in civic action provides opportunities to build social capital (Krasny et al., 2013).

Sense of Community

Sense of community is a feeling that members of a community have of belonging, of mattering to each other and to the group, and that their needs will be met through their commitment to be together (McMillan and Chavis, 1986). Sense of community includes four elements: *membership*, a feeling of belonging; *influ-ence*, a sense of making a difference to the group; *fulfillment of needs*, a belief that one's needs will be met through membership in the group; and *emotional con-nection*, a sense of shared history, places, and experiences.

When people are uprooted from rural communities and move to cities, or when a new highway disrupts social patterns in an urban neighborhood, a sense of community may be lost. People often seek out ways to re-establish a sense of belonging, having influence, fulfilling their needs, and connecting emotionally. This can be through destructive means such as joining gangs or through more positive activities such as participating in youth programs that focus on environ-mental learning and stewardship.

Whereas environmental education often focuses on local places and place-based education, recognition of the importance of community as part of place is growing (Smith and Sobel, 2010). Similarly, environmental education research has focused on sense of place (see chapter 7), which can be a predictor of envi-ronmental behaviors (Jorgensen and Stedman, 2006). Future research in envi-ronmental education may focus not just on how programs influence sense of place but also their impact on participants' sense of community and how sense of community influences civic environmental action. In addition, given the con-nection of sense of community to well-being and civic action, environmental educators may consider an explicit focus on creating feelings of belonging and influence, meeting participants' needs, and creating a sense of connectedness in their programs (see also chapter 17).

Collective Efficacy

Collective efficacy is defined as social cohesion, trust, and the willingness to take action for the betterment of one's community (Sampson, Raudenbush, and Earls, 1997). Traditionally, environmental education has focused on self-efficacy, which has to do with the belief that an individual has the capacity to take action that will produce desired outcomes. Collective efficacy helps us to understand collective rather than individual actions in urban environmental education.

A 1999 study of low-income neighborhoods in Chicago showed how col-lective efficacy is related to community well-being. The researchers drove a car with cameras mounted on both sides down thousands of miles of city streets, videotaping everything taking place along the way. It turned out that neighbor-hoods where there were indicators that residents were solving problems together had lower crime rates. For example, when researchers reviewed the camera foot-age and saw community gardens rather than blighted lots, they considered this evidence that people were working together. When such neighborhoods were compared against police statistics, the researchers discovered they also had lower crime rates (Sampson and Raudenbush, 1999). In a separate study of public housing tenants in New York City, researchers found that residents who started growing flowers and vegetables for an apartment beautification contest ended up organizing window watches to sound the alarm and mobilize when someone threatened to pick their flowers, and they assigned troublemakers among the children to guard their plantings from vandals. In short, what started as planting flowers grew into cleaning up and protecting newly prized common areas and gardens, all of which required cooperation and organizing (Lewis, 1972).

We may not think of community gardening as environmental education, yet similar to so many other civic ecology practices that integrate environmental stewardship with community well-being in cities, community gardening provides opportunities for environmental learning (Krasny and Tidball, 2015). Who has been to a community garden where children and adults were planting together and not seen the young people express curiosity, ask questions, and learn about a plant, bird, or bug? And through community gardening, young and older people demonstrate their willingness to take action to steward our urban public spaces, one goal of urban environmental education.

So if we expand urban environmental education to include learning that takes place through stewardship action like community gardening, in addition to more structured lessons in classrooms, then we can see how urban environmental education becomes part of a community demonstrating collective efficacy. We can think of collective efficacy as tending to one's surroundings, even when those surroundings include vacant lots, vandalized buildings, and other "incivilities" often found in cities (Sampson, Raudenbush, and Earls, 1997). These affronts to everyday life communicate an attitude of not caring, helplessness, and even hopelessness, not unlike the hopelessness some may feel about the environment. Taking action for the collective good can provide a remedy to these attitudes, instilling caring, efficacy, and even hope.

Discussion

So far we have made the case that social capital, sense of community, and collective efficacy are desirable outcomes for urban environmental education because they contribute to a community's well-being and its ability to act collectively for the common good. The question arises: How do we go about building these community assets? Urban environmental education approaches that build community assets include place- and community-based education (Smith and

Sobel, 2010), environmental action (Schusler and Krasny, 2010), positive youth development (see chapter 17), and community environmental education (see chapter 13). Such programs featuring students working alongside "community others" also add a unique dimension of meaning and authenticity to the learning process (Beames and Atencio, 2008).

Once the idea of learning based in collective action with local residents and in a specific place takes root, one might ask about particular settings and activities. Publicly owned and community-run green spaces, such as community gardens or city parks, can be places for school groups, youth in out-of-school programs, and residents to build assets while demonstrating collective action. Because community gardens, tree planting, and other civic ecology practices taking place in urban open space demonstrate the collective efficacy of a neighborhood, we can avoid pitfalls encountered in programs that assume local people are disadvantaged and have little agency in deciding how to take action. The human interactions among diverse individuals working together in a community garden or a cleanup along an urban river are foundational to building social capital and creating a sense of community.

Settings such as urban community gardens, and activities such as tree planting or shoreline cleanups, lead not only to community and environmental outcomes; they also foster learning (Krasny and Tidball, 2015). For the participants, these include learning lifelong skills (e.g., gardening) and applying abstract concepts from math, language arts, science, and geography. Beames, Higgins, and Nicol (2012) confirm that this approach "is not about choosing community development over mathematics or literacy" (p. 70); indeed, the two can symbiotically enrich each other through engaging students in authentic, real world contexts. This integrated pedagogy also can enhance local environments, which is a fundamental aim of environmental education. In short, urban environmental education that offers opportunities for diverse groups of people to come together and work hand-in-hand to develop community and environmental assets is well placed to strengthen a shared social fabric and foster learning in meaningful ways.

Conclusion

Relationships among environmental education, social assets like social capital and sense of community, and environmental action are not unidirectional. Rather we can think of them as reinforcing each other, or as "complex systems feedbacks." For example, urban environmental education can be a means of building social capital, and social capital can in turn lead to collective environmental action. Referring to the community gardening example, environmental learning and more formal environmental education lessons can be part of community gardening, and community gardening can build social capital when youths and adults forge trust and social networks through working together. This social capital in turn can foster further engagement in community gardening or other collective action, such as advocating for open space in cities. And when youths are engaged in advocacy, they have additional opportunities to build trust and networks, or social capital. Similarly, sense of community can both facilitate collective action and be built through engaging in collective action, including actions such as dune restoration or tree planting that provide opportunities for environmental learning in cities.

So how does all this apply to urban environmental education? The notion of sustainability bridges social and environmental outcomes, but specific pathways to sustainability are harder to come by. Such pathways are often obstructed by entrenched perspectives that position efforts to address community well-being as antithetical to those that focus on environmental enhancement. At the same time, research demonstrates that spending time in and stewarding nature—common urban environmental education activities—foster both individual and community resilience and well-being (Krasny and Tidball, 2015). In short, urban environmental education includes activities that bridge this community-environment divide. These urban environmental education programs integrate building community assets like social capital and sense of community, often through embedding learning in collective action and thus demonstrating a neighborhood's collective efficacy. Such programs provide one means for understanding how environmental education is more than learning, but also about building sustainable cities.

References

Ahn, T. K., and Ostrom, E. (2008). Social capital and collective action. In D. Castiglione, J. W. van Deth, and G. Wolleb (Eds.), *Handbook of social capital* (pp. 70–100). Oxford, UK: Oxford University Press.

Beames, S., and Atencio, M. (2008). Building social capital through outdoor education. *Journal of Adventure Education & Outdoor Learning, 8*(2), 99–112.

Beames, S., Higgins, P., and Nicol, R. (2012). *Learning outside the classroom.* New York: Routledge.

Chawla, L., and Cushing, D. F. (2007). Education for strategic environmental behavior. *Environmental Education Research, 13*(4), 437–452.

Jorgensen, B., and Stedman, R. C. (2006). A comparative analysis of predictors of sense of place dimensions: Attachment to, dependence on, and identification with lakeshore properties. *Journal of Environmental Management, 79*(3), 316–327.

Krasny, M., Kalbacker, L., Stedman, R., and Russ, A. (2013). Measuring social capital among youth: Applications in environmental education. *Environmental Education Research, 21*(1), 1–23.

Krasny, M. E., and Tidball, K. G. (2015). *Civic ecology: Adaptation and transformation from the ground up*. Cambridge, Mass.: MIT Press.

Lewis, C. (1972). Public housing gardens: Landscapes for the soul. In *Landscape for Living* (pp. 277–282). Washington, D.C.: USDA Yearbook of Agriculture.

McKenzie, M. (2003). Beyond "The Outward Bound Process:" Rethinking student learning. *Journal of Experiential Education, 26*(1), 8–23.

McMillan, D. W., and Chavis, D. M. (1986). Sense of community: A definition and theory. *Journal of Community Psychology, 14*(1), 6–23.

Putnam, R. B. (2000). *Bowling alone: The collapse and revival of American community*. New York: Simon & Schuster.

Sampson, R. J., Raudenbush, S. W., and Earls, F. (1997). Neighborhoods and violent crime: A multilevel study of collective efficacy. *Science, 277*(5328), 918–924.

Sampson, R. J., and Raudenbush, S. W. (1999). Systematic social observation of public spaces: A new look at disorder in urban neighborhoods. *American Journal of Sociology, 105*(3), 603–651.

Schusler, T. M., and Krasny, M. (2010). Environmental action as context for youth development. *Journal of Environmental Education, 41*(4), 208–223.

Sirianni, C., and Friedland, L. A. (2005). *The civic renewal movement: Community building and democracy in the United States*. Dayton, Ohio: Charles F. Kettering Foundation.

Smith, G. A., and Sobel, D. (2010). *Place- and community-based education in schools*. New York: Routledge.

TRUST AND COLLABORATIVE GOVERNANCE

Marc J. Stern and Alexander Hellquist

Highlights

- "Wicked" urban sustainability issues call for collaborative governance based on deliberation.
- Urban environmental literacy should include an understanding of governance and skills related to productive deliberation.
- Understanding mechanisms for the development of trust can enhance the potential for constructive deliberation and collaborative governance.
- Environmental educators can serve as both trainers and facilitators of multi-stakeholder collaboration in urban communities.

Introduction

Urban sustainability challenges are commonly characterized as "wicked" problems (e.g., Rittel and Webber, 1973). They are complex and contested, not least in terms of tensions within the social-ecological systems that cities constitute. They often involve unbalanced power relations between stakeholders with diverging interests. Moreover, their contributing factors commonly shift, making both causes and solutions difficult to define. Resolving wicked problems defies simple policy solutions and goes beyond the responsibility of a single organization or government authority. Urban sustainability efforts thus reflect challenges of "governance."

The concept of governance encompasses the structures, processes, and traditions through which people in a society share power and make decisions. It stretches beyond government interventions by state actors to include a wide array of stakeholders. Effective governance is the result of dynamic links and interactions between individuals and groups operating at different levels and scales, and it often blurs traditional lines of authority to spur collective action (see chapter 11). In the Western world, a shift away from "government" toward "governance," including in urban planning and policy making, began in the 1960s in reaction to public protests against massive, expert-driven resource exploitation. The acceptance of stakeholder participation and dialogue as crucial elements in governance related to complex urban issues is now prominent in legislation and practice in many countries. The trend is sometimes referred to as the "deliberative turn" in literature on urban governance and planning.

The deliberative turn highlights the importance of public participation, attention to both purposive and inadvertent forms of exclusion, the value of dialogue among stakeholders, and the creation of an environment in which the distorting effects of power are diminished, such that individuals can feel safe to express themselves freely (Parkins and Mitchell, 2005). Deliberative processes typically involve greater investments of time by public officials, relinquishing some control over decision making, respect and patience for diverging viewpoints, and responsiveness to the concerns of diverse participants. The messiness of these processes has often frustrated officials (Predmore et al., 2011). Some scholars have even argued for a return to publicly informed but expert-driven planning processes (Burton and Mitchell, 2006).

While acknowledging the need to improve existing methods for deliberation, we argue that deliberative processes are critical to generating the innovative ideas necessary for confronting wicked problems in urban sustainability. Successful deliberative processes support the sharing and vetting of divergent ideas, enabling a wider range of alternatives to be considered. They may also create a sense of ownership among participants and build relationships to catalyze carrying ideas forward into action. Moreover, whether we like it or not, in a networked society it is not possible to calmly return to more traditional forms of public involvement in decision making, such as merely informing the public about intended policies or simply recording sound bite comments from the public. Citizens and stakeholder groups expect to influence urban governance through new channels, and it is thus necessary to find innovative ways to involve them.

In this chapter, we examine the linkages between urban environmental education programs and urban environmental governance in light of the "deliberative turn." (See chapter 11 for an examination of how organizations that conduct environmental education contribute to governance networks.) Participants in urban environmental governance need certain skills beyond the technical knowledge of their trades, including abilities to think critically, to see connections that cross traditional disciplinary training or organizational boundaries, to solve problems collaboratively, and to work constructively with a wide diversity of stakeholders (Willard et al., 2010). While expert knowledge is critically important, it must be situated within the social, political, and economic fabric of the larger urban system, so that substantive knowledge can be clearly distinguished from normative values. As a result, science can play its appropriate role of narrowing uncertainty and making predictions, while value-based decisions are deliberated among stakeholders.

Roles for Environmental Education

For environmental education to be relevant and successful in addressing urban sustainability challenges, it must recognize the complexity of such challenges and of deliberation across traditional political, socioeconomic, sectoral (e.g., nongovernmental organizations, government), and disciplinary lines. We emphasize two key outcomes within this context. First, environmental education can build the urban environmental literacy required to tackle wicked sustainability issues through an expanded consideration of governance. Second, environmental education can improve the collaborative capacities of individuals in multiple roles, enhancing the potential of deliberative processes to produce long-term commitments and partnerships with the capacity to implement and adapt solutions. A critical aspect of improving collaborative capacities and deliberative processes is the development of trust.

Developing Urban Environmental Literacy

The term "environmental literacy" encompasses the knowledge, attitudes, dispositions, and competencies necessary to equip people to effectively analyze and address environmental problems (Hollweg et al., 2011). In urban settings, we argue first and foremost that this means defining "environment" as the social-ecological system in which people live, rather than any view of some "other" nature that may be separate from the lives of urban dwellers. The systems component of this definition stresses not only the interactions of environmental components, such as water or wildlife, but also of human components. This means going beyond traditional upstream-downstream considerations to examining more complex causal chains and feedbacks, which take into account interactions between policy choices, social programs, infrastructure challenges, and social and environmental impacts. A reconsideration of governance structures and processes is required, which replaces traditional views of government authorities or narrowly defined organizational lines with visions of what might be possible across government and nongovernment sectors.

For example, one initiative in southwestern Virginia is integrating the traditionally separate domains of energy efficiency and aging in a program that retrofits seniors' homes to comply with the American with Disabilities Act. The initiative aims to enable seniors to age in place without being forced into a nursing home, while simultaneously conducting energy audits and making improvements in energy efficiency. Addressing both issues together has not only saved costs but has opened up new sources of funding not previously available. The effort required a holistic view of governance processes, which enabled new connections to be made across government institutions (local housing, workforce training, and energy authorities, as well as a regional planning commission) and nongovernmental organizations.

Such systems thinking can apply at local scales as well. For example, the nonprofit organization Green Bronx Machine combines elements of environmental education, local food production, and workforce development to simultaneously address issues of poverty, youth nutrition, and community development in a single school district. Here the deliberative process involved interactions between school administration, the school board, teachers, students, parents, and local community organizations that could link students with opportunities beyond the schoolyard.

Urban environmental literacy should include tools to understand governance and deliberative processes. Sustainability challenges require not only reasoned consideration of existing alternatives (i.e., critical thinking), but also the ability to make new connections within existing structures and systems. These skills, however, will have limited impact if they are not also combined with the development of capacity to collaborate with others who do not necessarily see the world in the same way.

Enhancing Collaborative Capacities

Successful collaborative governance is based on the degree to which participants are invested in the process and willing to create a holistic solution that is greater than the sum of its parts. Too often, public participation and political discourse devolve quickly into "us vs. them" rhetoric and strategies designed to push a preconceived solution rather than to generate a solution based on the diverse ideas of multiple stakeholders (Predmore et al. 2011). Solutions enhanced through collaboration typically rely on social learning, in which participants experience a change in understanding based on their interactions (Reed et al., 2010). We believe that environmental education can enable social learning, both through training participants in collaborative problem solving and through direct facilitation.

Trust has long been recognized as a key ingredient that enables social learning and effective collaboration. Trust is defined as a willingness to accept vulnerability in the face of uncertainty (Rousseau et al., 1999). This willingness allows participants in collaborative governance to take risks, share more freely, and listen more openly. Stern and Coleman (2015) identified four forms of trust relevant to collaborative governance in the environmental arena: dispositional trust, rational trust, affinitive trust, and systems-based (or procedural) trust.

Dispositional trust refers to individuals' pre-existing tendencies to be generally trusting of others. Dispositional trust thus sets the baseline from which other forms of trust are developed or eroded. Those who show up to public involvement events associated with environmental issues commonly have low levels of dispositional trust (Smith et al., 2013). Thus, individuals involved in complex governance deliberations spanning multiple sectors often begin their interactions from a more skeptical stance than they might when surrounded by people who are more familiar.

The other three forms of trust can be directly affected by interactions throughout a deliberative process, including through carefully designed urban environmental education. Rational trust involves an explicit evaluation by the trustor about the likely outcome of placing their trust in someone. It is therefore typically based on perceptions of competence and consistent past performance of a potential trustee in relation to one's own goals. Within a deliberative process, this means demonstrating relevant knowledge, holding to promises, and completing incremental tasks in a timely and competent manner.

Similar to rational trust, affinitive trust is based on interpersonal interactions, but affinitive trust is not based on a calculation or prediction of a particular outcome. Rather, it is based on an affinity for a potential trustee. This affinity, or positive attraction, typically involves an assumption of shared values and can emerge from positive social experiences, perceptions of active listening, responsiveness, caring, or general values discussions. In collaborative governance settings, the practice of communicating underlying values, as opposed to simply stating preconceived positions, can often reveal common ground important to developing affinitive trust (Fisher and Ury, 1999). Both rational and affinitive trust are forms of interpersonal trust.

Systems-based trust involves trust in the system within which interactions take place, rather than trust in a particular entity. Research suggests that procedures that are highly transparent, are jointly developed, promote power sharing, and involve an equitable distribution of benefits and risks tend to promote high levels of systems-based trust (Stern and Baird, 2015). These conditions mirror those found by Ostrom (1990) as necessary for sustainable and equitable governance of shared resources (e.g., a town forest or irrigation system shared by multiple farmers).

Stern and Baird (2015) demonstrate that adequate and well-distributed supplies of all three actionable forms of trust—rational, affinitive, and systems-based—are necessary for collaboration to be resilient to changes over time. For example, if policies change (related to systems-based trust), interpersonal trust (rational or affinitive) can allow stakeholders to chart a new course while new procedures are developed. If interpersonal trust is lost, for example, through turnover of a highly trusted leader, systems-based trust may enable a group to continue to work together while new leadership is established. If someone fails to perform effectively (violates rational trust), an affinitive relationship can help to limit the damage while rational trust is rebuilt.

Environmental educators can play important roles in catalyzing the development of these three forms of trust, both through training participants and as facilitators of collaborative deliberation (Table 10.1). Understanding how trust comes about may equip environmental educators with skills necessary to serve

TABLE 10.1 Strategies for building trust in environmental education programs (based on Stern and Baird, 2015; and Stern and Coleman, 2014)

TYPE OF TRUST	DEFINITION	ENVIRONMENTAL EDUCATION STRATEGY	
		TRAINING PARTICIPANTS	FACILITATION
Rational	Trust based on an evaluation of the expected outcome of another participant's predicted behavior	Developing critical thinking skills, evaluating different sources of information, promoting effective argumentation based on objective information	Providing opportunities to demonstrate competence and reliability
Affinitive	Trust based on an affinity for another participant, typically through an assumption of shared values or positive social experience	Respecting multiple viewpoints, understanding the merits of alternative arguments, demonstrating uncertainty, practice in cooperative learning and genuine listening	Moving participants from their positions toward discussions of their values
Systems-based	Trust in procedures that decrease vulnerability of the individual	Discussing power distributions, education on participatory processes, team-building procedures	Developing transparent procedures for decision making upon which all participants agree

as a bridge across interest groups. Acknowledging the presence or absence of different forms of trust is a crucial component of the context analysis educators undertake in designing programs. It allows educators to tailor programs to participant needs and to create an atmosphere in which participants engage fully and deliberate productively about sustainability issues.

Conclusion

Our goal in this chapter has been to highlight the importance of deliberative processes in governance and to provide guidance for environmental educators wishing to catalyze collaborations necessary for addressing wicked problems. We argue that urban environmental education should include: (1) a focus on illuminating the possibilities of making new connections across traditionally separate organizations, agencies, and people; and (2) training and facilitation to enhance collaborative capacities for constructive deliberation through trust building. Our calls are not entirely new to the field; many practitioners are undoubtedly already employing these techniques, and researchers have previously highlighted the potential of environmental education to catalyze social capital development and collaborative action (e.g., Krasny et al., 2015).

We suggest that environmental educators orient their efforts in at least two particular ways to capitalize on these potentials. First, environmental educators can help others to see the complex networks of governance at play within any wicked environmental challenge (see chapter 11). This exposes multiple levers for potential action and may enhance feelings of empowerment as new opportunities are explored. Simultaneously, environmental educators can develop skills in structuring learning experiences and collaborative processes that engender enough trust to allow room for honest debate, knowledge sharing, values discussions, and innovation. This involves moving people away from stating hard-and-fast positions toward revealing their values and interests (Fisher and Ury, 1999), creating opportunities for demonstrations of competence (building rational trust), facilitating positive social interactions and helping participants to understand the perspectives of others (building affinitive trust), and jointly developing fair and transparent procedures for decision making (building systems-based trust).

Environmental education that integrates governance and deliberative processes involves engaging multiple perspectives and acknowledging uncertainty. Some urban issues might be solved through raising awareness or teaching technical solutions, but this is rarely sufficient in the case of wicked problems. Thus while environmental education programs that are prescriptive or stress immediate technical fixes (e.g., recycling) may influence environmentally responsible behaviors, they are unlikely to help participants generate the innovative solutions needed to address urban sustainability issues. For this reason, participatory approaches to environmental education heralded by such authors as Louise Chawla, Roger Hart, Arjen Wals, Jeppe Laessoe, and others (e.g., Reid et al., 2008) are critical. Further, environmental educators can play critical roles in helping students navigate the intersections between "expert" knowledge, local knowledge, and diverse public values. It may be at this intersection where environmental education can have the greatest impact on fostering urban sustainability.

References

Burton, E., and Mitchell, L. (2006). *Inclusive urban design: Streets for life*. London: Routledge.

Fisher, R., and Ury, W. (1999). *Getting to yes: Negotiating agreement without giving in.* 2nd edition. New York: Penguin.

Hollweg, K. S., Taylor, J. R., Bybee, R. W., Marcinkowski, T. J., McBeth, W. C., and Zoido, P. (2011). *Developing a framework for assessing environmental literacy.* Washington, D.C.: North American Association for Environmental Education.

Krasny, M. E., Kalbacker, L., Stedman, R. C., and Russ, A. (2015). Measuring social capital among youth: Applications in environmental education. *Environmental Education Research, 21*(1), 1–23.

Ostrom, E. (1990). *Governing the commons: The evolution of institutions for collective action.* Cambridge: Cambridge University Press.

Parkins, J. R., and Mitchell, R. E. (2005). Public participation as public debate: A deliberative turn in natural resource management. *Society and Natural Resources, 18*(6), 529–540.

Predmore, S. A., Stern, M. J., Mortimer, M. J., and Seesholtz, D. (2011). Perceptions of legally mandated public involvement processes in the U.S. Forest Service. *Society and Natural Resources, 24*(12), 1286–1303.

Reed, M. S., Evely, A. C., Cundill, G., et al. (2010). What is social learning? *Ecology and Society, 15*(4).

Reid, A., Jensen, B. B., Nikel, J., and Simovska, V. (Eds.) (2008). *Participation and learning: Perspectives on education and the environment, health and sustainability.* New York: Springer.

Rittel, H. W. J., and Webber, M. M. (1973). Dilemmas in a general theory of planning. *Policy Sciences, 4*, 155–169.

Rousseau, D. M., Sitkin, S. B., Burt, R. S., and Camerer, C. (1998). Not so different after all: A cross-discipline view of trust. *Academy of Management Review, 23*(3), 393–404.

Smith, J. W., Leahy, J. E., Anderson, D. H., and Davenport, M. A. (2013). Community/agency trust and public involvement in resource planning. *Society and Natural Resources, 26*(4), 252–271.

Stern, M. J., and Baird, T. D. (2015). Trust ecology and the resilience of natural resource management institutions. *Ecology and Society, 20*(2), 14.

Stern, M. J., and Coleman, K. J. (2015). The multi-dimensionality of trust: Applications in collaborative natural resource management. *Society and Natural Resources, 28*(2), 117–132.

Willard, M., Wiedemeyer, C., Flint, R. W., Weedon, J. S., et al. (2010). The sustainability professional: 2010 competency survey report. *Environmental Quality Management, 20*(1), 49–83.

11

ENVIRONMENTAL GOVERNANCE

Marianne E. Krasny, Erika S. Svendsen,
Cecil Konijnendijk van den Bosch,
Johan Enqvist, and Alex Russ

Highlights

- Environmental governance represents the involvement of any government, civil society, or business organization in making rules and decisions about environmental management and in formulating environmental policy.
- Organizations that conduct environmental education play a role in environmental governance networks in cities.
- Urban environmental education prepares participants to play a role in local policy and planning processes, but it lacks an explicit focus on environmental governance and governance networks.
- By understanding their organization's role in environmental governance, urban environmental educators and program participants can better position themselves to influence urban sustainability.

Introduction

Environmental governance is a term used to reflect how not just a single government entity, but multiple government agencies, civil society organizations (e.g., community-based, nonprofit, and national or international nongovernmental organizations), and for-profit businesses play a role in environmental management and policy. More specifically, environmental governance refers to the involvement of a range of government, civil society, and business actors in the process of making rules, decisions, and policies about commonly held environmental resources. Recently, governance has become increasingly decentralized and participatory, whereas previously governance exclusively by government agencies was the norm (Buizer et al., 2015). But what does environmental governance have to do with urban environmental education? The answer lies in the fact that many government agencies, civil society organizations, and businesses that play a role in environmental governance also conduct environmental education in cities.

In this chapter, we first introduce environmental governance and governance networks. Next we present research on the prevalence of organizations conducting environmental education in governance networks in Asian, European, and U.S. cities. We close by proposing how environmental education organizations can be effective contributors in urban environmental governance and provide practical suggestions for making environmental education's role in governance transparent to educators and participants. In so doing, we make the argument that environmental education organizations are actors in urban governance networks, and through organizational leaders and program participants becoming aware of this role, these organizations can become more strategic players in environmental governance. We feel that an explicit focus on governance will enable organizational leaders to target their partnerships and efforts to have a greater impact on urban sustainability and will enable youths and other participants to gain an understanding of critical concepts in environmental management and policy. By focusing on environmental education *organizations*, this chapter complements chapter 10, which addresses governance from the perspective of how environmental educators can build program participants' capacity for governance, including through enhancing trust.

Environmental Governance

Environmental activism and civil society involvement in environmental policy in Europe can be traced back to the late nineteenth century, particularly related to urban forests (Konijnendijk, 2008). More recently, environmental governance in the United States and Europe is part of a forty-year trend of growing involvement of civil society in environmental management and policy. During the 1970s, government agencies in the United States issued regulations, often in response to pressure from large environmental nongovernmental organizations (e.g., Sierra Club). Relationships between environmentalists and industry were adversarial and in a few cases became violent. In the 1990s, the ways U.S. society managed its resources started to change. Tired of conflict, people who depended on natural resources for their livelihoods (e.g., loggers) and those who appreciated forests and coastlines for recreational and aesthetic reasons sought common ground. At the same time, interest in new forms of civic engagement, including through volunteer stewardship activities like community gardening, water quality monitoring, and coastal cleanups, was spreading. A new civic environmental movement, in which civil society organizations engaged in hands-on stewardship and advocacy formed partnerships with government agencies and businesses, was born (Weber, 2003; Sirianni and Friedland, 2005).

As more civil society organizations have become involved in environmental management, innovative governance arrangements have emerged. These arrangements have moved away from government control and regulations to incorporate citizen participation, including not just government-directed efforts seeking stakeholder input, but also citizen-driven efforts to influence policies and practices. Further, civil society actors have become more professionalized and now draw on a suite of tactics and strategies (Fisher, Campbell, and Svendsen, 2012; Fisher and Svendsen, 2014). For example, in Bangalore, India, citizen-driven initiatives to protect and restore urban lakes have generated a city-wide water governance network of civic stewardship and advocacy groups. Because network actors live and work in communities around the lake, they are better placed than government authorities to monitor water quality and environmental degradation (Enqvist, Tengö, and Boonstra, 2016). As these decentralized governance networks play an increasing role in setting environmental policy, issues arise as to the role of various government and nongovernment actors, power relationships, accountability, and the functioning of partnerships (Buizer et al., 2015).

The Bangalore case illustrates the importance of governance networks—that is, actors and their interactions and relationships—in environmental governance. In the early 2000s, the environmental stewardship network in New York City included more than two thousand government, civil society, and business organizations that shared information and resources, often around specific resources such as community gardens or the Hudson River estuary. Government agencies, including the New York City Department of Parks and Recreation and New York State Department of Environmental Conservation, served as central "bridging" organizations facilitating the flow of resources and knowledge within environmental networks. Although less central than government agencies, nonprofit organizations also played important roles as information providers for other organizations. The New York City environmental network structure was characterized by so-called "loose ties" among civic environmental groups focused on specific resources and by strong ties between civil society and government actors (Svendsen and Campbell, 2008; Connolly et al., 2014). This linking of organizations focusing on different resources and operating at different levels creates the capacity to address environmental problems at multiple scales.

Governance networks are important because the actors bring diverse experiences and knowledge around managing local resources and because the ties between the players enable communication and learning across organizations. Bridging organizations often have broad knowledge of stewardship and stewardship actors across the city and can share knowledge across organizations as well as connect actors with complementary interests and concerns. In addition to sharing knowledge, member organizations and individual stakeholders create new understandings about resource management through informal processes such as trying out management approaches and observing results, or learning by doing (Olsson et al., 2007). Compared to government agencies, smaller community organizations have less bureaucracy and may have the capacity to change or innovate more quickly, but they often lack organizational and leadership continuity; thus governmental actors have important roles to play in facilitating discussions and providing continuity and stability. One can think of the large government institutions in a governance network as the more rooted or stable "trees" and the smaller organizations as the more mobile or adaptable "bees" (cf. Young Foundation, 2012).

Information sharing and diverse actors in governance networks allow cities to adapt, which is critical to addressing wicked problems like climate change and associated sea level rise, flooding, and heat waves (Armitage and Plummer, 2010). Government actors can provide incentives for and recognize adaptation efforts, whereas civil society and business organizations often create the practice innovations. For example, the state of Maryland in the United States issued regulations to reduce the impact of development on storm water runoff. In response, heavily urbanized Prince George's County teamed up with a private company to launch the storm water management public-private Clean Water Partnership, which supports local job creation and training and hires minority-owned businesses to install urban green infrastructure projects. The White House (the U.S. Presidency) recognized this partnership as "among the most innovative in the nation" (Prince George's County, 2016). Important to environmental education, this project's career training and related learning opportunities enable youths to gain skills in building green infrastructure.

Environmental Education Organizations

In cities in India, Europe, and the United States, organizations that conduct environmental education are actors in environmental governance networks, leading to outcomes important to urban sustainability. For example, in Bangalore,

India, members of a green space governance network mentioned raising public awareness and putting environmental issues on the urban agenda as their most important achievements. This growing awareness can be attributed to such network activities as creating platforms for diverse citizens to discuss needed changes in green space management, and campaigns in different neighborhoods to share alternative visions for the city. Together with other manifestations of civic engagement in Bangalore and India more broadly, the network activities have influenced media reports, authorities' behavior, and public opinion such that open consultations for major public projects are now expected and questioning traditional development pathways is commonplace (Enqvist, Tengö, and Bodin, 2014).

Similarly, 25 percent of civil society organizations engaged in green space governance in twenty European cities provided education, and 40 percent encouraged city residents to experience green spaces or nature (Buizer et al., 2015). The emphasis on education varied from 7 percent of urban park agencies, 45 percent of urban farming initiatives, and 66 percent of conservation organizations, which saw conservation actions "as a way to promote environmental awareness and education." Examples of these environmental outreach programs come from Helsinki, Finland, and Linz, Austria, where civil society organizations created and shared web-based maps of public fruit trees and edible shrubs.

In New York City, more than two thousand stewardship organizations are organized around city parks, neighborhood open space, community gardens, the New York Harbor estuary, and other urban resources. In the early 2000s, more than half of these actors were small community organizations, nearly a third were larger nonprofits, with a smaller number being government agencies operating at the federal, state, or local level and for-profit businesses. When a subset of the groups was asked about the resources they provide to the community, four out of eleven resources were related to education, including providing information or data, hands-on trainings and curricula, and engaging students or interns. Further, when asked about their social and environmental impacts, nearly 70 percent of the organizations said they provide environmental education, whereas more than 60 percent mentioned engaging youth and providing educational experiences (Svendsen and Campbell, 2008). Finally, both government agencies and civil society organizations central to the networks, including the City Department of Parks and Recreation, State Department of Environmental Education, Brooklyn Botanic Garden, New York Restoration Project, and Grow NYC (Connolly et al., 2014), conduct education and interpretation programs ranging from longer-term summer camps and after-school community gardening programs to public fishing days and garden contests.

The fact that government and civil society organizations conduct environmental education in cities is nothing new. Scholars have documented the role of community gardens in science, cultural, and civic education (Krasny and Tidball, 2009) and how organizations whose missions focus on youth and community development engage youth in water quality monitoring, community gardening, invasive species removal, and other environmental stewardship or civic ecology practices in the Bronx (Kudryavtsev, 2013). But a closer look at environmental education *organizations*, as opposed to programs and curricula, reveals how the field of environmental education can contribute to urban sustainability not just through its ongoing teaching activities, but also through purposeful participation in governance networks.

Implications for Environmental Education

The good news for environmental education is that organizations that conduct environmental education are already part of governance networks. Further, education-focused organizations can make important contributions to governance networks, including their expertise in teaching, communication, and learning by doing. Given the importance of environmental governance networks in addressing urban sustainability issues, a purposeful focus on the role of environmental education actors in such networks is important. Below we first outline ways in which organizations that conduct environmental education—including community gardens, youth and community development organizations, museums, botanical gardens, city parks, environmental nongovernmental organizations, state agency-run camps, and amusement parks (e.g., Disney)—are already engaged in environmental governance. We close by suggesting how environmental educators might incorporate governance into their education programs.

Organizations that conduct environmental education in cities are often engaged in a number of governance and related management and planning activities. These include lobbying for environmental regulations; information campaigns to inform local communities about sustainability issues and possible solutions; green infrastructure planning, design, and implementation; and monitoring wildlife populations and water quality through citizen science programs. Youth participants in environmental education programs become involved in these and related activities. For example, the UNESCO Growing Up in Cities program engages children in impoverished neighborhoods in planning local green space in cities around the world; the U.S. Garden Mosaics program engages youths and adults in managing and learning about community gardens; and participants in the Cornell University BirdSleuth program monitor bird populations in the United States and Latin America. Given the interest in education among government, civil society, and private-sector organizations, as well as in learning by doing as a means to generate urban sustainability innovations, opportunity exists for environmental education organizations at the local, state, national, and international level to form additional partnerships. Environmental organizations can bring to the table knowledge and pedagogical strategies backed up by educational research, as well as their own networks of participants and physical resources such as nature centers or camps.

As a means to strengthen existing networks, organizations that conduct environmental education can be training grounds for other network actors (e.g., about pedagogy, youth development) and for their own program participants. Focusing on participants, educators can point out how governance-related activities youth are already engaged in—such as decision making, planning, hands-on stewardship, and monitoring—involve multiple government agency, nonprofit, and private-sector partners. They can further incorporate into these activities discussions and activities to help participants understand the roles of governance networks and their organizational actors.

Although we are not aware of environmental education organizations purposefully incorporating governance in this way, we present several strategies to do so. Youths could use an environmental or youth organization website to generate a list of collaborators. For example, the partners listed on the website for an urban environmental education organization along the shores of the Bronx River include New York City public high schools; Bronx community organizations and businesses; scientific, technical, and environmental organizations (ranging from local to national in scale); boat-related organizations; and cultural and public organizations (http://www.rockingtheboat.org).

Alternatively, educators might ask program participants to list all the individuals from different organizations they have come into contact with during their environmental education program, such as government scientists, youths from other organizations, and parks department staff. Program participants could consider the missions of these organizations and brainstorm potential governance networks of which their organization is a part, including not only environmental networks but also those focused on youth and community development. Educators and youths also might acquaint themselves with forms of participation in urban green space and other types of environmental governance, such as conserving, managing, monitoring, restoring, advocating, and educating the public (Connolly et al., 2014). They could next identify where their organization plays or could play a role and how their activities might best contribute to governance networks focused on green space, community development, and other sustainability issues.

Conclusion

Environmental education programs seek to foster deliberation and decision-making skills and build trust among participants (see chapter 10). We contend that these activities, which foster participants' ability to engage in local policy making, can be complemented by activities to make transparent the role of the environmental organizations and their participants as governance actors. Understanding environmental governance—and how organizations, including those that conduct environmental education, contribute to governance networks—is critical to understanding environmental management and policy processes in cities. As educators and participants understand their roles and those of their organizations, they may more effectively position themselves and their organizations as actors in governance networks, which are critical to generating adaptations and innovations needed to address social and environmental change and sustainability in cities.

References

Armitage, D., and Plummer, R. (2010). *Adaptive capacity: Building environmental governance in an age of uncertainty.* Berlin: Springer-Verlag.

Buizer, M., Elands, B., Mattijssen, T., van der Jagt, A., Ambrose, B., Gerőházi, É., Santos, A., and Steen Møller, M. (2015). *The governance of urban green spaces in selected EU-cities.* Green Surge, E.U.

Connolly, J. J., Svendsen, E., Fisher, D. R., and Campbell L. (2014). Networked governance and the management of ecosystem services: The case of urban environmental stewardship in New York City. *Ecosystem Services, 10,* 187–194.

Enqvist, J., Tengö, M., and Boonstra, W. (2016). Against the current: Rewiring rigidity trap dynamics in urban water governance through civic engagement. *Sustainability Science, 11*(6), 919–933.

Enqvist, J., Tengö, M., and Bodin, Ö. (2014). Citizen networks in the Garden City: Protecting urban ecosystems in rapid urbanization. *Landscape and Urban Planning, 130,* 24–35.

Fisher, D. R., Campbell, L., and Svendsen, E. S. (2012). The organisational structure of urban environmental stewardship. *Environmental Politics, 21*(1), 26–48.

Fisher, D. R., and Svendsen, E. S. (2014). Hybrid arrangements within the environmental state. In S. Lockie, D. A. Sonnenfeld, and D. R. Fisher (Eds.) *Routledge international handbook of social and environmental change* (pp. 179–189). London: Routledge.

Konijnendijk, C. C. (2008). *The city and the forest: The cultural landscape of urban woodland.* The Netherlands: Springer.

Krasny, M. E., and Tidball, K. G. (2009). Community gardens as contexts for science, stewardship, and civic action learning. *Cities and the Environment, 2*(1), 8.

Kudryavtsev, A. (2013). Urban environmental education and sense of place. PhD dissertation. Cornell University, Ithaca, N.Y.

Olsson, P., Folke, C., Galaz, V., Hahn, T., and Schultz, L. (2007). Enhancing the fit through adaptive comanagement: Creating and maintaining bridging functions for matching scales in the Kristianstads Vattenrike Biosphere Reserve Sweden. *Ecology and Society 12*(1), 28.

Prince George's County. (2016). Clean Water Partnership. http://thecleanwaterpartnership.com.

Sirianni, C., and Friedland, L. A. (2005). *The civic renewal movement: Community building and democracy in the United States.* Dayton, Ohio: Charles F. Kettering Foundation.

Svendsen, E. S., and Campbell, L. (2008). Urban ecological stewardship: Understanding the structure, function and network of community-based land management. *Cities and the Environment, 1*(1), 4.

Weber, E. P. (2003). *Bringing society back in: Grassroots ecosystem management, accountability, and sustainable communities.* Cambridge, Mass.: MIT Press.

Young Foundation. (2012). Social innovation overview: A deliverable of the project: The theoretical, empirical and policy foundations for building social innovation in Europe (TEPSIE). European Commission – 7th Framework Programme, DG Research, Brussels, Belgium.

Part III
EDUCATIONAL SETTINGS

12

NONFORMAL EDUCATIONAL SETTINGS

Joe E. Heimlich, Jennifer D. Adams,
and Marc J. Stern

Highlights

- Nonformal environmental education, in which learners themselves decide to engage, occurs in city parks, zoos, libraries, nonprofit education centers, and other settings.
- The diverse social roles of urbanites create rich "learningscapes" for environmental learning.
- Urban nonformal environmental education involves relating environmental content to the everyday lives of urban learners, ensuring learner autonomy, and integrating the institutions of environmental education providers within the broader array of social institutions in the urban environment.

Introduction

The vast array of resources available in almost any urban setting challenges the notion that urbanites do not have access to nature and to environmental education. Parks, zoos, aquariums, nature centers, gardens, arboreta, and other institutions provide nature access, as do many nongovernmental organizations and governmental agencies providing environmental education and outreach programs for urbanites. While actual access to green spaces is often negatively correlated with income (Lee and Maheswaran, 2011), myriad opportunities exist to engage in environmental education, even in dense and economically challenged urban communities. Indeed, urban, nonformal environmental education can occur within the cityscape in all sorts of ways. This chapter will define the types of urban nonformal educational opportunities, situate them in the lives of urbanites using the concept of "learningscapes," and examine the pedagogy of nonformal environmental education for urban audiences.

Nonformal Urban Environmental Education

For decades, educators have engaged in discussion about what to call organized learning that happens outside of formal schooling. Informal, nonformal, incidental, everyday, free-choice, all are valid terms, and all have slightly different meanings in terms of contexts and ways in which educational messages are constructed and presented. Here, we use nonformal as defined by Mocker and Spear (1982), and later clarified in science and environmental education, as learning contexts where someone other than the learner decides what is to be learned (or creates a program), but the learner decides whether or not to engage.

In most cities, on any day, individuals have scores of opportunities to participate in environmental learning. It might be a community meeting about energy conservation offered by the local electric utility, a water conservation program offered by the water and sewer agency, or a lecture offered by a nongovernmental organization such as Audubon Society, Sierra Club, or the Nature Conservancy. It could also be an environmental issues café (discussion) at a science museum or hands-on activity at a nature center. We suggest five general categories of nonformal environmental education providers: government, quasi-governmental organizations, environmental organizations, businesses/industry, and community institutions. The government providers include environment regulators and managers, whereas quasi-governmental programs occur through universities and publicly supported organizations that have environmental and nature education missions. In addition to business, other providers include nature centers and zoos, plus nongovernmental organizations and environmental and youth community groups.

Nonformal environmental education can be categorized along three dimensions (Table 12.1). The "choice" spectrum involves the motivations of the participants. At one end of the spectrum may be interest-focused citizens actively seeking solutions to a particular environmental problem. At the other end might be a school field trip to a nature center or park where students have minimal choice, or programs where a participant may simply be accompanying someone else who decided to participate. The second dimension involves the goals of the participants. These range from none at all to satisfying a general curiosity to

TABLE 12.1 Types of nonformal urban environmental education programs according to participant choice and goals and provider goals

TYPE OF NONFORMAL PROGRAM	CHOICE IN PARTICIPATION	TYPICAL GOALS OF PARTICIPANTS	TYPICAL GOALS OF PROVIDERS
School field trips or related programs	None	Entertainment Academic achievement Content knowledge	Providing content knowledge Influencing conservation behavior Teaching critical thinking
Casual visit to a community institution (e.g., nature center)	Variable	Social experience Educational	Specific content Environmental conservation or protection attitudes and behaviors
Specific programs (e.g., an extension or outreach presentation or stewardship activity)	High	Knowledge of topical or contextual information Skills development Social experience Addressing a specific problem	Specific content or skill development Environmental conservation or protection behaviors
Recreational programs	Variable	Exercise Fun Social experience	Health Environmental awareness Conservation behaviors

learning about a particular environmental problem to entertainment. The third dimension involves the goals of the nonformal program provider. These goals relate to the provider's mission and range from influencing conservation-related behaviors to providing safe recreational opportunities to building support for the organization.

Urban Environmental Learningscapes

Most environmental learning occurs outside the context of formal schooling. Such learning happens across experiences and settings and is grounded in the context of a person's life (Lave and Wenger, 1991). To understand nonformal environmental education, we situate the learner not only in the setting, but consider their identity and social role in a given context. Social role theory (Biddle, 1979) tells us that we each may assume a range of different roles, sometimes called identities, from parent to child, professional to hobbyist, friend to colleague, enthusiast to expert. We enact different roles in which various aspects of our selves become dominant. The present role of an individual affects what he or she pays attention to and his or her interpretation of the experience (Feather, 1982). For example, while in the role of a parent, we may experience a nature center visit entirely differently than we might on an individual visit. The effect of one's role on one's lens and interpretation of the experience will determine what is most likely to be learned.

People move through life engaging in varied and not always linear or connected endeavors. One might go to the symphony one evening and kayaking on the river the next morning. Another day might include gardening and playing basketball on the neighborhood courts. Individuals have the potential to make meaning across collective experiences. This is part of a learningscape, an individual's movement through life in various social roles and how the individual connects experiences and makes meaning and learns cumulatively across and among all experiences. Nonformal environmental education programs can help individuals connect the many experiences of their lives and facilitate meaning across experiences. Environmental education providers in urban areas who make these connections explicit can help learners make connections to environmental issues, possibly leading to greater interest and action for engaging in sustainable, urban living.

A learner's identity influences the way he or she moves through learning, while learningscapes influence the identity of the learner. For example, a community member notices the unsavory color and smell of the local urban lake and wonders if renting the new pedal boats would be safe. She visits the Environmental Protection Agency website and learns about a public program on the toxicity of the blue-green algal bloom. After participating in this nonformal educational program, she posts what she learned on a community blog, affording others access to this information and asking them to take actions. The identity of this person has possibly moved from concerned citizen to community advocate, as she has begun to encourage others to express concern and seek to remedy this situation (Stapleton, 2015).

Tying identity to agency helps develop an environmental identity, with agency referring to the power to act within certain circumstances (Adams and Gupta, 2015). Fostering agency around environmental issues, with attention to existing identities and relationships to the environment, is a key objective for nonformal environmental education providers seeking to foster public advocacy. By having programs and learning materials tied to increasing agency (through learning about issues and providing avenues to work toward change), nonformal institutions influence environmental identities of individuals and groups.

Clearly, not every experience of an individual adds to his or her environmental understanding or identity. A modified Delphi study of environmental education stakeholders revealed that many environmental learnings throughout one's life are not always tied to nature, but to other relevant concerns such as health, family, safety, leisure, and security. Although the core of environmental education is literacy enabling individual environmental knowledge, affect, and action benefiting self and the environment, environmental education includes public health, environmental justice, social equity, diversity, justice, and other concerns, many of which are intensified in the urban context.

Learning in Urban Nonformal Environmental Education

Within the variety of nonformal programs, pedagogical approaches vary drastically. Although participants may be physically captive in some settings (e.g., school programs or drop-off programs for kids), they are rarely cognitively captive. The absence of clear consequences or assessment frees participants to engage only to the extent interest or curiosity is piqued or an affective connection is made with the provider. For providers seeking to achieve the broader goals of environmental education, including enhancing knowledge, skills, attitudes, and dispositions related to environmental problem solving, three theoretical models may be particularly relevant: the elaboration likelihood model, self-determination theory, and reference group theory.

The elaboration likelihood model (Petty and Cacioppo, 1986) originates from persuasive communication research and has relevance for educators seeking to change environmental attitudes. Its utility for understanding education with noncaptive audiences lies in the two routes to persuasion it describes: central and peripheral. The *central* route to persuasion involves explicit cognitive processing ("elaboration") of the message by a message recipient. In other words, the person draws upon prior experience and knowledge to scrutinize and evaluate issue-relevant arguments presented in the communication. This cognitive processing can result in a well-articulated attitude integrated in the person's belief structure. Attitudes developed via this route tend to be relatively accessible, persistent over time, predictive of behavior, and resistant to change. For central route processing to occur, the person must be motivated and able to process the message. When motivation or ability to process arguments is low, the context in which the information is provided may take precedence and still work to persuade the person. This *peripheral* route processing, however, only tends to influence the message recipient as long as the environmental cue is in place. For example, one might pick up trash when in the presence of others who do so, but might not when alone unless the behavior was internalized through central route processing.

With noncaptive audiences whose familiarity with environmental topics may be limited, motivating central route processing is highly dependent upon a few elements. First, does something within the program command attention?

Moscardo's (1999) work on promoting mindfulness in visitors suggests that novelty, multisensory engagement, and choice can enhance openness to new ideas. Meanwhile, other scholars from the constructivist tradition stress the importance of highlighting the relevance of the subject matter to the lives of participants. This suggests the importance of an appropriate blend of novelty and familiarity in a setting that engages participants in meaningful ways and in which participants retain sufficient autonomy to pursue their own interests.

To illustrate, NorthBay Adventure Center serves inner-city Baltimore middle-school-age youth in a novel environment on Chesapeake Bay in Maryland. For most participants, the hour-plus journey to NorthBay is their first time leaving the city. Located on the beach in the midst of a state park, NorthBay also includes a large gymnasium for sports and a multimedia theater where environmental themes from lessons learned during the day are translated into analogous lessons about the participants' home environments. For example, after learning about invasive species during the day, participants attend an evening show focusing on crime and drugs in inner-city communities. NorthBay educators explicitly discuss environment as the place where students are, rather than some place distant or pristine "out there," further helping participants link lessons to their home lives (Stern, Powell, and Ardoin, 2010).

Self-determination theory (Ryan and Deci, 2000) further stresses the importance of autonomy for learners. The theory and associated research demonstrate that people's feelings of autonomy, competence, and relatedness are keys to intrinsic motivation, which enhances learning and central route processing. Nonformal environmental education programs may address each of these elements through responsiveness to learner interest and through allowing learners to make choices within programs (autonomy); focusing beyond content knowledge toward skills development and application, and drawing upon relevant prior knowledge, skills, and known situations (competence); and creating supportive and collaborative environments in which innovation, risk taking, and open exploration are encouraged (relatedness). In urban settings, connecting content to locally relevant situations and drawing on community concerns may be particularly important to counteract traditional conceptualizations of canned nature programs that don't connect meaningfully to audiences whose definitions of "nature" or the "environment" may not match those of providers.

Urban populations are diverse along multiple dimensions of interest, culture, and socioeconomic status, and nonformal programs vary in their potential for reaching different segments of the population. For example, those attracted to university outreach programs may not be the same people who visit their local nature centers. Moreover, large proportions of the population may be largely unaware of or uninterested in environmental education opportunities in their communities, or may engage in programs without even being aware it is environmental education. Recently, a study of the perceived values of nature centers to their local communities (Browning et al., in review) discovered that these centers, and presumably similar community institutions, may be valued well beyond their traditional forms of environmental programming and leisure provision. Community members also valued centers for their roles in enhancing civic engagement and community resilience, suggesting that activities such entities might normally consider "mission creep" might actually be more valuable than commonly assumed (Heimlich, 2009).

Reference group theory (Merton, 1968) helps us understand how linkages within the urban community can enhance public trust and subsequently the diffusion and impact of nonformal environmental education programs. Trust for providers of various forms of environmental programming is an important factor driving their success (Stern and Coleman, 2015). We draw our values, opinions, and resulting assessments largely through comparison to others we feel are important or whom we trust. One might think of reference groups in an urban environment as a complicated Venn diagram of influences upon an individual, ranging from family members to other community members to politicians and celebrities. Through active engagement in community realms beyond those typically inhabited by "environmental types," providers of environmental education may build trusting relationships that serve as gateways for nontraditional audiences to become curious about environmental programming. Through broader engagement with a diversity of community members, providers may become part of the reference groups of an ever broadening array of people, initiating not only program participation, but also larger conversations about the role of environmental education across sectors. In the typically dense social networks and diverse learningscapes of urban communities, these bridging activities (e.g., volunteering at a local literacy event or providing a venue for a community concert) may have exponential impacts.

Conclusion

We propose that effective nonformal environmental education programs for urban audiences do not resemble isolated nor formal education presentations or lectures. Rather, they engage urban community members in activities directly relevant to the environments in which they live, including the built environment. They engage people in learning about environmental issues and problems faced in daily life, from the everyday to the extraordinary. They stress skills for navigating environmental issues in local spaces. Whether in the zoo, museum, or library; at work, home, or in transit; with friends, alone, or with family, we are engaged with the environment in all aspects of our lives, and opportunities for nonformal environmental education surround us. We propose that urban environmental education providers have unique opportunities for connecting beyond traditional audiences due to the dense and diverse networks of programs within urban environments, ranging from youth sports leagues to literacy clubs and neighborhood watches. Building relationships across sectors can not only bring people to programs but can also enhance the impact of urban environmental education by integrating environmental content with what nontraditional audiences might find more relevant, leading to a greater consciousness and potential motivation for addressing environmental issues. Building relationships with community organizations can also open up environmental education to social issues, thus reflecting current scholarship in university environmental and sustainability oriented departments that focuses on *integrated* social-ecological systems. Finally, by building these relationships, nonformal providers are better situated to facilitate participants' connections among the many experiences they encounter through their everyday life.

References

Adams, J., and Gupta, P. (2015). Informal science institutions and learning to teach: An examination of identity, agency and affordances. *Journal of Research in Science Teaching.* http://dx.doi.org/10.1002/tea.21270.

Biddle, B. J. (1979). *Role theory: Concepts and research.* New York: Academic Press.

Browning, M. E. M., Stern, M. J., Ardoin, N. M, and Heimlich, J. E. (in review). The values of nature centers to local communities. *Environmental Education Research.*

Feather, N. T. (1982). *Expectations and actions: Expectancy-value models in psychology.* Mahwah, N.J.: Lawrence Erlbaum Associates.

Heimlich, J. E. (2009). Environmental education evaluation: Reinterpreting education as a strategy for meeting mission. *Journal of Evaluation and Program Planning, 33*(2), 180–185.

Lave, J., and Wenger, E. (1991). *Situated learning: Legitimate peripheral participation.* Cambridge: Cambridge University Press.

Lee, A. C. K., and Maheswaran, R. (2011). The health benefits of urban green spaces: A review of the evidence. *Journal of Public Health, 33*(2), 212–222.

Merton, R. K. (1968). *Social theory and social structure.* New York: The Free Press.

Mocker, D. W., and Spear, G. E. (1982). *Lifelong learning: Formal, nonformal, informal, and self-directed.* Information Series No. 241. Columbus, Ohio: ERIC CSMEE.

Moscardo, G. (1999). *Making visitors mindful: Principles for creating sustainable visitor experiences through effective communication.* Urbana, Ill.: Sagamore Publishing.

Petty, R. E., and Cacioppo, J. T. (1986). The elaboration likelihood model of persuasion. *Advances in Experimental Psychology, 19*, 123–205.

Ryan, R. M., and Deci, E. L. (2000). Self-determination theory and the facilitation of intrinsic motivation, social development and well-being. *American Psychologist, 55*(1), 68–78.

Stapleton, S. (2015). Environmental identity development through social interactions, action, and recognition. *Journal of Environmental Education, 46*(2), 94–113.

Stern, M. J., and Coleman, K. J. (2015). The multi-dimensionality of trust: Applications in collaborative natural resource management. *Society and Natural Resources, 28*(2), 117–132.

Stern, M. J., Powell, R. B., and Ardoin, N. M. (2010). Evaluating a constructivist and culturally responsive approach to environmental education for diverse audiences. *Journal of Environmental Education, 42*(2), 109–122.

13

COMMUNITY ENVIRONMENTAL EDUCATION

Marianne E. Krasny, Mutizwa Mukute,
Olivia M. Aguilar, Mapula Priscilla Masilela,
and Lausanne Olvitt

Highlights

- Community environmental education uses environmental learning and action to foster community wellness in cities and other settings.
- Social learning encompasses a diversity of learning theories, all of which focus on learning through interaction with others.
- Communities of practice and cultural historical activity theory are two social learning frameworks useful in understanding community environmental education.

Introduction

Community environmental education prioritizes community wellness above environmental outcomes. Rather than learning in, about, and for the environment being an end in itself, environmental learning becomes a means toward achieving community wellness and healing. In this way, community environmental education is aligned with youth and community development, participatory, and resilience approaches in environmental education. Although the priority is social rather than environmental, in reality community environmental education programs generally result in positive impacts for both communities and the environment.

124

Recognizing that community environmental education is an emerging field lacking a clear definition (Aguilar, 2016; Aguilar, Price, and Krasny, 2015), here we use a definition developed in the U.S. urban context (Price, Simmons, and Krasny, 2014): "Community environmental education aims to enhance a community's wellness through thoughtful environmental action. It fosters collaborative learning and action, taking into account the social, cultural, economic, and environmental conditions of a community."

The term community also has multiple definitions, including those built around a common location, social connections or belonging, cultural identity, and interests (Delanty, 2003). Our use of the term integrates local (e.g., a neighborhood), common interests (e.g., youth development, organic food production), and relational or belonging aspects of community, which is consistent with our focus on community wellness. We define community wellness as social, environmental, and economic conditions that support health and quality of life, including the presence of healthy green spaces, food and water, and opportunities to engage in healthy activities with others. Although environmental education focusing on community wellness can occur anywhere, much of our understanding of community environmental education comes from work in cities.

Because building connections among people is critical to achieving community wellness, a learning theory that emphasizes how learning occurs through interaction with others is useful in elucidating the learning process and outcomes of community environmental education. Social learning encompasses a group of theories that have in common a focus on learning through interactions with others and with the environment (Wals, 2007). Two social learning theories used in understanding environmental education include communities of practice and cultural historical activity theory. For example, Aguilar and Krasny (2011) applied communities of practice theory to understanding how learning occurs in environmental after-school programs in small cities in Texas, and Krasny and Roth (2010) applied cultural historical activity theory to watershed programs occurring near Victoria, British Columbia. Importantly, these two theories privilege not just the knowledge and perspectives of professionals, but also of community members and of youth participants in environmental education programs. For the urban environmental educator, these theories enable understanding of how learning occurs in programs designed to foster individual and organizational transformations leading to community wellness.

In this chapter, we apply community of practice theory to a youth program focusing on water quality in the United States and cultural historical activity theory to two programs in South Africa, one involving organic agriculture and the other medical wastes. Although the South African cases may seem foreign to Western environmental educators who commonly work with youth audiences, lessons drawn from these cases about identifying and resolving contradictions through interactions among academic, professional, and practical knowledge holders, leading to transformations and outcomes consistent with community wellness, are relevant to community environmental education more broadly.

Communities of Practice

Originally developed to understand how people learn a craft or skill through interactions with more skilled craftsmen, communities of practice theory examines individual and group identity formation and transformation as a learning process. According to Wenger (1998), a community of practice is a place where people with a common interest or concern engage and become members, agree on and pursue a particular enterprise (e.g., community wellness), and cultivate a common repertoire (e.g., cultural values). The framework considers learning as a social process that occurs as individuals participate in groups associated with a specific physical, historical, and cultural context, often resembling an apprenticeship focused around a common interest or concern (Lave and Wenger, 1991). Researchers have used this framework to identify apprenticeship-like approaches to learning, while others have examined individual identity and power differentials as a result of participation in communities of practice.

Water Watchers: An Environmental Education Community of Practice in Austin, Texas

Water Watchers (organization name changed to protect participants' privacy) is an environmental education program that engages low-income youth in Austin, Texas. Its mission is to "advance personal and academic achievement through environmental monitoring, education, and adventure." It provides an example of how program staff's attention to multiple elements of a community of practice fosters youth engagement. During the academic year after the school day ends, program staff members transport students to various sites to test water quality, and then to program headquarters, where students socialize, share food, and do homework with peers who tested a different site. During the summer, staff members transport students to their water monitoring sites, after which they go swimming or on a field trip. Through this process, Water Watchers has developed a community of practice, including *membership, common enterprise,* and *shared culture* (Aguilar, in revision).

A community of practice relies on consistent *membership* with multiple entry points for joining. Water Watchers offers meetings through the year, provides transportation and a stipend (thus encouraging attendance), offers multiple activities and volunteer opportunities, and brings in speakers and community members. This allows students to participate for different reasons: they like science, they want to be with friends, their teacher recommended them, or they simply want something to do after school.

The program common *enterprise* revolves around youth development—including academic achievement, social support, agency, and empowerment—and around environmental stewardship, both of which foster community wellness. While students often identify the program enterprise as one of water quality monitoring and socializing, they also acknowledge that the program has given them a voice and feelings of respect and acceptance. The program leaders feel students should leave the program "prepared to create a life for themselves that will be better," and thus they ask students to develop goals not only for program participation, but also for their school and family lives. Students work as mentees until they pass a test to become mentors. Mentors in turn develop confidence in their skills as they help newcomers with water testing procedures. Students also apply their water quality knowledge in new arenas, like canoeing and service learning. Finally, the community of practice includes trajectories that enable members to expand their academic and social skills and bridge with other communities of practice.

Water Watchers also projects a shared *culture* of respect for each participant and of helping each other. This culture is reinforced when students depend on one another for a successful water test and through overnight camping and trips to learn about colleges. For example, an African American male who had recently opened up about his homosexuality on an all-boys overnight trip found acceptance rather than ridicule in the Water Watchers community. Another student admitted that high school was a difficult place to feel accepted, but Water Watchers made it easier for her to find a sense of belonging.

In addition to consistent membership, common enterprise, and shared culture, Water Watchers provides for needs like food, financial assistance in the form of a stipend, and a base for homework and recreation. These services result in a "safe space" and enable a "sense of belonging" for students, many of whom come from unstable homes. In short, Water Watchers empowers participants by improving their social and educational skills, and it fosters community wellness through these youth development outcomes and through monitoring water quality.

Cultural Historical Activity Theory

Cultural historical activity theory is based on the idea that humans change or learn when they engage in productive activity within a particular cultural and historical context and environment and, in doing so, change that environment. Productive activity occurs within an activity system, which is made up of a goal or outcome for the activity, tools, rules, objects, subjects, community, and division of labor, as well as the interaction of these elements (Engeström, 1987). Learning occurs through interaction of the learner with other components of this system.

Learning also occurs when contradictions between different elements of the activity system generate conflicts, for example when rules specifying how to conduct an activity are not consistent with project goals. This can lead to transformations or expanding the activity to include new rules, tools, or goals. Further, one activity system may produce outcomes that are used by another activity system, such as when knowledge produced through a water monitoring activity system is used by policy makers in a legislative activity system. In short, a learning activity system is dynamic and has multiple interactions among its elements and with other activity systems, which can lead to transformation of the activity system and related learning.

Expansive Learning in Organic Agriculture Learning System, Durban, South Africa

In 2008, Rhodes University, which has cultural knowledge that functions as activity system "tools," and the South African Qualifications Authority, which makes educational policies and standards and thus provides "rules," began implementing the Researching Work and Learning program in environmental education. The Isidore Organic Network and its marketing arm, Earth Mother Organic, constituted one research site (Mukute, 2010). In trying to address growing demand for organic produce in Durban, these organizations faced challenges meeting organic standards, getting certified as organic producers, and becoming profitable. Cultural historical activity theory, in particular its focus on collaborative learning, transformations of current practice, and contradictions, is useful in understanding how the organic farmer group and its stakeholders sought to overcome obstacles.

Through collaboration with Rhodes University researchers, members of the organic agriculture organizations used a series of steps to contribute to expansive social learning at the local level and potentially to education nationally. They analyzed Isidore and Earth Mother Organic agriculture and agribusiness

practices, which surfaced key challenges and their underlying causes (contradictions). Then they collectively developed and implemented a solution to address
the contradictions.

More than twenty organic farmers, trainers, and marketers jointly defined key
challenges, surfaced their causes, and developed solutions in an expansive learning process. They identified the goal of their collaborative learning as human
health, profit, and environmental sustainability, which could only be enabled by a
qualitatively new practice. The research participants decided to work on the contradiction between organic regulations (rules) and local social-ecological conditions (community). They concluded that this contradiction was caused by lack of
collaborative linkages in the organic sector, which in turn was explained by diffi-
culties in making a profit (part of which would be used for collective learning and
innovation); by historically constructed cultural barriers among organic value
chain actors and associated low levels of trust; by a strong culture of individualism fostered by past failures of cooperatives; and by inadequate infrastructure to
support the organic farming movement, including collection centers, training,
inspection, and certification.

Responding to this contradiction, the project conducted a workshop that led
to the formation of a Green Growers Association consisting of organic farmers,
trainers, marketers, certifiers, and the municipality, with the goal of linking and
coordinating learning and actions of the Durban-area organic farming community. The project also identified eleven stakeholder groups and accompanying activity systems that needed to be intentionally engaged, including agro-
processors, suppliers of agricultural tools, consumer groups, funding partners,
research organizations, universities, and colleges (Figure 13.1). The second
model solution was the identification and adoption of the International Fed-
eration for Organic Agriculture Movements' Participatory Guarantee System,
which would enable the local organic farming community to set, implement,
monitor, and certify local organic production using agreed-upon criteria. The
Green Growers Association recruited organic inspectors and an information
technologies specialist to adapt international organic farming standards, communication, and marketing.

While the above process helped the Durban organic agriculture community
learn jointly and generate solutions to agricultural challenges, it also revealed
that organic trainers and mentors needed higher-order skills to perform their
tasks. In addition, the study concluded that agricultural cognition was made up
not just of the knowledge of trainers, but also of farmers, farm workers, inspectors, and marketers, which should be drawn on and developed (Mukute, 2010).
Finally, it recommended the formation of local long-term collective learning,
innovation, and action structures. These insights were shared with the South

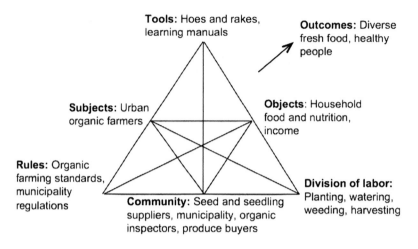

FIGURE 13.1. Urban organic farmers activity system, Durban, South Africa. Diagram adapted from Engeström, 1987.

African Qualifications Authority and Rhodes University, which influence education policy in South Africa. The insights and recommendations demonstrate a link between local and national level learning processes, which could strengthen environmental education impacts across multiple scales.

Knowledge-Sharing Practices in Community Home-Based Care, South Africa

Community home-based care in South Africa is in high demand due to the HIV/AIDS pandemic and related diseases, which result in waste that poses a public health risk if not disposed of correctly. Typically, health care waste includes swabs, adult diapers, and used dressings, needles, and surgical gloves. Young children have been seen playing with surgical gloves found dumped on a vacant plot, inflating them, filling them with water, and drinking out of them.

Different community players contribute toward achieving sustainable health care waste management. Some partners enforce waste-management regulations, some produce health care waste, while others sort, manage, and dispose of waste. Cultural historical activity theory sees these players as interacting in activity systems that are dynamic and multivoiced and as individuals whose ideas and practices can be transformed through ongoing dialogue in expansive learning processes.

Research revealed that problematic waste-management practices in home-based care facilities were linked to limited knowledge and knowledge sharing

(Masilela, 2015). It became clear that environmental education processes were needed to strengthen environmental management practices. For example, health care waste is commonly disposed of in domestic waste bins or illegally burned, but environmental health officers lacked knowledge about such practices. Similarly, community home-based caregivers, despite extensive experience in nursing and palliative care, did not know how to dispose of waste generated outside of a clinic. Although senior managers seem to hold more detailed knowledge about health care waste management, channels to disseminate this knowledge to environmental health officers or community home-based caregivers were nonexistent. The result: impoverished waste pickers rummaging through piles of domestic garbage in search of items to recycle or resell faced risks of encountering health care waste.

Three workshops provided the basic framework for an expansive learning process in which the managers of home-based care facilities, environmental health officers, and waste inspectors identified their strengths and weaknesses and collaborated to seek long-term solutions. The voices of waste pickers and caregivers were brought into the workshops through interview transcripts and photographs, enabling stakeholders to develop a richer perspective on the complexity and contested nature of the problem. The workshops created opportunities for people with diverse skills and backgrounds to build common knowledge and develop new practices around a shared outcome (i.e., improving waste management). Participants learned about daily practices related to health care waste management ("who does what"); gained insight into tensions and contradictions; and asked "why," "how," "where," and "what" questions to clarify misconceptions.

The health care waste-management activity system suggests lessons for community environmental education more broadly. Environmental sustainability challenges in urban settings require collaboration among multiple players who need access to contextually relevant knowledge. Processes that stimulate dialogue and the production, circulation, and reflexive critique of knowledge within and across activity systems, such as the workshops addressing health care waste management, create opportunities for expansive learning leading to sustainability innovations.

Conclusion

The communities of practice framework allows us to examine social learning that occurs through participation in a community focused on a common enterprise. Cultural historical activity theory enables us to see how activities expand through encountering challenges or contradictions, resulting in learning at higher levels.

A focus on learning through interactions also suggests equitable knowledge sharing, which is important to urban environmental education. It reveals a subtle change in perspective from expanding existing outreach programs to simply being more inclusive of nontraditional audiences, such as low-income youth, farmers, or community health care workers. Instead, the focus is on the knowledge and experience youths, farmers, and health care workers, alongside university scientists and professional environmental educators, bring to the table. Recognizing and honoring each actor's assets not only uncovers information and ideas potentially useful in addressing sustainability issues, it also empowers less powerful community members. For these reasons, recognizing assets is a critical component of social learning and of urban environmental education that seeks to foster community wellness and environmental sustainability.

References

Aguilar, O. M. (2016). Examining the literature to reveal the nature of community EE/ESD programs and research. *Environmental Education Research.*

Aguilar, O. M., and Krasny, M. E. (2011). Using the community of practice framework to examine an after-school environmental education program for Hispanic youth. *Environmental Education Research, 17*(2), 217–233.

Aguilar, O., Price, A., and Krasny, M. E. (2015). Perspectives on community environmental education. In M. Monroe and M. E. Krasny (Eds.). *Across the spectrum: Resources for environmental educators.* Washington, D.C.: NAAEE.

Delanty, G. (2003). *Community.* London: Routledge.

Engeström, Y. (Ed.). (1987). *Learning by expanding: An activity-theoretical approach to developmental research.* Helsinki: Orienta-Konsultit.

Krasny, M., and Roth, W.-M. (2010). Environmental education for social-ecological system resilience: A perspective from activity theory. *Environmental Education Research, 16*(5–6), 545–558.

Lave, J., and Wenger, E. (1991). *Situated learning.* Cambridge, UK: Cambridge University Press.

Masilela, K. (2016). Draft MEd thesis. Rhodes University, Grahamstown, South Africa.

Mukute, M. (2010). Exploring and expanding farmer learning in sustainable agriculture workplaces. PhD dissertation, Rhodes University, Grahamstown, South Africa.

Price, A., Simmons. B., and Krasny, M. E. (2014). Principles of excellence in community environmental education. Unpublished document.

Wals, A. E. J. (2007). *Social learning towards a sustainable world: Principles, perspectives, and praxis.* Wageningen, the Netherlands: Wageningen Academic Publishers.

Wenger, E. (1998). *Communities of practice: Learning, meaning and identity.* Cambridge: Cambridge University Press.

14

SCHOOL PARTNERSHIPS

Polly L. Knowlton Cockett, Janet E. Dyment,
Mariona Espinet, and Yu Huang

Highlights

- Urban schools can use local environments to serve as stimulus, context, and content for teaching and learning about sustainability.
- School curricula and teacher pedagogies both limit and enable what is possible through urban environmental education.
- When schools establish rich and sustaining partnerships with local communities, opportunities for urban environmental education are significantly enhanced.

Introduction

Urban schools—any public, private, or charter school delivering formal primary or secondary education—are key institutions in shaping vibrant and sustainable cities. Imagining such cities depends on the assumptions and ideologies of those involved in the transformation of urban sites and on moving beyond perceiving urban schools as problematic institutions (Pink and Noblit, 2007). Globally, a steady process of urbanization results from migration from rural and conflict areas. This trend points to the urgent need to develop programs—including environmental education—that target schools as pivotal in serving diverse, translocated, and often marginalized students. Such urban environmental education can also empower those who live in challenging circumstances to work together to improve social-ecological well-being and foster "citizens that are informed and motivated to live more sustainably, be responsible stewards of the environment, and help ensure future generations' quality of life" (Alberta Council for Environmental Education, 2015).

A variety of programs that encourage student engagement in environmental initiatives have supported schools worldwide. Two foremost international initiatives are the Eco-Schools program established in Europe in 1992 and the Green Schools Alliance introduced in the United States in 2007. They provide environmental education programs and environmental management systems for school facilities and grounds, and they award schemes that promote and acknowledge actions for the environment and transitioning toward sustainability. Further, United Nations Agenda 21 acknowledges local jurisdictions as being best positioned to tailor programs to the individual needs of schools and communities.

In this chapter we build on the definition of urban environmental education as "any environmental education that occurs in cities" (Russ and Krasny, 2015, p. 12) by acknowledging the importance of overarching curricular goals set by formal educational institutions. The following sections present "socio-ecological refrains" adapted from Knowlton Cockett (2013), which incorporate stewardship, pedagogy, interrelationships, and heritage and which highlight the role schools can play in shaping sustainable cities through urban environmental education. These refrains promote a connectedness to place through (1) the use of the local environment to stimulate learning, (2) the development of curricula and pedagogies that embrace the development of sustainable cities, and (3) the establishment of links with the community to foster relationships, stewardship, and resiliency. Case studies from Canada, Australia, China, and Spain illustrate these refrains, as well as show how schools are engaged more broadly in green school initiatives.

Local Environments as Stimulus, Context, and Content

Creating learning environments where students can develop as citizens with pronounced understandings of sustainability is a major educational challenge. While much emphasis has been placed on incorporating sustainability into formal schooling, recent scholarship shows that significant sustainability learning can happen beyond the four corners of the classroom (Knowlton Cockett, 2013; Russ and Krasny, 2015; Tidball and Krasny, 2010). Urban contexts that can be used to deliver urban environmental education typically include nature centers, parks, community gardens, resource recovery centers, and landfills. Extending to other vital urban settings such as hospitals, jails, shelters, government housing, immigrant organizations, businesses, and women's and seniors' centers provides meaningful opportunities for schools to form partnerships aimed at integrated urban sustainability education. Such partnerships can stimulate learners in schools to understand environmental, political, social, cultural, and economic dynamics of systems.

Through such partnerships, urban environmental education presents concrete social-ecological issues that develop student problem-solving skills and recognizes urban communities as powerful landscapes to guide learners' understandings, confidence, and competence in relation to sustainability. In our case studies, we present examples of students working with park managers, landscape architects, and naturalists to understand the management of invasive species to support native biodiversity. Other examples involve partnering with scientific organizations in a constructed wetland on a former coal mine site and studying water issues in municipal river systems. We also present a case where a network of schools works with city administrators and universities to develop food systems and seed banks and to expand agroecology into urban settings. In each case, urban students are working within their local social-ecological contexts.

Curriculum and Pedagogy Oriented Toward Sustainable Cities

The presence of sustainability and environmental education in the curriculum varies dramatically around the world. In some countries, sustainability or environment is a stand-alone curriculum; in other countries, it is a cross-curricular interdisciplinary area; in yet other countries, there is a notable silence in relation to sustainability (Dyment, Hill, and Emery, 2014). Irrespective of curricular mandates, teachers can identify urban environments as sites for learning involving hands-on or embodied interactions within a particular place. These experiences are often framed by inquiry-based learning that positions students as investigators, designers, scientists, and gardeners (Stine, 1997).

Teacher understanding of pedagogies that support learning outside the classroom is a vital factor in enabling children to use urban spaces to learn about sustainability (Skamp, 2007). Teaching in urban landscapes requires new and different pedagogies involving letting go of some control and structure afforded by inside spaces and allowing for risk taking with students. Luckily, potential green school activities abound. Students might utilize mathematical concepts such as perimeter or area to determine the capacity of a rooftop to harvest water into tanks. Outdoor sites such as community gardens may provide inspiration for personal writing, artwork, or science activities. In these contexts student learning is focused toward specific features of the urban environment and may be guided by the curriculum or the teacher, or it emerges organically from the place itself.

Establishing Community Links to Foster Relationships and Stewardship

School Agenda 21 and green schools programs seek to promote socially and environmentally sustainable schools and municipalities by helping urban schools collaborate with their communities. Despite these mainstreaming efforts, some urban schools experience challenges emerging from the collaboration (Sandäs, 2014). School Community Collaboration for Sustainable Development, a European Union–funded multilateral network supported by the Environment and School Initiatives network, conducted an international comparative cross-case study (Espinet, 2014) to investigate challenges schools face including funding, effective networking, cultural background, and political orientation.

To promote sustainability, schools can adopt unconventional approaches to teaching and learning that invite community actors to cross boundaries and establish vital relationships with other actors and with their place (Wals, van der Hoeven, and Blanken, 2009). For example, in our case studies from China and Canada, students are communicating their learning back to the public via websites and interpretive signage. In our case studies from Australia and Spain, several nearby schools developed networks to obtain shared funding or to have older students mentor younger students, in each case working with community partners toward a common goal.

Four Case Studies

Natureground and Whispering Signs in Calgary, Alberta, Canada

The Centennial Natureground, situated on the grounds of an urban kindergarten to grade 6 school in Calgary, Alberta, Canada, is a publicly accessible, reclaimed and reconstructed sustainable mini-ecosystem featuring native plants. The plants have been rescued and transplanted from natural areas undergoing urban development and directly sowed from native seeds or planted as seedlings for the purposes of holistic education and enjoyment. The area, established by students and volunteers in 2004, is maintained through local stewardship by classroom students during the academic year and community members during the summer. These stewards keep invasive species at bay, thus fostering urban biodiversity and supporting pollinators such as bees, birds, and bats. Classes regularly visit the area for curriculum-related ecological studies and as a space to read, journal, and sketch. The Natureground also features biofiltration basins, swales, and culverts to capture rainwater and snowmelt, thus reducing and filtering storm water runoff that would otherwise carry pollutants from paved roads straight into open waterways.

Whispering Signs is a curriculum-connected project consisting of a site-specific set of interpretive signs within the Natureground and an adjacent fragment of native shortgrass prairie. Students, teachers, parents, and community members worked together over several years to produce the original art, poetry, and text for thirty-four beautiful and provocative signs for school-based and public education. For example, an alphabet sign shows a common white-tailed jackrabbit changing its coat over the seasons, during a variety of weather conditions, and under different heights of the sun over the course of a year, all concepts within the school curriculum (Figure 14.1). Latitude, longitude, and elevation are indicated on each sign and give rise to spatial geography lessons and orienteering activities. These signs stem from a place-based literacy project conducted in the area, where students researched, represented, and communicated information about plants, animals, and physical features of the landscape. Throughout these and other green school projects, participants developed meaningful interrelationships and became increasingly connected to place.

Constructed Wetlands and Frogs in Australia's Latrobe Valley

An unusual urban environmental initiative is found in a surprising place in Australia: the heart of the Latrobe Valley in Gippsland, Victoria. This region supplies electricity through brown-coal-fired power generation. Socially and economically disadvantaged, this area has huge open-cut brown coal mines, massive power lines, transformer stations, and puffing chimneys of large and small power stations. The Latrobe Valley has poor air quality and high pollution levels.

A local primary school, however, began using the Morwell River wetlands as a site for teaching and learning about the complex social, cultural, economic, and environmental aspects of this contested area (Somerville and Green, 2012). The wetlands have been constructed in the river overflow site that was relocated to make way for the coal mine, and they encompass pools, banks, islands, and many creatures and plants, including frogs, trees, shrubs, and grasses. The primary

FIGURE 14.1. Jackrabbits through the seasons in Calgary, Alberta, Canada. Credit: Polly L. Knowlton Cockett.

school has been involved in the wetlands since they were constructed and students have monitored the plants and animals that have found "home" there. Shortly after the wetlands were created, three local schools applied for a science grant and received $20,000 to set up a wetlands study and develop a curriculum model. The schools worked with the Amphibian Research Centre to develop the Frog Census Program based on the belief that frogs are the gateway to understanding the wetlands.

The wetlands are visited regularly by all school grades, and curriculum links are made across subject areas. Younger students study life cycles of frogs and raise tadpoles in a mini-wetlands constructed on their school ground. Middle-year students monitor the wetlands and older students measure water quality and identify micro- and macro-organisms. From an eyesore to a healthy ecosystem, these constructed wetlands have become enriched with educational opportunities for students.

"Water-Loving" Studies on the Long River in Beijing, China

The high school affiliated with the Beijing Institute of Technology is located on the southern bank of the Long River, which is an indispensable part of the Beijing city water system. Influenced by the green school movement, which has been supported by the national government in China since 1996, the school has been promoting a series of local environmental education activities since 2001 (Liu and Huang, 2013). For example, in the context of general water inquiries, teachers have established "water-loving" student groups. These grade-level groups carry out many projects, such as investigating water usage in their school and households, as well as researching the watersheds surrounding their campus.

Under teachers' guidance, members of "water-loving" groups study water issues relevant to the school and the Long River system. After preliminary investigations and analyses, students undertake Long River water surveys and launch environmental fieldwork integrating aspects of geography, biology, chemistry, and physics. As young scientists (Figure 14.2), the students design their research, divide their work reasonably, and rethink obstacles they encounter, while constantly discussing and revising plans with others. Teachers and students also use information technology to record and share students' research processes and results and use data they collect as resources in information technology courses. Then they create "water-loving" actions on a website, such as conservation measures and water quality monitoring, which provides a convenient way to locate and express their research process and results. Thus, this project-based learning provides rich information technology curriculum resources and offers a medium

FIGURE 14.2.   Investigating the Long River in Beijing, China. Credit: Guochun Zhang.

of communication about project results and actions. These two stages of "Integrated Curriculum of Practical Activity" complement and promote each other.

Through these activities on the Long River, the "water-loving" theme is effectively spread and sets up a series of "water-loving" actions. The activities also have been playing an important role in motivating students to explore their academic and sustainability-related interests and laying a foundation for future inquiries. In addition, teachers update their own pedagogical understandings, thus enhancing the capacity for adapting and implementing curriculum reform.

School Agroecology and Community Collaboration, Sant Cugat del Vallès, Catalonia, Spain

The Science Education Department at the Autonomous University of Barcelona and the Municipal Environment Department of Sant Cugat del Vallès in Catalonia, Spain, collaborated for seven years to enhance the School Agenda 21 program in the city. Established in 2001, the program involved urban schools in the city's effort to promote sustainable development, and it established links between schools and the community for the development of a new field of study called School Agroecology (Llerena, 2015). The program built an urban school network involving all public urban schools from pre-K to secondary level, university researchers, local administrators, and environmental educators with the aim of empowering students, teachers, and the community to develop agroecological food production and food consumption (Espinet and Llerena, 2014).

One of the collective projects was to transform school and community food gardens as places to grow endangered native plants (Figure 14.3). After consultation with a regional seed bank, each school chose a specific native plant to grow;

FIGURE 14.3. Nurturing native plants in Sant Cugat del Vallès, Catalonia, Spain. Credit: Mariona Espinet and Lidia Bassons.

students then harvested and preserved seeds and shared seeds among different school and community actors to be grown in their own food gardens. Through a service-learning approach, secondary students visited primary students to teach seed preservation. Seed exchanges became an event where donor schools provided not only a sample of seeds but also storytelling, drama, or visualizations about growing practices. Once schools started getting seeds from several plants, they built seed banks inside their schools. In so doing, urban public schools, with the help of the community, became authentic urban agents of native plant preservation. One result of this urban environmental education project has been the creation of a new professional niche: the agroenvironmental educator responsible for promoting and maintaining urban environmental education activities focused on the food system at the interface between the school and the city.

Conclusion

As demonstrated by our urban case studies, ongoing green school actions—whether learning about life cycles, monitoring water quality, or seed harvesting—guide students' understanding of their environment. Within the complex networks of urban settings, students also become directly engaged in urgent and interrelated global movements, for example pertaining to food security, as well as in global initiatives such as Local Action for Biodiversity or BiodiverCities. Thus, socioecological refrains, involving place-based, curriculum-connected, community-engaged, collaborative practices, serve as effective frameworks for urban primary and secondary schools to provide students with rich, meaningful experiential learning opportunities fostering systems thinking, stewardship, and sustainability.

References

Alberta Council for Environmental Education. (2015). *Mission and vision.* Canmore, Alberta, Canada: ACEE.

Dyment, J. E., Hill, A., and Emery, S. (2014). Sustainability as a cross-curricular priority in the Australian curriculum: A Tasmanian investigation. *Environmental Education Research, 21*(8), 1105–1126.

Espinet, M. (Ed.). (2014). *CoDeS selected cases of school community collaboration for sustainable development.* Vienna, Austria: Austrian Federal Ministry of Education and Women's Affairs.

Espinet, M., and Llerena, G. (2014). School agroecology as a motor for community and land transformation: A case study on the collaboration among community actors to promote education for sustainability networks. In C. P. Constantinou,

N. Papadouris, and A. Hadjigeorgiou (Eds.). *Proceedings of the ESERA 2013 Conference: Science Education Research For Evidence-based Teaching and Coherence in Learning* (p. 244–250). Nicosia, Cyprus: ESERA.

Knowlton Cockett, P. (2013). In situ conversation: Understanding sense of place through socioecological cartographies. PhD dissertation, University of Calgary.

Liu, J., and Huang, Y. (2013). Practices and inspirations on a school-based curriculum for ESD. *Research on Curriculum, Textbook and Teaching Method, 33*(3), 98–102. (In Chinese.)

Llerena, G. (2015). Agroecologia escolar. Doctoral dissertation, Universitat Autònoma de Barcelona.

Pink, W. T., and Noblit, G. W. (Eds.). (2007). *International handbook of urban education*. Dordrecht: Springer.

Russ, A., and Krasny, M. (2015). Urban environmental education trends. In A. Russ (Ed.). *Urban environmental education* (pp. 12–25). Ithaca, N.Y., and Washington, D.C.: Cornell University Civic Ecology Lab, NAAEE and EECapacity.

Sandäs, A. (2014). Travelling through the landscape of school-community collaboration for sustainable development. In C. Affolter and M. Reti (Eds.). *Travelling guide for school community collaboration for sustainable development.* ENSI i.n.p.a.: CoDeS Network.

Skamp, K. (2007). Understanding teachers' "levels of use" of learnscapes. *Environmental Education Research, 15*(1), 93–110.

Somerville, M., and Green, M. (2012). Place and sustainability literacy in schools and teacher education. Paper presented at Australian Association for Research in Education, Sydney, Australia.

Stine, S. (1997). *Landscapes for learning: Creating outdoor environments for children and youth.* Toronto: John Wiley & Sons.

Tidball, K. G., and Krasny, M. E. (2010). Urban environmental education from a social-ecological perspective: Conceptual framework for civic ecology education. *Cities and the Environment, 3*(1), article 11.

Wals, A., van der Hoeven, N., and Blanken, H. (2009). *The acoustics of social learning: Designing learning processes that contribute to a more sustainable world.* Utrecht, the Netherlands: Wageningen Academic Publishers.

15

SUSTAINABLE CAMPUSES

Scott Ashmann, Felix Pohl,
and Dave Barbier

Highlights

- Sustainable university campuses address aspects of urban sustainability related to infrastructure, teaching and learning, and connections to the community.
- The built environment and lifestyles are particularly crucial for urban campuses, given their location in areas of highly concentrated buildings and dense human population.
- Urban environmental education trends such as the City as Classroom, Problem Solving, and Environmental Stewardship are evident at many urban campuses.
- Learning and sustainability programs at urban campuses impact, and are impacted by, their local communities.

Introduction

University campuses have potential as change makers in urban environmental education. Sustainable campuses implement "green" practices in their research, teaching, outreach, facilities, and open spaces now and in planning for the future. Best practices for sustainability are still progressing, which creates an opportunity to challenge what has been and what can be.

Environmental paradigms are evolving constantly, challenging the foundations of modern culture. Universities like Stanford have divested their endowment from fossil fuels, and Microsoft and other businesses with ties to universities have implemented self-induced carbon taxes and are pushing to become fueled by 100 percent renewable resources. With millennials leading the way, consumers are propelling a new sharing economy. Exposed to these ways of thinking, today's students will be the educators and leaders who will guide our communities and society into the future. In this chapter, we first describe aspects of sustainable urban campuses, and then examine the impact urban sustainable campuses can have on their students and local communities. In so doing, we focus on elements of infrastructure, learning, and community through the lens of urban environmental education trends (see chapter 30), namely City as Classroom, Problem Solving, and Environmental Stewardship.

Aspects of Sustainable Campuses

Urban campuses have the capacity to be leaders in sustainability efforts both internal to the university and in the community in which they reside, including by spurring contemporary urban design in their surrounding neighborhoods (Wiewel and Perry, 2008). By making these efforts visible, understandable, relatable, and approachable, a whole community can experience the university's progression toward sustainability. Adopting accepted protocols, such as the American College and University Presidents' Climate Commitment aimed at reducing greenhouse gas emissions by 80 percent by the year 2050, or the Sustainability Tracking, Assessment and Rating System, which provides a self-reporting framework to measure the performance of university sustainability initiatives, can help to institutionalize and document the campus's efforts.

Developing a sustainable campus takes into account multiple organizational dimensions. Thomashow (2014) describes nine elements of a sustainable campus including energy, food, and materials (elements of infrastructure); governance, investment, and wellness (elements of community); and curriculum, interpretation, and aesthetics (elements of learning). These elements can function as a guide for the development of strategies and the evolution of a sustainability narrative pertaining to an urban campus. In addition, trends in urban environmental education such as City as Classroom, Problem Solving, and Environmental Stewardship (see chapter 30) can be connected with Thomashow's elements. We explore these connections further in the next three sections.

Elements of Infrastructure

Campus landscapes and facilities play a large role in sustainability as they are the most immediate physical representations of the university and also reflect its philosophy (Orr, 1994). For decades, campus master plans tried to cram in as many buildings as possible. Starting in the early 2000s, however, environmentally responsible design (particularly the use of green space) was no longer novel, but expected (Franklin, Durkin, and Schuh, 2003). Creating sustainable campuses and demonstrating effective resource-management practices that exceed regulatory compliance give urban colleges and universities an opportunity to use the campus to teach, to showcase progressive principles, and to serve as a model for the community at large. Green buildings, responsible purchasing, sustainable transportation, zero-carbon and zero-waste goals, sustainability classes, green landscaping, and opportunities for students to access nature are examples from urban campuses that can serve as models for local communities. Visits to the campus by school groups and community members to learn about these and other resources is just another example of using the "city as classroom." For example, in Germany, at Technische Universität München (Figure 15.1), visitors

FIGURE 15.1.   The physical campus boundaries at Technische Universität München's main location, which occupies a city block in the center left, blend with the surrounding neighborhood just as sustainability programs and initiatives can impact, and be impacted by, the community in which a university resides. Credit: Maximilian Dörrbecker, Wikimedia Commons.

can participate in a program where campus facilities are used to investigate building services engineering and renewable energies, building physics and energy efficiency, and building technology and life cycle engineering.

Another example comes from the University of Wisconsin–Milwaukee in the United States, where community members and school groups visit the campus to learn about the university's sustainability initiatives. Campus gardens provide the campus community with healthy, affordable, and local produce; teach the skills and share the joys of food gardening and healthy eating with individuals both on and off campus; and cultivate sustainable lifestyles. Community organizations and members of the public also visit the campus to learn about green roofs and environmentally friendly landscaping, which reduce the heat island index, storm water runoff, and the need for pesticides and which maintain wildlife habitat and native species. Tours also showcase the campus green cleaning program, which features cleaning with biodegradable products and low-maintenance flooring that utilizes cleaning machines where ionized water molecules pick up dirt.

The whole-of-university approach adopted by some urban campuses (McMillin and Dyball, 2009) seeks to connect the core functions of curriculum, research, and operations, each of which can influence teaching and learning. The educational focus shifts from the classroom to the whole university, beginning with its physical layout and buildings and sometimes extending beyond campus boundaries. This whole-of-university approach can provide guidance to urban areas if the parallels between university and city, student and resident, and curriculum and daily activities are made explicit.

Elements of Learning

Embedding sustainability concepts into the curriculum, faculty research projects, infrastructure development, and policies enable urban campuses to demonstrate their resolve to be sustainable. For example, the Department for Social Responsibility and Sustainability at the University of Edinburgh in Scotland offers training for all its students and staff members who are interested in learning how to work and live in a more sustainable manner. The university offers multiple degrees, courses, student societies, and forums related to sustainability topics and provides students with work-based placements and volunteer opportunities to apply their sustainability-related skills and knowledge. University of Edinburgh staff members are challenged to make their area of work more sustainable through the support of campus programs and by treating the "University as a Living Lab," that is, using their own academic and research capabilities to solve sustainability problems relating to campus infrastructure and practices.

At City University of Hong Kong, Thomashow's (2014) ideas related to curriculum, interpretation, and aesthetics are combined in the Extreme Environments project. This project investigates how the sciences and arts can work together to collect and analyze climate change data in creative and innovative forms. Although university students in the Sustainable Design course conduct research in remote science stations in Antarctica, the media art and design products they create based on their experience offer ways for the scientific community and the general public to visualize data and gain better understandings of critical concepts. For example, at the Freeze Frame exhibition in 2014, students used images, videos, and scientific datasets to explore how climate change is impacting the Earth's most isolated landscape. Student artworks on display included a mobile game application of penguin behaviors that looks like a daily newspaper; a visualization of lichen growth and color displayed inside four mirrors arranged above a compass; and a sculptural presentation of iceberg texture, shape, and geometry using recyclable materials. Although the exhibit may not present information immediately relevant to Hong Kong residents, its novelty may capture their interest and thus help them learn about climate change.

Elements of Community

Whereas Thomashow (2014) focuses on the development of community internal to the university, in this chapter we look at community as a way of linking the university to the community in which it resides. What happens on an urban campus can be shared with the community to assist in solving problems and addressing issues, not only through community member visits to the campus but also through outreach, student service learning, internships, and faculty research. These are important means of information sharing since the community often looks to the urban campus as a partner and fellow community member.

Urban campuses where research and teaching directly address the complex problems of urbanization and democratization become resources for the urban centers in which they reside. With respect to sustainability issues, universities can offer technical advice on energy conservation, recycling, transportation, and water usage; behavior intervention strategies; social psychology topics, such as value orientations, motivation, and worldviews; social marketing; and program development and evaluation (as an example, see Chan et al., 2012). Going beyond providing research expertise, technical advice, or technology transfer, these efforts can nurture long-term partnerships in which the campus plays an important role in urban transformation. An authentic campus-community partnership focuses on building trust, honesty, transparency, respect, and equity, leading to the coproduction and application of knowledge for positive local change (Klopp, Ngau, and Sclar, 2011). Below we discuss outreach and engaged research programs that illustrate these elements of campus-community partnerships.

Outreach programs at urban campuses typically focus on strengthening economic, cultural, educational, or social services in the local community and improving the quality of life for residents. The principles of effective outreach programs include (a) paying attention to the needs of participants, (b) keeping in mind the context in which the outcomes of the program will be implemented, (c) providing high-quality resources and learning experiences, (d) making the value of the program transparent, (e) hiring staff members with the proper credentials and passion for what they do, and (f) evaluating the program so as to determine elements to keep and modify. For example, the Innovative Small Farmers' Outreach Program at Lincoln University in Missouri in the United States focuses on urban food production in St. Louis and Kansas City and helps residents with limited resources access nutritious produce. Urban campuses not just in the United States but in other countries, such as Keio University in Tokyo, University College London, and Curtin University in Perth, Australia, have the responsibility to provide outreach education that contributes to urban sustainability and resilience as part of their university mission, goals, and initiatives.

In the Missouri and other outreach efforts, universities establish partnerships with community organizations (e.g., community gardens). These partnerships draw on faculty expertise, professional networks, and the university's material resources (i.e., infrastructure), as well as the experience and knowledge of the partner organizations. How can university-community partnerships be structured so they are both effective and efficient? Grounded in an ideology of community participation and empowerment, McNall et al. (2009) describe the four qualities that create and sustain partnerships: (a) cooperative goal setting and planning; (b) shared power, resources, and decision making; (c) group cohesion; and (d) partnership management. A prime example of a university teaming up with a community to address local sustainability concerns is occurring in South Florida. In 2012, the University of Miami launched the Urban and Environmental Sustainability Initiative to address the region's declining natural resources, accelerating urban growth, poverty, hunger, and environmental degradation. University students and faculty members, national and local scholars, activists, local practitioners, and community members gathered to discuss issues of sustainability and to create community-university collaborations that address problems from multiple perspectives. This initiative created a transdisciplinary, cross-sector dialogue that translated new knowledge into the implementation of more sustainable practices and public policy.

Research related to sustainability issues has been described as problem- and solution- oriented and committed to both scientific rigor and social relevance (Brundiers and Wiek, 2011). Two large-scale research initiatives that involve students, faculty, and community members in addressing sustainability problems are the Transdisciplinary Case Studies for Sustainable Development project at the Swiss Federal Institute of Technology in Zurich (Scholz et al., 2006) and the Sustainable Learning Classroom Model at four academic institutions in Vancouver, British Columbia, Canada. In these examples, the students and faculty members apply knowledge and skills developed at the university to a community-based issue.

Undergraduate and graduate students involved in research and outreach gain real-world experience and provide organizations with different types of assistance (Lucas, Sherman, and Fischer, 2013). The community-engaged research model described by Peters and Gauthier (2009) takes the concept of service learning to a higher level in academia using a dialogic approach in which researchers and community members collaboratively determine the focus of a research project based on the needs of community members and scholars. Community members often contribute to data collection and analysis, thus ensuring that data are relevant to their needs.

In 2007, Debra Rowe, president of the U.S. Partnership for Education for Sustainable Development, described her vision of sustainability education that includes students being regularly assigned to sustainability problems presented by city government, businesses, nonprofit organizations, and other institutions. One way to carry out this vision is through undergraduate internships, which enable students to gain knowledge and understanding of local urban sustainability issues and prepare them to become future urban leaders. Internships often reflect the Problem Solving and Environmental Stewardship trends in urban environmental education (see chapter 30).

Conclusion

Campus sustainability programs have only begun to be change makers. Yet they are already highly regarded resources by campus and community alike. Communities bring to universities real-world problems, many of which involve sustainability issues. These issues impact the curriculum taught to students and foster the development of campus-community partnerships. Effective partnerships are based on engaging in honest communication, ensuring transparency in intentions and work, shared decision making, using creativity to address challenges that emerge, and ongoing evaluation of progress. Environmental education in cities can thus greatly benefit from harnessing the power that lies within a university campus's academic, infrastructural, and community-related resources.

References

Brundiers, K., and Wiek, A. (2011). Educating students in real-world sustainability research: Vision and implementation. *Innovative Higher Education, 36*(2), 107–124.

Chan, S., Dolderman, D., Savan, B., and Wakefield, S. (2012). Practicing sustainability in an urban university: A case study of a behavior based energy conservation project. *Applied Environmental Education and Communication, 11*(1), 9–17.

Franklin, C., Durkin, T., and Schuh, S. P. (2003). The role of the landscape in creating a sustainable campus. *Planning for Higher Education, 31*(3), 142–149.

Klopp, J., Ngau, P., and Sclar, E. (2011). University/city partnerships: Creating policy networks for urban transformation in Nairobi. *Metropolitan Universities, 22*(2), 131–142.

Lucas, C. M., Sherman, N. E., and Fischer, C. (2013). Higher education and nonprofit community collaboration: Innovative teaching and learning for graduate student education. *International Journal of Teaching and Learning in Higher Education, 25*(2), 239–247.

McMillin, J., and Dyball, R. (2009). Developing a whole-of-university approach to educating for sustainability. *Journal of Education for Sustainable Development, 3*(1), 55–64.

McNall, M., Sturdevant Reed, C., Brown, R., and Allen, A. (2009). Brokering community-university engagement. *Innovative Higher Education, 33*(5), 317–331.

Orr, D. W. (1994). *Earth in mind: On education, environment, and the human prospect.* Washington, D.C.: Island Press.

Peters, M., and Gauthier, K. (2009). Integrating community engaged research into existing school of education graduate research courses. *Collected Faculty Scholarship.* Paper 8.

Rowe, D. (2007). Education for a sustainable future. *Science, 317*(5836), 323–324.

Scholz, R. W., Lang, D. J., Wiek, A., Walter, A. I., and Stauffacher, M. (2006). Transdisciplinary case studies as a means of sustainability learning: Historical framework and theory. *International Journal of Sustainability in Higher Education, 7*(3), 226–251.

Thomashow, M. (2014). *The nine elements of a sustainable campus.* Cambridge, Mass.: MIT Press.

Wiewel, W., and Perry, D. C. (2008). *Global universities and urban development: Case studies and analysis.* Armonk, N.Y.: M. E. Sharpe.

Part IV
PARTICIPANTS

16

EARLY CHILDHOOD

Victoria Derr, Louise Chawla, and Illène Pevec

Highlights

- Early childhood environmental education in cities draws on ideas of John Dewey's progressive education, Reggio Emilia preschools, environment education in the built environment, and education for sustainability.
- Urban environmental education facilitates children's contact with and learning about urban nature and the built environment.
- Successful models for early childhood environmental education develop citizenship and promote sustainability.
- A variety of approaches, including participatory planning, forest kindergartens, mobile preschools, and school gardens, can be integrated into urban early childhood education.

Introduction

Early childhood—which is generally defined as ages three through eight—is a foundational period when children rapidly move through milestones in physical, cognitive, social, emotional, and language development (McCartney and Phillips, 2006). Cities offer unique environments for learning because they present young children with high densities of people from different backgrounds and cultures, buildings and public spaces that may reflect hundreds or even thousands of years of human history, and political systems that regulate environmental behaviors and decision making. In parks and along riverbanks, in vacant lots and gardens, the natural world weaves its presence. This chapter begins by identifying successive schools of thought in early childhood education that have encouraged the exploration of urban environments by young children. These traditions have pursued similar aims: creative self-expression, democratic decision making, collaborative learning among peers and multiple generations, communication skills, and a deepening of children's experiential, place-based learning. This chapter illustrates diverse ways these aims can be achieved in cities, including participatory planning and design, mobile preschools, greening the grounds of schools and child care centers, gardening, and forest and nature schools in metropolitan areas. It draws on examples from both resourced and poorly resourced schools and child care centers in the Global North and South.

Supportive Teaching Philosophies

In the 1890s, John Dewey's progressive education sought to prepare children to adapt to an ever-changing world through democratic processes of problem solving (Zilversmit, 1993). Central to this philosophy was the ideal of community, that children need opportunities to work with others in a spirit of empathy and service to the world. Dewey's lab school demonstrated that essential skills like reading, writing, and mathematics could be taught by following children's own interests in communication, investigation, constructing things, and artistic expression. Dewey's ideas encouraged project-based learning, which in some schools extended to explorations of local urban and natural environments.

The Reggio Emilia approach to preschool education, which grew out of the ruins of World War II in northern Italy, shared many goals of progressive education. It too sought to replace authoritarian systems of education with more tolerant, communal, equitable, and child-centered values that nurture democracy (Hall and Rudkin, 2011). Adopted by all municipal preschools in the city of Reggio Emilia, its influence has spread worldwide.

Because progressive education and the Reggio Emilia approach encouraged community democratic processes and projects that were motivated by children's own interests, they opened spaces for investigation of the urban environment. Learning about the city and shaping it through participatory processes of urban design and planning were central aims of the built environment education movement that arose in the United Kingdom in the 1960s and 1970s. In 1969, the Skeffington Report to government made community consultation an integral part of planning. The Town and Country Planning Association responded by

launching the "Bulletin of Environmental Education," which advocated education to make people more aware, knowledgeable, and responsible for their interactions with the environment "in a manner explicitly constructed to enable them
to work with others to take greater control of the shaping and management of
their own world" (Bishop, Kean, and Adams, 1992, p. 51). In combination with
progressive initiatives in British primary schools that included learning through
direct experience, team teaching, and field trips into neighborhoods, built environment education led to systematic curricula that brought architects, planners,
artists and other experts into classrooms and sent students into the city to investigate and give input on local issues.

Ideals of community and democracy that run through progressive education,
the Reggio Emilia approach, and built environment education persist in current
expressions of education for sustainability in early childhood education. As Phillips (2014) observed in her discussion of education for sustainability, even very
young children want to do "real things" that contribute to solving social and environmental problems. Integration of social and environmental systems, which is
characteristic of education for sustainability, is also evident in the current international movement to naturalize grounds and plant gardens in schools and child
care centers as a means to bring nature into urban children's lives (Danks, 2010).

Taken together, these pedagogical approaches suggest a set of more specific
strategies that can inform early childhood environmental education in cities
(Table 16.1). Below we illustrate these approaches and strategies using case
studies of participatory planning and design and garden education.

TABLE 16.1 Early childhood approaches, exemplified by case studies in this
chapter

	PARTICIPATORY PLANNING AND DESIGN	GARDEN EDUCATION
Creative self-expression	Art-based methods, including murals, *nicho* boxes, videos, three-dimensional models	Songs, storytelling, cultural exchange
Collaborative learning	Peer-to-peer and multigenerational learning through dialogue with city leaders and designers	Multigenerational and multicultural exchanges
Experiential, place-based learning	Field trips and research about sites	Native plants and foods, ethnobotanic gardens
Development of empathy	Recommendations for wildlife habitat in urban spaces including butterfly gardens and creek restoration	Community service, cultural exchange
Sample recommendation	Tree houses near the library and creek to view and read about nature	Dissipation pond for rain catchment and water play

Participation in Planning and Design of Urban Spaces

Growing Up Boulder is a child-friendly city initiative that was formed in 2009 and is a formal partnership between the city of Boulder, Boulder Valley School District, and the University of Colorado's Program in Environmental Design. While the initiative engages children of all ages, its work with young children (ages three to eight) has included participatory design of city parks, playgrounds, large-scale public spaces, neighborhoods, and open space. Growing Up Boulder fosters creative self-expression and collaborative learning through its methods of engagement, from *nicho* boxes (multimedia boxes inspired from Latin American folk art) and murals to three-dimensional models of recommended redesigns, which allow children to effectively express their ideas (Derr and Tarantini, 2016).

A critical aspect of Growing Up Boulder's work with young children is developing partnerships in which teachers understand the value of participation in early childhood. One such partnership has been with the Boulder Journey School, a Reggio Emilia school. The school's philosophies of honoring children's own modes of expression, instilling a "pedagogy of listening," and promoting children's right to active citizenship (Hall and Rudkin, 2011) support participatory design and planning with children ages four to five. For example, Boulder Journey School students contributed to the redesign of Boulder's Civic Area, a public space in the city's downtown, through field trips, drawings and photographs, a presentation to city council, and participation as jurors in the city's design competition (Derr and Tarantini, 2016).

Growing Up Boulder has also partnered with third graders (ages eight to nine) from an ethnically and economically diverse school that utilizes the International Baccalaureate curriculum. Projects have included neighborhood design for increased density as well as redesign of public space (Derr and Kovács, 2017). The most recent project focused on resilience in partnership with Mexico City, as part of the Rockefeller Foundation's 100 Resilient Cities network. The project allowed creative self-expression and collaborative learning both within and across schools, through video and mural exchange.

In Growing Up Boulder projects, children consistently consider the rights of others and show empathy toward other people and nature (Chawla and Rivkin, 2014; Derr and Tarantini, 2016). For example, in considering parks and open space, Boulder Journey School students researched physical features of insects and developed simple costumes of antennae and wings (Figure 16.1), and in the classroom, teachers projected large insect shadows on a wall so that children could experience the scale at which humans appear to insects. In their recommendations, students showed concern that insects might be hurt by visitors

FIGURE 16.1.   Children demonstrate empathy by dressing as insects on a field trip to a city park. Credit: Tina Briggs.

on trails and wanted to protect the insects and their homes. Growing Up Boulder has found that desires for nature protection and enhancement emerge across projects and ages, in early childhood and beyond (Chawla and Rivkin, 2014).

Children's Access to Nature in the City

Early childhood education can provide many opportunities for children to interact with nature, by exploring natural areas in the city, greening schoolyards, and cultivating school gardens.

Bringing Children to Nature

In an effort to increase young children's access to nature, many Canadian and European cities have established forest schools in which urban children walk to nearby forests or green spaces for some or all of their day (Elliott et al., 2014). Forest schools reach preschool through second grade and are integrated into both private and public school settings. In forest schools, children visit the same place on a regular basis, thus coming to know it and its cycles intimately. Teachers respond to children's interests by listening to and writing down children's ideas and then deepening students' knowledge of nature and place. In Canada, forest schools also employ aboriginal specialists who integrate stories and cultural knowledge into place-based education (Elliott et al., 2014).

In response to shrinking school grounds that lack natural play areas, cities in Scandinavia and Australia have created mobile preschools, in which children ride a bus to natural areas and cultural places in the city. From their research with a mobile preschool in Sweden, Gustafson and van der Burgt (2015) caution that while this model may foster independence and increase children's access to urban places, such programs face practical limitations from changes in weather conditions, the frequent need for outdoor toilets, and discussion of rules of behavior for different physical settings. This model provides a contrast to forest schools, which provide routine opportunities for learning through repeated visits to the same place.

Bringing Nature to Children

Naturalized child care centers in North Carolina in the United States are similar to forest schools in bringing nature to children where they learn and play. Moore and Cosco (2014) have found that community and ecosystem health fosters physical activity and a diversity of play types. Research comparing behaviors before and after naturalizing school grounds found children spent more time outdoors in all seasons; teachers created more vegetable gardens; children exhibited decreases in negative social behaviors, increases in imaginative play, and increases in play among peers with different abilities; and the community expressed increased pride about school grounds.

Perhaps the largest movement to increase children's access to nature within the city is school gardens. As the following examples illustrate, gardens embody a whole-systems approach to understanding life's interconnections and involve children in interacting with plants and animals as they care for them. Tending a garden helps children to develop an ethic of caring and to connect with themselves, the seasonal cycles, and the creatures that share the garden (Noddings, 2005). Integrating stories about plants, insects, and animals into environmental education engages children in life's wonders on a metaphorical and affective level. Songs tied to natural cycles deepen children's relationship with what they plant by allowing children to sing, dance, and act as part of their experience.

Gardens at Day Care Centers: Puebla, Mexico, and Rocinha, Rio de Janeiro, Brazil

A small international organization, A Child's Garden of Peace, partnered with Casa Cuna, the only free day care in Puebla, Mexico, to create a garden and nature education program on the day care's grounds (Figure 16.2). Secondary schools

FIGURE 16.2. Multigenerational planting at a day care center in Puebla, Mexico. Credit: Illène Pevec.

and universities in Puebla (population two million) require several hundred hours of community service from their students. As a service project, about sixty youths prepared the Casa Cuna ground for planting. None had ever held a shovel or planted a garden. They worked with children aged two to five to plant herbs, vegetables, flowers, and fruit trees. Everyone learned together. The garden also includes a shade structure where children rest and participate in garden-inspired art and music activities. Children's senses lead their garden explorations. The youth and children water the garden daily, discover what has bloomed or become ripe for picking, and carry the harvest to the school kitchen.

When early childhood centers lack land for a garden, large pots filled with soil can provide planting space. In Rocinha, Brazil's largest favela where more than 100,000 people live on a granite hillside, the Associação Social Padre Anchieta Day Care has no land except the building's footprint. The school's roof provides a small outdoor play area, and one ten-square-foot area bordered by a six-inch raised edge became a small garden with the addition of compost donated by a local environmental group. Children used the small plot and large plastic pots to plant garlic, onions, beets, lettuce, collards, herbs, and flowers, which in turn enhanced nutrition and flavor of meals, attracted pollinators, and added color and life to the day care, creating a sanctuary from street dangers.

Educational Gardens: Vancouver, British Columbia, Canada

The "Spirit of Nature" garden was initiated by two University of British Columbia students at the Grandview/U'uquinakuh Elementary School and Grandview Terrace Childcare Centre in 1998. Children, teachers, and neighbors engaged in all phases of planning and implementation. Models created by children inspired a landscape architecture student's one-acre design that included a butterfly garden, wild bird habitat, ethnobotanic garden, school vegetable garden, community garden, an outdoor classroom modeled after an indigenous longhouse building, and a dissipation pond. The dissipation pond—in which sand and crushed shells mimic a coastal beachfront and absorb falling rainwater—represents a compromise between children, who wanted a pond, and the school board, which prohibited it for liability reasons (Bell, 2001). The rain catchment system provided a superb play space, affording opportunities for dam building and leaf sailing on rainy days. The Vancouver Coastal Health Authority has funded a garden coordinator/classroom educator since 2001. Lessons for early grades integrate science, culture, and math. For example, students make graphs to measure seedling growth and use an abacus fence to count harvests. The librarian also hosts story times that thematically link garden eating with books about the plants being eaten.

Gardens can facilitate cross-cultural knowledge exchange in diverse urban communities. Elders who live adjacent to the garden in Grandview's public housing created a book titled "The Web of Life" to share their childhood garden experiences as indigenous peoples of Canada and as immigrants from other countries. The First Nations' school members also held a community-wide ceremony in which native chiefs, dancers, and singers came in full regalia to bless the gardens and longhouse, with its totem poles carved on site. As they play in the native maple tree's shade or under the longhouse roof on a rainy day, children experience wildlife attracted by the native plants and engage in a cultural environment honoring local heritage (Pevec, 2003).

Conclusion

This chapter describes educational approaches that encourage children's exploration of built and natural settings in cities. These approaches provide opportunities for children to express empathy for other living beings and respect for diverse cultures. Through the participatory design of a playground, a garden space, or a public park, children develop a sense of agency and competence and increase their understanding of the processes that shape a city. Through field trips and gardening, they learn about natural cycles and systems. These experiences lay a foundation for the development of environmental responsibility and stewardship. According to the ideas of John Dewey, Reggio Emilia preschools, and built environment education, social and environmental challenges cannot be solved through authoritarian, technocratic decision making. Successful problem solving requires the intelligence, creativity, and collaborative resourcefulness of all sectors of society, including young children. Early childhood is the time to begin teaching these skills. By bringing children out of their child care centers and classrooms into the built and natural spaces of their cities, and by involving children in naturalizing built surroundings, urban environmental education contributes to cities where human constructions and natural processes can productively coexist for all ages.

References

Bell, A. (2001). *Grounds for learning: Stories and insights from six Canadian school ground naturalization initiatives.* Canada: Evergreen.
Bishop, J., Kean, J., and Adams, E. (1992). Children, environment and education. *Children's Environments* 9(1), 49–67.

Chawla, L., and Rivkin, M. (2014). Early childhood education for sustainability in the United States of America. In J. Davis and S. Elliott (Eds.), *Research in early childhood education for sustainability: International perspectives and provocations* (pp. 248–265). London: Routledge.

Danks, S. (2010). *Asphalt to ecosystems.* Oakland, Calif.: New Village Press.

Derr, V., and Kovács, I. G. (2017). How participatory processes impact children and contribute to planning: A case study of neighborhood design from Boulder, Colorado, USA. *Journal of Urbanism: International Research on Placemaking and Urban Sustainability, 10*(1), 29–48.

Derr, V., and Tarantini, E. (2016). "Because we are all people": Outcomes and reflections from young people's participation in the planning and design of child-friendly public spaces. *Local Environment: The International Journal of Justice and Sustainability.*

Elliott, E., Eycke, K., Chan, S., and Müller, U. (2014). Taking kindergarteners outdoors: Documenting their explorations and assessing the impact on environmental awareness. *Children, Youth and Environments, 24*(2), 102–122.

Hall, E. L., and Rudkin, J. K. (2011). *Seen and heard: Children's rights in early childhood education.* New York: Teachers College Press.

Gustafson, K., and van der Burgt, D. (2015). 'Being on the move': Time-spatial organization and mobility in a mobile preschool. *Transport Geography, 46,* 201–209.

McCartney, K., and Phillips, D. (Eds.). (2006). *Blackwell handbook of early childhood development.* Malden, Mass.: Blackwell Publishing.

Moore, R., and Cosco, N. (2014). Growing up green: Naturalization as a health promotion strategy in early childhood outdoor learning environments. *Children, Youth and Environments, 24*(2), 168–191.

Noddings, N. (2005). *The challenge to care in schools: An alternative approach to education.* 2nd edition. New York: Teachers College Press.

Pevec, I. (2003). Ethnobotanical gardens: Celebrating the link between human culture and the natural world. *Green Teacher, 70,* 25–28.

Phillips, L. G. (2014). I want to do real things: Explorations of children's active community participation. In J. Davis and S. Elliott (Eds.), *Research in early childhood education for sustainability: International perspectives and provocations* (194–207). London: Routledge.

Zilversmit, A. (1993). *Changing schools: Progressive education theory and practice, 1930–1960.* Chicago: University of Chicago Press.

17

POSITIVE YOUTH DEVELOPMENT

Tania M. Schusler, Jacqueline Davis-Manigaulte,
and Amy Cutter-Mackenzie

Highlights

- Positive youth development is an assets-based approach for cultivating competencies essential to personal well-being.
- When environmental education enables children and youths to contribute to improving urban environments, it can not only increase cities' sustainability and resilience but also foster young people's personal growth.
- Participatory action research, peer education, and youth civic engagement are three educational approaches that can lead to positive change for both urban environments and youths living within them.

Introduction

Environmental education is often associated with environmental learning and pro-environmental behaviors. Some approaches to environmental education, however, also enable young people's personal growth through the development of confidence, self-efficacy, and other assets that support an individual's well-being. This chapter explores the intersection of urban environmental education and positive youth development. It can inform teachers, environmental educators, science educators, youth workers, and others who want to advance environmental learning and advance a positive developmental trajectory for young people in varied educational settings, such as school classrooms, after-school programs, community organizations, youth development organizations, churches, camps, nature centers, science centers, museums, and gardens.

We begin by defining positive youth development and applying it to environmental education. We then describe three programs from the United States and Australia to illustrate different pedagogies for integrating positive youth development in environmental education aimed at urban sustainability. By "youth," we refer to the transitional period between childhood and adulthood, which varies across cultures. The United Nations defines youth as individuals age fifteen to twenty-four, but others include children younger than fifteen or young adults older than twenty-four in their definitions. The programs we describe also included some children younger than fifteen.

Positive Youth Development in Environmental Education

A paradigm shift in the youth development field has occurred, from a focus on reducing specific problems like unintended pregnancy or drug use to "positive youth development," which builds upon young people's strengths to develop competencies essential to well-being. Among multiple frameworks describing positive youth development, one of the most comprehensive describes four categories of personal assets promoting well-being: physical (e.g., good health habits); intellectual (e.g., critical thinking, good decision making); psychological (e.g., positive self-regard, emotional self-regulation); and social (e.g., connectedness, commitment to civic engagement) (Eccles and Gootman, 2002). In addition to its emphasis on strengthening assets, positive youth development acknowledges that developmental experiences do not occur as isolated events, but they occur throughout young people's daily lives as they interact with peers, family, and nonfamilial adults in schools, after-school programs, and their broader communities.

Settings that promote positive youth development in the United States have been found to share similar characteristics (Eccles and Gootman, 2002):

- Physical and psychological safety (e.g., safe facilities, safe peer interactions);
- Appropriate structure (e.g., clear and consistent expectations);
- Supportive relationships (e.g., good communication);
- Opportunities to belong (e.g., meaningful inclusion);
- Positive social norms (e.g., rules of behavior, values and morals);
- Support for efficacy and mattering (e.g., responsibility granting, meaningful challenge);

- Opportunities for skill building; and
- Integration of family, school, and community efforts.

The more of these features within an urban environmental education program, the more likely that positive youth development outcomes will result. All features need not be present, however, and some might require adaptation to be culturally relevant in other countries.

Youths' physical and psychosocial development is also influenced by the quality of the urban environment, such as environmental toxins, noise, indoor air quality, and access to green space (Evans, 2006). Urban environmental education can enable young people to play a role in ameliorating environmental conditions that negatively impact well-being. Around the globe, youths have demonstrated their capacity to assess and act to improve environmental conditions in cities (Hart, 1997; Chawla, 2002). When youths have genuine opportunity to address environmental concerns, they can develop valuable personal assets and also increase their own and others' well-being by enhancing urban environments (Figure 17.1). In short, urban environmental education can promote positive

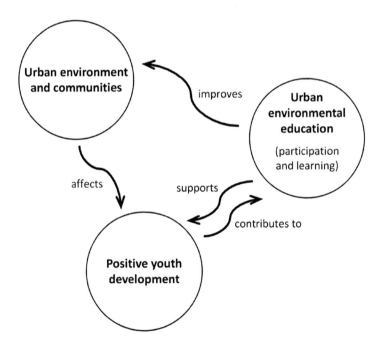

FIGURE 17.1. Urban environmental education that encompasses young people's participation in improving urban environments can build assets promoting their well-being, while also changing environmental conditions that impact youth development.

youth development, and youths, in turn, can positively contribute to urban sustainability and resilience.

Studies suggest that when youths participate in programs where they act positively for the environment, they themselves grow positively in various ways (Schusler and Krasny, 2010). For example, Hawaiian students working together to select, investigate, and act on a local environmental issue improved their critical thinking; reading, writing, and oral communication skills; familiarity with technology; self-confidence; and citizenship competence (Volk and Cheak, 2003). A food justice education program in New York City proved a valuable developmental experience for youth because it offered somewhere to belong, an opportunity to be pushed toward developing one's potential, to grapple with complexity, to practice leadership, and to become oneself (Delia, 2014). The evaluators of two environmental service-learning programs in East Africa, Roots & Shoots and Wildlife Clubs of Uganda, found that youths in both programs most valued forming relationships with club members, leaders, and community members as an outcome of environmental education (Johnson-Pynn and Johnson, 2010).

While more research is needed into the opportunities and barriers inherent to integrating positive youth development with urban environmental education, the two can be synergistic when programs are intentionally designed with both in mind. To illustrate the synergy that arises between urban environmental education and positive youth development when youths are offered genuine opportunity to effect environmental change, we describe three programs below. The first involves young people in participatory action research through a child-framed approach. The second develops young people's leadership capacities as peer educators. The third facilitates youth civic engagement through local environmental action. In each urban environmental education example, young people were given the opportunity to understand and effect change in urban environments and, as a result, also developed assets promoting their own well-being (Figure 17.1).

Youths as Co-researchers

Children and youths are experts on their own lives, yet research involving children is often conceived of and led by adults. Barratt Hacking, Cutter-Mackenzie, and Barratt (2013) call for including children as researchers rather than objects of investigation. To that end, the project "Is 'Nature' Diminishing in Childhood?"

Implications for Children's Lives" engaged young people in Australia in research about childhood and nature from their own perspectives. The project used a child-framed methodology incorporating qualitative and quantitative research in five distinct stages. It involved ten children ages nine to fourteen as co-researchers in each of two sites, one urban and the other an urban fringe suburb.

Stage 1 involved training sessions where the children learned about qualitative research, specifically ethnography (participant observation, semistructured interviews) and arts-based methods (photography, video, mapping), which enabled the children to study themselves and local culture (Cutter-Mackenzie, Edwards, and Widdop Quinton, 2015). One child's description of this experience was typical: "I am excited about being able to voice my opinion. . . . There are lots of young people who are passionate to be heard, but this is the only project I have heard of or taken part in that allows them to do so." Such opportunity to be heard may contribute to positive developmental assets, such as self-efficacy and a sense of social integration.

In stage 2, children conducted research over two months examining nature deficit disorder within their own cultural settings. The children received a device with Wi-Fi and GPS for mapping everyday experiences, appropriate research protocols, and a secure dropbox for uploading data. The latter encouraged children not only to take responsibility for their data but also to begin preliminary analysis (Barratt Hacking, Cutter-Mackenzie, and Barratt, 2013). Stage 3 involved children analyzing their data during research think tanks completed over one intensive session. Participants presented, discussed, mapped, and analyzed their findings. Focus group interviews with the children co-researchers and their parents or guardians also served to triangulate the research findings.

Stage 4 incorporated an online survey that the children co-researchers co-developed with Cutter-Mackenzie. Finally, stage 5 centered on disseminating the young people's research to academics, practitioners, and other children. The young people prepared ways to communicate their findings including a documentary and photomontage (Figure 17.2).

Together the stages of this child-framed methodology highlight how youth can genuinely engage as research collaborators. Through such experiences, children may develop positive developmental assets, such as self-efficacy, connectedness, and research, critical thinking, and communication skills. The results of children's research also may enhance understanding of children's experiences of nature in ways that can inform design and management of urban environments (Figure 17.1).

FIGURE 17.2. Photomontage designed and created by young co-researcher showing what she described as "nature by road" with photos taken at different times throughout the day. She explained that roads in her community both connected (like "blood lines") and disconnected children to nature. Credit: Graciella Mosqueira.

Youths as Peer Leaders

Peer education involves people with similar characteristics or experiences learning from each other. Used successfully in the health field, it also can be effective in other arenas, including environmental issues (de Vreede, Warner, and Pitter, 2014). Evidence suggests that educating teens to facilitate learning experiences for younger youths can have positive developmental impacts for both younger program recipients and "teens as teachers" (Lee and Murdock, 2001). This strategy provides teens with ownership over the direction of program activities, leading to investment in the outcome of their work (Larson, Walker, and Pearce, 2005).

A peer education or "teens as teachers" strategy was piloted in a 4-H environmental education initiative in New York City during the summer of 2015. 4-H is the youth development component of the Cooperative Extension System at many U.S. public universities. Twenty New York City 4-H teens attended the 4-H Career Exploration Conference at Cornell University, where they participated in science and leadership minicourses led by faculty and staff. During the closing assembly, New York City 4-Hers engaged more than four hundred peers and adult volunteers in creating "Pollinator Seed Bombs" as part of the National Pollinator Initiative, a U.S. presidential directive to conserve pollinators and thus protect the nation's food supply. Seed bombs are compressed bundles of clay, compost, or soil containing seeds that can be tossed into a bare patch of land to grow new plant life (http://kidsgardening.org). The 4-H teens and adult vol-unteers pledged to share their new knowledge and seed bombs with friends and 4-H clubs in their respective communities. One New York City 4-H peer educator reflected, "I could see action being taken to improve the world and I was proud to have been a part of it!" This illustrates how participating as an environmental peer educator contributed to this teen leader's self-efficacy and feelings of mat-tering, which are positive developmental assets.

When they returned home, the New York City 4-H teens also served as "teen teachers" for the 4-H Exploring Your Urban Environment summer day camp

FIGURE 17.3. In New York City, "teen teachers" in the 4-H Exploring Your Urban Environment program guided younger children releasing butterflies as part of their environmental stewardship project. Credit: Teishawn W. Florestal-Kevelier.

program (Figure 17.3). The teens were trained to implement a five-week program with younger youths in eight community agencies in New York City. The teen leaders connected 392 youths to their communities through service-learning opportunities that promoted environmental stewardship and community beautification. In a survey assessing program impacts, all thirty-five teen teachers agreed or strongly agreed with the statement, "I can make a difference in my community through community service"; such commitment to community service is a social asset for positive youth development. Teens' psychological assets were also enhanced as reflected by their agreement or strong agreement with the statement, "I am more confident in helping others." These results align with our conceptual framework (Figure 17.1), highlighting the positive impact that connecting youths to their environment in meaningful ways can have for the youths as well as their environment and communities.

Youths as Civic Actors

Youth civic engagement refers to young people developing their civic capacities by actively collaborating with others to shape society. One form of youth civic engagement is environmental action, whereby learners collectively analyze a problem and act to solve it. Environmental action can involve directly improving the environment, such as planting native vegetation to restore habitat in a city park, or can indirectly influence others to act through education or policy advocacy. Critical to environmental action is shared decision making; participants collaborate in defining a problem and then envision and enact solutions (Jensen and Schnack, 1997; Hart, 1997). Adults can experience tensions in sharing decision-making power; navigating these tensions is essential to ensuring genuine opportunity for youths' participation and positive development (Schusler, Krasny, and Decker, 2016).

A youth development specialist and an environmental educator collaborated in an after-school program to facilitate a project in which seven middle school students produced a documentary about "Green Homes" in the city of Ithaca and surrounding towns in upstate New York. The adult leaders chose the project focus—producing a video about green building—and invited youths to participate. The youths then made decisions with educators' guidance throughout all facets of video production over seven months, from planning to filming, editing, and debuting to area residents their eighteen-minute documentary. The role of the adult leader and youth participants in decision making in this project reflects the results of a study on youth environmental action programs, in which educators spoke about striking a balance between providing needed guidance as well as opportunities for youth to assume decision making and leadership (Schusler, Krasny, and Decker, 2016).

The students' video featured three local homes demonstrating building with natural materials, recycled materials, and renewable energy. It also included a "green home" for dogs and cats at the Tompkins County Society for the Prevention of Cruelty to Animals. The "pet home" highlighted the use of recycled materials, natural lighting, a geo-exchange heating and cooling system, and native landscaping.

Youths reported gaining knowledge about green building and being motivated to do more. As one youth said, "it's really inspired me to look more at our environment and what I can do to help." They also spoke of developing skills in video production, problem solving, communication, teamwork, interacting with adults, persisting to complete a long-term project, and being patient. They valued the opportunity to contribute to their community. As one reflected, "This is going to have an impact on how people build their homes. People that see [the video], at least they're going to do some of the minor things talked about. And maybe when they see that kids have done something like this, people will give the kids much more respect in the community." This form of indirect environmental action—youths acting to try to influence residents to make environmentally friendly choices—demonstrates one way that young people develop assets while educating others toward increased urban sustainability (Figure 17.1).

Conclusion

Participatory action research, peer education, and youth civic engagement are three approaches that have been used in urban environmental education to advance sustainability and foster positive youth development. These three approaches are not mutually exclusive; for example, youth environmental action often involves young people as researchers to understand a situation before proceeding in collective action to change it for the better; it thus integrates participatory action research and civic engagement. All three approaches value young people's capabilities, build upon their strengths, and offer opportunity for genuine, meaningful participation with the potential for impact on their communities and the environment. They also require adult leaders who provide a caring environment and appropriate levels of guidance, expectations, and freedom for youth to take on leadership and other responsibilities. Through such experiences, young people can contribute to creating more sustainable and resilient cities while developing valuable physical, intellectual, psychological, and social assets that enhance personal well-being.

References

Barratt Hacking, E., Cutter-Mackenzie, A., and Barratt, R. (2013). Children as active researchers: The potential of environmental education research involving children. In R. B. Stevenson, M. Brody, J. Dillon, and A. E. J. Wals (Eds.), *International handbook of research on environmental education* (pp. 438–458). New York: Routledge/AERA.

Chawla, L. (Ed.) (2002). *Growing up in an urbanizing world*. Paris: UNESCO Publishing.

Cutter-Mackenzie, A., Edwards, S., and Widdop Quinton, H. (2015). Child-framed video research methodologies: Issues, possibilities and challenges for researching with children. *Children's Geographies, 13*(3), 343–356.

Delia, J. E. (2014). Cultivating a culture of authentic care in urban environmental education: Narratives from youth interns at East New York Farms. Master's thesis, Cornell University.

de Vreede, C., Warner, A., and Pitter, R. (2014). Facilitating youth to take sustainability actions: The potential of peer education. *Journal of Environmental Education, 45*(1), 37–56.

Eccles, J., and Gootman, J. A. (Eds.). (2002). *Community programs to promote youth development*. Washington, D.C.: National Academy Press.

Evans, G. W. (2006). Child development and the physical environment. *Annual Review of Psychology, 57*, 423–451.

Hart, R. A. (1997). *Children's participation: The theory and practice of involving young citizens in community development and environmental care*. London: Earthscan.

Jensen, B. B., and Schnack, K. (1997). The action competence approach in environmental education. *Environmental Education Research, 3*(2), 163–178.

Johnson-Pynn, J. S., and Johnson, L. R. (2010). Exploring environmental education for East African youth: Do program contexts matter? *Children, Youth and Environments, 20*(1), 123–151.

Larson, R., Walker, K., and Pearce, N. (2005). A comparison of youth-driven and adult-driven youth programs: Balancing inputs from youth and adults. *Journal of Community Psychology, 33*(1), 57–74.

Lee, F. C. H., and Murdock, S. (2001). Teen as teachers programs: Ten essential elements. *Journal of Extension, 39*(1). http://www.joe.org/joe/2001february/rb1.php.

Schusler, T. M., and Krasny, M. E. (2010). Environmental action as context for youth development. *Journal of Environmental Education, 41*(4), 208–223.

Schusler, T. M., Krasny, M. E., and Decker, D. J. (2016). The autonomy-authority duality of shared decision-making in youth environmental action. *Environmental Education Research*. http://dx.doi.org/10.1080/13504622.2016.1144174.

Volk, T. L., and Cheak, M. J. (2003). The effects of an environmental education program on students, parents, and community. *Journal of Environmental Education, 34*(4), 12–25.

18

ADULT EDUCATION

Philip Silva and Shelby Gull Laird

Highlights

- Adult learning theories suggest ways to engage adults in urban environmental education through action-oriented projects and enrichment opportunities.
- Adult urban environmental education includes programs with predetermined outcomes as well as those that enable participants to define their own learning goals.
- Many programs draw on learning theory to integrate both instrumental and emancipatory goals.

Introduction

"You can't teach an old dog new tricks." Though this timeworn adage suggests that adults are incapable of learning, we know this to be false. Most adults continue to learn throughout their lives. Indeed, many individuals seek out new knowledge for personal growth or to transition through life events (Knowles, 1984). Most environmental education—urban and otherwise—focuses on children and young adults, either in a classroom setting or through field trips to nature centers, museums, public gardens, or other similar settings. In this chapter we explore opportunities for developing urban environmental education experiences for adults.

Theories and documented practices of adult education offer rich conceptual and practical frameworks for urban environmental education, extending and in some cases strengthening the work that has been done with children, adolescents, and young adults. Adult education can include teaching and learning in formal settings, such as continuing education offered through colleges and universities, adult literacy and high school equivalency programs, and a variety of workshops, lectures, professional development opportunities, and other one-off learning events sponsored by government agencies, nongovernmental organizations, and even for-profit businesses. It also includes the teaching and learning that happens informally through apprenticeships, community-based activism, and other forms of spontaneous and collaborative learning through doing.

Recognizing that a single chapter cannot account for the diversity of approaches in adult education, we focus on a narrow selection of themes that harmonize with current issues and trends in urban environmental education. We begin with a brief introduction to the core ideas of three influential adult education scholars and go on to briefly describe two cases of adult environmental education in cities. We conclude by exploring both theory and practice through the binary categories of "emancipatory" versus "instrumental" environmental education and consider the implications for urban environmental educators working with adults.

Keystone Thinkers in Adult Education: Freire, Knowles, and Vella

Adult education is a wide-ranging field of theory and practice with no shortage of influential thinkers and doers to call upon. One could go as far back as Plato's "Dialogues" to find documented evidence of adults struggling to learn from each other. Here we introduce three keystone thinkers in adult education from the second half of the twentieth century: the Brazilian educator Paulo Freire (1921–1997), his North American contemporary Malcolm Knowles (1913–1997), and Jane Vella (born 1931), who synthesized and expanded on Freire's and Knowles' work to make it accessible and applicable to a new generation of adult educators.

Paulo Freire's influence on both the theory and practice of adult education is international in scope. Though Freire's "Pedagogy of the Oppressed" is nearly fifty years old, his progressive views on teaching and learning in adulthood continue to challenge and inspire adult educators. Freire's ideas about adult education evolved while he developed literacy programs for working class adults in northeastern Brazil in the 1940s and 1950s. His early writing shed light on what he called "the banking myth of education," or the notion that teachers can simply "deposit" static information into the minds of passive students. Freire called on educators to engage students in an active process of "conscientization," working side by side to critically decode the conditions of oppression in their lives and create useful knowledge to change the world and "regain their humanity" (2005, p. 48). Freire's pedagogy emphasized learning-in-action, linking theory and practice in an inextricable process he named "praxis."

Malcolm Knowles also crafted an approach to adult education that urged instructors to put the needs and aspirations of their students first. Knowles' views on adult education were grounded in his experience leading informal adult learning programs through the Young Men's Christian Association (YMCA) in the 1940s. Knowles believed the theory and practice of adult education merited its own field of study and he popularized the concept of "andragogy" for adults as a complement to "pedagogy" for children. In his "Andragogy in Action" (1984), Knowles wrote, "Because adults are motivated to learn after they experience a need in their life situation, they enter an educational activity with a life-centered, or problem-centered orientation to learning. For the most part, adults do not learn for the sake of learning; they learn in order to be able to perform a task, solve a problem, or live in a more satisfying way" (p. 11). Like Freire, Knowles believed that adult education should honor the knowledge, skills, and wisdom every adult student brings to the classroom or workshop. His "problem-centered orientation to learning" offered another conceptual route to empowering adult students and incorporating their motivations to learn into the educational experience.

Jane Vella's "Twelve Principles for Effective Adult Learning" (2002) are inspired, in large part, by her reading of Freire and Knowles and her own formative experience working in education for community development in Tanzania from the mid-1950s to the early 1970s. Vella's work synthesizes insights from a wide range of thinkers in adult education, as well as from cognitive psychology and community organizing. Her approach is mainly geared toward workshops, training sessions, and courses that allow educators to purposively plan and design a learning experience.

Vella calls on educators to show respect for learners as decision makers by inviting them to participate in a needs assessment that shapes the content of a new course or workshop. Educators, according to Vella, should honor the need for immediacy in adult learning; everything should tie back to the immediate needs and aspirations of the learners. Immediacy, in turn, grows from opportunities for students to experience praxis or hands-on learning by doing through direct engagement with ideas, feelings, and actions. Accountability comes from completing discrete and accomplishable tasks that give students immediate feedback on their accomplishments. Teamwork in small groups fosters relationships among students and between students and teachers, while the concept of role development encourages students to find their own voices and develop a strong self-awareness of the part they play in dialogue with others. Thoughtful sequencing of content and tasks in a workshop can create a safe environment for adults to propose, discuss, and debate new ideas without risk of embarrassment.

We do not offer Vella's principles and practices as the final word in adult education. Rather her principles offer a window into a set of concepts and concerns that synthesize the work of many adult education theorists. These include not only Freire and Knowles but also the philosopher John Dewey, the psychologist Kurt Lewin, the activist Myles Horton, the sociologist Jack Mezirow, and the cultural critic bell hooks, to name just a few. We turn next to short descriptions of adult urban environmental education programs that reflect the work of Vella and other scholars.

Examples of Adult Urban Environmental Education

Examples of urban environmental education for adults come in a variety of forms, each one shaped by its own implicit and explicit assumptions about effective teaching and learning in adulthood. Here we offer two examples that help illustrate the differences between formally designed learning experiences on the one hand and informal, learn-as-you-go experiences on the other. Keep in mind that this conceptual split is just one of multiple ways to divide up the different cases of urban environmental education under way throughout the world, and some cases will fit within these categories more easily than others. These categories, then, are constructions, thinking tools that help us draw tidy boundaries around phenomena in an untidy world (Lincoln and Guba, 2013), and they shouldn't be confused with normative benchmarks for assessing the value or "fit" of different kinds of real-world cases.

Brooklyn Urban Gardener, New York City

Brooklyn Urban Gardener works with adults who want to become knowledgeable ambassadors for horticultural initiatives throughout Brooklyn, a borough of more than 2.5 million people. The training takes place indoors at the Brooklyn Botanic Garden and outside at nearby community gardens (Figure 18.1). The principles and practices of Vella's dialogue education guide the design of the sessions, which give learners knowledge that is immediately useful and applicable to their gardening and urban horticulture practices. The topics, which are mostly chosen by educators at the botanic garden, include composting, vegetable

FIGURE 18.1. Brooklyn Urban Gardener students learn about street trees on the sidewalk outside Brooklyn Botanic Garden. Credit: Nina Browne, courtesy of Brooklyn Botanic Garden.

gardening, urban forestry, pest management, and community organizing. The sessions also invite participants to share their pre-existing knowledge of urban horticulture during small group tasks. Outside the sessions, participants work together on a community volunteer project and perform thirty hours of service before receiving their Brooklyn Urban Gardener certificate.

Camley Street Natural Park Volunteers, London

Camley Street Natural Park is a two-acre green space wedged between a major railway and a former industrial canal in the heart of London. Volunteers created the park in the early 1980s, transforming a former coal dump facility into a tiny patchwork of woodlands, wetlands, and meadows (Figure 18.2). The London Wildlife Trust, a city-wide conservation organization, sponsors a small staff of educators and administrators at the park, but volunteers continue to perform much of the day-to-day labor involved in managing the site. The adult volunteers learn about what does and doesn't work in their ongoing management of the site

FIGURE 18.2. Volunteers at Camley Street Natural Park surveying their work to maintain the grounds. Credit: Alex Russ.

through repeated trial and error. For example, as real estate redevelopment along nearby Regent's Canal intensifies, volunteers and park managers are working to adapt the site to meet the changing habitat needs of nearby fauna.

Emancipatory and Instrumental Adult Urban Environmental Education

The New York City and London examples illustrate best practices in that they are distinctively adult urban environmental education experiences that require a working knowledge of adult education theory and practice to successfully implement. While the Brooklyn Urban Gardener program explicitly draws on Vella's approach to craft a sequence of preplanned workshops, the volunteers at Camley Street find more incidental and informal opportunities to learn on the job. Wals et al. (2008) propose three overarching approaches to environmental education that help us interpret these key differences between the Brooklyn Urban Gardener program and the volunteer initiatives at Camley Street: (1) instrumental approaches wherein desired behavioral outcomes of an activity are known in advance—usually by the teacher or instructor—and designed as a step-by-step experience in a workshop, classroom lesson, or tutorial; (2) emancipatory approaches that are more open-ended and iteratively responsive to the complex and emergent needs of the learners; and (3) approaches that combine instrumental and emancipatory approaches.

According to Wals and colleagues, instrumental environmental education "assumes that a desired behavioral outcome of an [environmental education] activity is known, (more or less) agreed on, and can be influenced by carefully designed interventions" (p. 56). In contrast, emancipatory environmental education tries "to engage citizens in an active dialogue to establish co-owned objectives, shared meanings, and a joint, self-determined plan of action to make changes they themselves consider desirable" (pp. 56–57). The critical distinction between instrumental and emancipatory approaches is whether the learning agenda is mostly prescribed for the learners by an educator ahead of time, or whether the learners actively shape the educational agenda, often in response to a problem they perceive in society or the world at large.

Instrumental approaches to adult urban environmental education can take various forms. Many large urban parks and public gardens offer formal workshops, tours, and multiweek certification programs that invite adults to learn about forest ecology, botany, horticulture, birding, garden design, boating, and other topics; these programs prepare adults to become volunteer urban stewards, much like the Brooklyn Urban Gardener program described above. The "Citizen Pruner" program sponsored by the nonprofit organization Trees New York offers another "instrumental" example (Campbell and Wiesen, 2009). This five-week workshop series trains adults to take care of street trees in the public right-of-way. The workshops include topics such as basic tree botany, soil amendment, watering, and safe limb pruning. The instruction is mostly lecture-based, with some fieldwork for teaching participants to prune dead, diseased, and damaged branches from street trees. Professionals in urban forestry, horticulture, and other branches of urban public space maintenance may avail themselves of continuing education and training opportunities. Whether their aim is recreational or vocational, or a combination of the two, adults enter into these instrumental environmental education experiences knowing that the goals and objectives have been predefined and the outcomes of the process are, for the most part, nonnegotiable.

Emancipatory forms of urban environmental education for adults can emerge from self-organized efforts to manage natural resources in cities (much like the volunteers at Camley Street in London), from social movements advocating policy changes related to environmental injustices, or from participatory action and related research approaches. Krasny and Tidball (2015) label self-organized environmental stewardship initiatives typically found in cities "civic ecology practices," noting the collaborative nature of these practices and the opportunities they afford adults to engage in social learning. Civic ecology practices include community gardening, street tree stewardship, urban waterway restoration, trash removal initiatives, and other hands-on efforts to create and maintain social-ecological systems in cities. Participants in civic ecology practices engage in field-based "learning by doing," developing an understanding of the strengths and weaknesses of adaptations in practice over time.

Adult city dwellers may also encounter opportunities for emancipatory forms of urban environmental education when they band together to address inequities in the spatial distribution of toxic land uses under the broad heading of environmental justice (Sandler and Pezzullo, 2007; Corburn, 2005). Activists fighting the development of power plants, incinerators, landfills, and highways in low-income neighborhoods come to learn about the public health, urban planning, and political dimensions of their struggles. They learn to use technologies in mapping, environmental sensing, and participatory design (Wylie et al., 2014; Al-Kodmany, 2001) to investigate and reveal problems resulting from the siting of undesirable land uses, following which they learn to pose environmentally sustainable and socially equitable alternatives to plans crafted by municipal officials and business leaders.

Emancipatory environmental education for adults in cities also can take the form of original research or investigative journalism. Participants "learn" about the world through a process of experimentation and discovery that leads to novel insights useful for creating change in the world. Examples range from learning how to grow healthier vegetables in a community garden to investigations that lead to preventing the construction of an incinerator in a low-income neighborhood. In these cases, emancipatory adult learning about environmental topics resembles John Dewey's pragmatism (1927) and the tenets of action research (Lewin, 1946), participatory action research (Fals-Borda, 1991), and community-based participatory research (Bidwell, 2009). In all emancipatory traditions, learning prioritizes creating new and useful knowledge rather than assimilating and reconstructing existing knowledge passed along from other sources.

Conclusion

Both instrumental and emancipatory forms of urban environmental education geared toward adults have conceptual roots in the work of Paulo Freire, Malcolm Knowles, and Jane Vella, among others. Freire's work has been particularly influential throughout the world in adult education. Urban environmental education experiences targeting adults are well-suited to emancipatory education efforts, including with marginalized groups working toward environmental and social justice outcomes. Knowles and Vella have tried to bring the sensibilities of responsible teaching and learning to adult educational experiences, thus adding an instrumental component. These scholars provide basic principles and guidelines to aid urban environmental educators in developing best practices that integrate emancipatory and instrumental approaches.

As urban environmental educators it is essential that we tailor our lessons to meet the needs of our students. In the case of adult learners, we have at our disposal multiple tools to engage, motivate, and enlighten. Through the use of andragogic methods such as relationship building, engagement in action, and a focus on the needs of the learner, adult urban environmental education efforts can help promote environmental literacy and action. Though the education of children today is important to the future, the education of adults can have a more immediate impact on the emergence of sustainable cities around the world.

References

Al-Kodmany, K. (2001). Visualization tools and methods for participatory planning and design. *Journal of Urban Technology, 8*(2), 1–37.

Bidwell, D. (2009). Is community-based participatory research postnormal science? *Science, Technology & Human Values, 34*(6), 741–761.

Campbell, L., and Wiesen, A. (Eds.). (2009). *Restorative commons: Creating health and well-being through urban landscapes* (USFS General Technical Report NRS-P-39). Washington, D.C.: U.S. Government Printing Office.

Corburn, J. (2005). *Street science: Community knowledge and environmental health justice.* Cambridge, Mass.: MIT Press.

Dewey, J. (1927). *The public and its problems.* New York: H. Holt and Company.

Fals-Borda, O. (1991). *Action and knowledge: Breaking the monopoly with participatory action research.* New York: Apex Press.

Freire, P. (2005/1970). *Pedagogy of the oppressed* (rev. ed.). New York: Continuum.

Knowles, M. S. (1984). *Andragogy in action: Applying modern principles of adult learning.* San Francisco: Jossey-Bass.

Krasny, M. E., and Tidball, K. G. (2015). *Civic ecology: Adaptation and transformation from the ground up.* Cambridge, Mass.: MIT Press.

Lewin, K. (1946). Action research and minority problems. *Journal of Social Issues, 2*(4), 34–46.

Lincoln, Y. S., and Guba, E. G. (2013). *The constructivist credo.* Walnut Creek, Calif.: Left Coast Press.

Sandler, R., and Pezzullo, P. C. (Eds.). (2007). *Environmental justice and environmentalism: The social justice challenge to the environmental movement.* Cambridge, Mass.: MIT Press.

Vella, J. (2002/1994). *Learning to listen, learning to teach: The power of dialogue in educating adults.* San Francisco: John Wiley & Sons.

Wals, A. E. J., Geerling-Eijff, F., Hubeek, F., van der Kroon, S., and Vader, J. (2008). All mixed up? Instrumental and emancipatory learning toward a more sustainable world: Considerations for EE policymakers. *Applied Environmental Education & Communication, 7*(3), 55–65.

Wylie, S. A., Jalbert, K., Dosemagen, S., and Ratto, M. (2014). Institutions for civic technoscience: How critical making is transforming environmental research. *The Information Society, 30*(2), 116–126.

19

INTERGENERATIONAL EDUCATION

Shih-Tsen Nike Liu and Matthew S. Kaplan

Highlights

- Adding an intergenerational component to environmental education programs enriches the learning experience for participants of all ages.
- Whereas multigenerational approaches to environmental education aim to include or accommodate different generations, intergenerational approaches seek to promote dialogue, collaborative learning, and mutual understanding.
- Across the globe, intergenerational environmental education programs are being implemented in diverse urban settings, including schools, parks, urban gardens, and community and environmental centers.

Introduction

In 1977, the Tbilisi intergovernmental conference on environmental education endorsed a set of guiding principles for environmental education. Some principles, including considering the environment in its totality, viewing environmental learning as a continuous lifelong process, and taking a historical perspective into account, lend support for intergenerational approaches to environmental education. This set of approaches to environmental education is particularly pertinent in cities, where working toward sustainable development involves addressing a host of complex environmental, historical, and social issues.

A child who has limited firsthand experience with the process of urbanization and accompanying economic, demographic, and environmental changes may have difficulty gaining a cognitive understanding and an emotional appreciation of the environmental challenges facing cities. Environmental education programs, resources, and materials certainly contribute to such learning. Learning is enhanced, however, when the child has direct access to the living experience and perceptions of older people who can share their experiences of changes in the urban environment over time. At the root of an intergenerational paradigm for environmental education is activating environmental learning through facilitating interactions across generations.

Background

Intergenerational programs have been defined broadly as social vehicles that create purposeful and ongoing exchange of resources and learning among older and younger generations (Kaplan, Henkin, and Kusano, 2002). With regard to urban environmental education, the focus of intergenerational programs turns to ways in which young people, older adults, and the generations in the middle can work together to explore, build awareness, gain understanding, and improve the urban environment.

Environmental education funding, research, and program design tend to target young people as the primary audience (Kaplan and Liu, 2004). One of the most significant social changes of our time, however, is the rapidly expanding number of older adults. In countries experiencing rapid urban development, such as Taiwan, Japan, and the United States, older adults will soon become the largest segment of the population.

This demographic shift can be viewed positively. Contrary to negative age-related stereotypes, many older adults living in cities are healthy, lively, and actively engaged in civic affairs, including in volunteer initiatives aimed at protecting the urban environment. Notable accounts of environmental initiatives aimed at reaching and involving the older adult population (Ingman, Benjamin, and Lusky, 1999; Benson, 2000) include older adult environmental volunteerism in the United States (Pillemer et al., 2016) and in Australia (Warburton and Gooch, 2007). But the level of engagement of older adults in environmental education initiatives targeting younger generations still has room to grow. The relative disconnection of older adults from schools, environmental centers, and other settings that educate people about the environment represents a missed opportunity for strengthening community relationships in urban communities and instilling in children and youths a deeper sense of environmental awareness and connection.

Scholars have documented the potential benefits of intergenerational environmental education (Ballantyne, Fien, and Packer, 2001; Vaughan et al., 2003). The adults in some studies, however, were passive learners who were not utilized as educators or colearners during the learning process. The intergenerational initiatives highlighted in this chapter go beyond the goal of multigenerational inclusion or simply including members of different generations. An ideal intergenerational program creates opportunities for people of different age groups to learn about each other's knowledge, experiences, skills, and perceptions. As participants learn about the impact of the environment in each other's lives, they gain an awareness of common concerns. This contributes to an understanding of the interrelationships among people and the environment and a sense of how to work collaboratively to influence environmental policies and practices (Kaplan and Liu, 2004).

Why Consider Intergenerational Environmental Education?

From an environmental education perspective, inclusion of an intergenerational component helps to broaden the pool of people who care and are knowledgeable about the natural environment and have the skills to take effective action to help sustain it. As multigenerational groups of participants share their views, experiences, and knowledge with regard to the natural environment, they also gain insights into one another's lives and recognize common interests in preserving and caring for the environment.

Benefits for Environmental Education

In cities, the student-teacher ratio is commonly high and the teachers' workload is heavy. In many countries, particularly in urban areas, the proportion of older adults in the population is growing. Well-designed intergenerational programs provide an institutional anchor and vehicle for taking advantage of this demographic trend; educated, civically engaged older adults who care about future generations and wish to make a contribution to their environmental learning can be recruited, trained, and engaged as human resources in support of environmental education programs (Kaplan and Liu, 2004).

Benefits for Children

Many urban children do not live near their grandparents and have limited contact with older adults. Older adults in an intergenerational activity can serve as role models for younger participants to observe and imitate, which are important forms of learning (Bandura, 1977). Older adults also have life experiences that can make environmental content in textbooks more relevant and meaningful to young learners. For instance, older adults can readily share how they use natural resources with children in a community festival. Children learn things such as how to conserve water by using remaining bathwater to water flowers. As another example, while teaching topics such as chemical pollution hazards, an older adult who used to work as a toxics prevention agent or suffered from past pollution accidents can share his or her own experiences. Such conversation helps children to relate to environmental issues and to view environmental health risks from a lifespan perspective (Schettler et al., 1999). Environmental educators can structure intergenerational dialogue to nurture such long-term environmental perspectives (cf. Wright and Lund, 2000).

Benefits for Older Adults

Intergenerational programs provide older adults with opportunities to stay active, expand their social networks, and make valued contributions to society (Kaplan, Henkin, and Kusano, 2002). A powerful motivation for older adults to volunteer for environmental stewardship activities is wanting to leave a legacy, both for the Earth and for their grandchildren (Warburton and Gooch, 2007); a desire to leave a legacy could also motivate older adults to volunteer in environmental education programs.

Benefits for the City

Intergenerational programs tend to involve a broad spectrum of organizational partners and collaborators, thereby extending the reach and influence of environmental education and action across cities. The Lincoln Place "Futures Festival" held in Pittsburgh provides an example of how a collaborative planning process involving residents of all ages, and representatives of local community organizations and agencies from multiple sectors, can broaden the visioning process to encompass the natural as well as the built environment. The process of having to reach consensus and integrate their diverse ideas into large murals encouraged participants to work together to create age-inclusive, economically vibrant, and ecologically sustainable visions for the future of Lincoln Place (Kaplan et al., 2004).

What Do Intergenerational Environmental Education Initiatives Look Like?

Intergenerational environmental education initiatives can take place in multiple urban settings including schools, environmental education centers, parks, playgrounds, community centers, retirement centers, city streets, community gardens, and even vacant lots. Such educational initiatives can also be launched by different organizations and interorganizational partnerships. A school that wants to let students know about the history of a local urban forest, for example, can partner with a local historical society whose members include older adult residents willing to share the history of the site and discuss factors that influenced changes. An urban environmental center wanting to hold an air pollution monitoring fair that attracts residents of all ages can work with youth service and senior volunteer organizations to establish intergenerational teams working together to develop, set up, and staff interactive exhibits at the fair.

Educators across the globe are creating models to stimulate intergenerational dialogue and colearning about the natural environment. For example, Tanaka (2007) describes a school-based project in Japan in which students and adult volunteers developed a miniature biosphere to heighten their environmental awareness and appreciation. Chand and Shukla (2003) describe an intergenerational biodiversity contest in India designed to enhance learning about plants and promote values of conservation and respect for traditional ecological knowledge. Garden Mosaics is a science education and national outreach program developed by Cornell University that combines community action and intergenerational learning. Through interviewing elder gardeners, youths ages ten to eighteen learn about the mosaic of plants, planting practices, and cultures in urban community and other gardens (Figure 19.1). Youth participants balance what they learn from elder gardeners with learning from "Science Pages" developed at Cornell, which explain key science principles behind the practices youths observe and learn about from elders in the gardens (Kaplan and Liu, 2004).

Two additional examples, one from formal education in Taiwan and the other from nonformal education in the United States, illustrate elements of intergenerational urban environmental education programs (Table 19.1). The first program took place at He-cuo Elementary School in Taichung, Taiwan's third largest city. The teachers and principals invited senior adults from the community to participate in a series of intergenerational activities. The senior volunteers' opinions were taken into account throughout the planning process. Over the ten years of the program, new activities and volunteer recruits were continually integrated. On a city tour, children learned about old trees in the He-cuo community and listened to the elders' stories about the trees. In other activities, participants observed juxtaposed

FIGURE 19.1. Young people and an educator in Abraham House, the Bronx, New York City, learn from an elderly gardener (right) in a community garden. Credit: Alex Russ.

TABLE 19.1 Urban intergenerational environmental education programs in Taiwan and the United States

	HE-CUO ELEMENTARY SCHOOL	SHAVER'S CREEK ENVIRONMENTAL CENTER
Country	Taichung, Taiwan	Pennsylvania, the United States
Organization	School	Environmental education center
Setting	Downtown area	Suburban recreation area
Program approaches	Subject class, extracurricular activity, community family fair, and special day event	4-day summer camp for children from urban areas
Elderly participants	Community senior residents	Members of retirement centers
Young participants	Elementary school students	Fifth grade students signed up by their teachers
Main subject	Community environment and traditional artistry	Nature conservation and urban development
Examples of urban resources	Plants and animals, life style, and community changes over time	Traditional living style and urban development issues

old and new photos to learn about environmental changes over time, and students learned about differences between rural and city lifestyles through displays of traditional farmers' equipment. These and other activities combined to have an impact on student, teacher, and even nearby residents' awareness of community changes associated with urbanization. The program also helped students weave this historical context into their sense of local identity.

The second example is a four-day-residential program located at the Shaver's Creek Environmental Center, approximately fourteen miles south of downtown State College, Pennsylvania. The researchers conducted an experimental study to determine the effectiveness of an intergenerational program versus a monogenerational program (Liu and Kaplan, 2006). In the intergenerational condition, a group of older adult volunteers participated in the program as colearners and assistant instructors working with students to teach about traditional tools, such as darning eggs (an egg-shaped piece of wood inserted into the toe or heel of a sock during mending), and to share environment-friendly living habits. In another activity, the students were asked to discuss the possibility of converting the Environmental Center into a shopping mall. Students recognized that the development would have negative environmental consequences. At that point one of the senior volunteers shared a pertinent example from personal experience; residents of her childhood community successfully organized against a massive development plan that entailed replacing natural woodland with an airport. Such real-life stories helped students to better understand the process of community change and the potential influence of local residents.

How to Implement Intergenerational Environmental Education Initiatives?

Beyond program activities per se, organizational partnerships have a bearing on program structure and success. The critical step is to invite local leaders, stakeholders, and senior volunteers to join the planning process of the environmental education program. In the above example, the He-cuo Elementary School recruited older adult participants from local organizations including a Salvation Army center, a Taoism temple, a women's club, a traditional orchestra, and a puppet performance museum. These organizations have had a long-term relationship with the He-cuo School starting at the beginning of the environmental education activities. They also help with school functions such as student enrollment, holiday festivals, and student club advising, thereby broadening the school-community partnership beyond the environmental education program. Other organizations in urban areas can make good partners for helping to recruit local youths as well as older adults, such as 4-H clubs, scout troops, after-school programs, universities, animal shelters, and senior and community centers.

In order to build partnerships, environmental educators can seek out organizations with similar or complementary interests and objectives. For instance, a university may hold a class for elders about urban plants, and the adult students can partner with an elementary school's nature class. Or the older members of a community photography club can be invited to play a role in an intergenerational activity aimed at enhancing environmental awareness.

Integration of an intergenerational component into environmental education activities also introduces complexities and considerations with regard to program design. The following principles contribute to productive group dynamics and learning effectiveness in intergenerational programs (Kaplan and Liu, 2004):

1. Prepare participants of both generations before the program begins.
2. Draw upon both the youths' and adults' experiences and talents.
3. Promote extensive dialogue and sharing among participants.
4. Focus on the relationship among participants as well as the task.
5. Pay attention to safety for different age groups.
6. Design tasks that require the active participation of both generations to be completed.

Conclusion

Sustainability is an intergenerational concept. Meadows, Meadows, and Randers (1993) define a "sustainable society" as "one that can persist over generations; one that is far-seeing enough, flexible enough, and wise enough not to undermine either its physical or its social system of support." When considering how natural resources are used/misused over time, as well as strategies to preserve and enhance the environment, it is important to engage in long-term thinking and strategic policy making. Environmental educators can structure intergenerational dialogue to nurture such a long-term perspective of the environment (cf. Wright and Lund, 2000). At the same time, older adults who volunteer in such programs gain opportunities to stay active, contribute, and connect meaningfully with young people in their communities.

References

Ballantyne, R., Fien, J., and Packer, J. (2001). School environmental education program impacts upon student and family learning: A case study analysis. *Environmental Education Research, 7*(1), 23–27.

Bandura, A. (1977). *Social learning theory.* Englewood Cliffs, N.J.: Prentice Hall.

Benson, W. (2000). Empowerment for sustainable communities: Engagement across the generations. *Sustainable Communities Review, 3,* 11–16.

Chand, V. S., and Shukla, S. R. (2003). "Biodiversity contexts": Indigenously informed and transformed environmental education. *Applied Environmental Education and Communication, 2*(4), 229–236.

Ingman, S., Benjamin, T., and Lusky, R. (1999). The environment: The quintessential intergenerational challenge. *Generations, 22*(4), 68–71.

Kaplan, M., Henkin, N., and Kusano, A. (Eds.). (2002). *Linking lifetimes: A global view of intergenerational exchange.* Lanham, Md.: University Press of America.

Kaplan, M., Higdon, F., Crago, N., and Robbins, L. (2004). Futures Festival: An intergenerational strategy for promoting community participation. *Journal of Intergenerational Relationships, 2*(3/4), 119–146.

Kaplan, M., and Liu, S.-T. (2004). *Generations united for environmental awareness and action.* Washington, D.C.: Generations United.

Liu, S.-T., and Kaplan, M. (2006). An intergenerational approach for enriching children's environmental attitudes and knowledge. *Applied Environmental Education and Communication, 5*(1), 9–20.

Meadows, D. H., Meadows, D. L., and Randers, J. (1993). *Beyond limits.* White River Junction, Vt.: Chelsea Green Publishing Company.

Pillemer, K., Wells, N. M., Meador, R. H., Schultz, L., Henderson Jr., C. R., and Cope, M. T. (2016). Engaging older adults in environmental volunteerism: The Retirees in Service to the Environment program. *The Gerontologist.* http://dx.doi.org/10.1093/geront/gnv693.

Schettler, T., Solomon, G., Valenti, M., and Huddle, A. (1999). *Generations at risk: Reproductive health and the environment.* Cambridge, Mass.: MIT Press.

Tanaka, M. (2007). Effects of the "intergenerational interaction" type of school biotope activities on community development. In S. Yajima, A. Kusano, M. Kuraoka, Y. Saito, and M. Kaplan (Eds.), *Proceedings: Uniting the generations: Japan conference to promote intergenerational programs and practices* (pp. 211–212). Tokyo: Seitoku University Institute for Lifelong Learning.

Vaughan, C., Gack, J., Solorazano, H., and Ray, R. (2003). The effect of environmental education on schoolchildren, the parents, and community members: A study of intergenerational and intercommunity learning. *Journal of Environmental Education, 34*(3), 12–21.

Warburton, J., and Gooch, M. (2007). Stewardship volunteering by older Australians: The generative response. *Local Environment, 12*(1), 43–55.

Wright, S., and Lund, D. (2000). Gray and green? Stewardship and sustainability in an aging society. *Journal of Aging Studies, 14*(3), 229–249.

20

INCLUSIVE EDUCATION

*Olivia M. Aguilar, Elizabeth P. McCann,
and Kendra Liddicoat*

Highlights

- Inclusivity refers to diversifying our field so as to value the multiple agendas, frameworks, and approaches that bring new perspectives to our work.
- Urban environmental education presents unique opportunities to address issues of inclusivity and access because urban environments bring together multiple cultures and people with different abilities and ways of knowing.
- Recognizing the complexity of diversity and the systemic nature of power and privilege serves as the foundation for cultural competency in urban environmental education.
- Inclusivity is important because it addresses issues of equity and allows sharing of multiple perspectives, which can lead to innovation in addressing sustainability issues.

Introduction

Throughout the history of environmental education, groups have been marginalized, or excluded from the dominant discourse or practice, in curriculum and programming (Lewis and James, 1995). Often these groups consist of populations already struggling for equity, resources, and access. Yet to be effective in improving environmental conditions while ensuring just, equitable, and democratic engagement, educators must be inclusive of class, race, ethnicity, age, ability, culture, gender identity, sexual orientation, and other socially constructed indicators of "difference" in our society. This goes beyond diversifying our field to valuing the multiple agendas, frameworks, and approaches that bring new perspectives to our work, what we refer to as inclusivity. Creating culturally relevant learning environments and understanding that "culture" is both multifaceted and dynamic in regards to the values, beliefs, attitudes, and experiences shared by people (Bennett, 2014) is also crucial to this work. It requires ensuring that our field and practices are physically, emotionally, and socially accessible.

With more than half the world's population living in urban areas, urban environmental education presents a unique opportunity to address issues of inclusivity and access. In cities, educators can reach large numbers of people; utilize a vast array of human, natural, and built resources; and engage students in learning about urban social-ecological systems dynamics. Students can also learn about urban living and sustainability themes, such as building design, energy, transportation, waste, and food. At the same time, a more inclusive approach to environmental education has the potential to create more sustainable cities by bringing together the diverse perspectives needed to address sustainability problems and by calling attention to community issues and resources (Russ and Krasny, 2015). As effective urban environmental education requires learning from and alongside difference, and thus valuing difference, this chapter explores ways we can broaden our perspectives and audiences in an urban context by examining (1) the dynamics of exclusion and marginalization in environmental education, (2) the opportunities for inclusivity and accessibility in the urban context, and (3) a reflective process necessary for equitable and just environmental education.

A Complex History

The conservation and preservation movements helped shape environmental education but also often marginalized cultures, peoples, and voices. These movements emphasized the separation between people and nature and focused largely on land and animals over people and health, which misrepresented the interests of many (Lewis and James, 1995). Similarly, a dominant focus on Western, scientific, and positivistic approaches to knowledge acquisition prevented some groups from fully participating and contributing to the environmental education field by marginalizing other ways of knowing and doing, particularly those of indigenous peoples (Aikenhead, 1996) and migrants coming to cities from agricultural backgrounds. Critically examining the history of the narratives and voices present and missing from environmental education agendas and curricula provides opportunities to expand and improve upon our work.

One such opportunity to expand our practice is to engage with environmental justice issues (see chapter 6), which have been historically lacking in environmental education realms (Haluza-DeLay, 2013). Environmental hazards and climate change disproportionately impact poor and marginalized groups in societies across the globe. By not effectively engaging in justice issues, Haluza-DeLay (2013) argues that "environmental educators have reduced the scope of environmental sustainability and missed opportunities to connect with more people and potential allies among a broader reach of civil society organizations and other educators" (p. 394). Further, some contend the historically marginalized voices—particularly of women, indigenous peoples, youth, elders, and residents of lesser-developed countries—represent new leaders who can contribute innovative solutions to the world's environmental challenges (Suzuki, 2003). Engaging and learning alongside these leaders can facilitate social change and enable environmental education to embrace the lived experiences of all community members.

For community members with disabilities, two additional historical factors complicate their opportunities for participation in environmental education experiences. Proponents of wilderness preservation and primitive outdoor recreation have often mounted objections to increasing physical accessibility on ideological grounds without considering the many creative ways that sites can be made accessible without destroying habitats and significantly altering visitor experiences (Sax, 1980). For example, in the United States, requirements for accessibility in outdoor settings are new and only apply to federal agencies (U.S. Access Board, 2014). Similarly, the push to move from explicitly separate to more inclusive classes and programs has come later for individuals with disabilities than for some other marginalized groups and is still as much a result of legislative requirements as societal expectations. By intentionally designing inclusive programs, urban environmental education has the opportunity to be at the forefront of rapidly shifting approaches in education and recreation (Devine, 2012).

Opportunities for Inclusion in the Urban Environment

The urban context provides unique opportunities to strengthen both inclusivity and environmental education practices by increasing accessibility using emotional, physical, and social means. On an emotional level, urban contexts allow for urban participants to remain close to their surroundings, which can reduce emotional stress and psychological barriers associated with wild spaces and include meaningful ways to engage in learning. Environmental education implemented in wild spaces, day and residential camps, or simply away from backyard spaces, can lead to an understanding about the environment as "out there" (Haluza-DeLay, 2001) and create anxiety for those experiencing "biophobia" about "nature" or "wilderness" (Madfes, 2004). When educators take advantage of the local urban environment for pedagogical purposes (see chapter 22), the context is not only culturally relevant through being rooted in the everyday sociocultural context of learners, it is also less intimidating. For example, a topic like environmental justice may capture the everyday experience of urban participants and allow them to engage meaningfully with environmental issues.

In a physical sense, shifting environmental education from remote wilderness areas to urban parks, backyards, community centers, gardens, and restoration sites has the potential to make environmental education accessible to people of all abilities and backgrounds. Urban parks and gardens often have paved or hard-packed trails and are located near public transportation or city streets. Reducing this transportation barrier alone can increase the ability of youths to participate. Incorporating technology and social media, for example through citizen science programs, can also increase access for those unable to travel to distant or hard-to-reach places.

Socially, urban environments bring together a range of cultures, abilities, and knowledge. For instance, older adults often serve as volunteers, civic leaders, and learners who offer opportunities for intergenerational dialogue and action (see chapter 19). Intergenerational learning opportunities can also lead to greater civic engagement in youth with the proper guidance and collaborations (Krasny and Tidball, 2009a). Additionally, engaging older adults in environmental volunteerism and other forms of environmental learning may enhance their social interactions, health, and well-being (Pillemer et al., 2010). Urban educators can capitalize on culturally relevant resources and opportunities for intergenerational exchange, through programs that incorporate community gardening, political activism, green employment, healthy living, and environmental quality, among others. These opportunities allow the local concerns of community members to be addressed through environmental problem solving, and they contribute to community resilience.

A Reflective Practice

We have already suggested that environmental education must be inclusive to be effective and that urban environmental education might be well-positioned to be inclusive. Still, the move toward inclusivity and a more just and equitable society requires constant evaluation and reflection. It also requires understanding the relationships among environment, race, class, gender, physical ability, and institutions, which reflect systemic dynamics of power and privilege. To be effective environmental educators, we must challenge our assumptions about other groups, approach learning in holistic ways, and recognize other ways of knowing beyond cognition, such as emotional, spiritual, social, and kinesthetic/physical understanding. Therefore, "intercultural competence"—the cognitive, affective, and behavioral skills and qualities needed to effectively and appropriately interact in various cultural contexts (Bennett, 2014)—is critical to our work. Competencies include cultural self-awareness, knowledge of other cultures, curiosity, open-mindedness, tolerance of ambiguity, empathy, active listening skills, conflict resolution skills, and capacity to build relationships, among others (Bennett, 2014). Cultural competency is hard work and is ongoing. It begins with understanding one's own privilege and understanding the systemic dynamics of privilege.

Enhancing our ability to create respectful, inclusive learning environments is an enduring responsibility. Dialogue with community members and considering aspects of culture in programming is a starting point. For instance, environmental education programs may have a multilingual staff and may offer written materials in multiple languages. They may employ educators with training and experience working with people with disabilities who serve as a resource for other staff members. Cultural competence, however, is much more than language and staff composition. It is about valuing and truly learning from the lived experiences of others.

Example Programs

The following cases illustrate how some urban environmental education programs are incorporating inclusive practices. An urban water-monitoring program in Austin, Texas, provides an example of a program that is listening to and addressing the local needs and concerns of its youth. An urban nature center in Milwaukee, Wisconsin, exemplifies the importance of attending to program missions and priorities to create a more physically inviting nature center. Finally, studies of neighborhoods in Cuba, Spain, and the United States show the importance of attending to issues of identity and well-being in low-income and marginalized communities.

Austin, Texas, United States

Educators leading a water-monitoring, after-school program in the ethnically diverse city of Austin, Texas, consistently reflect on their assumptions about how an environmental education program can lead to a more just and equitable society for low-income students. The program's goals are to "advance personal and academic achievement through environmental monitoring, education and adventure." The program directors listened to the concerns of the community and asked how they could expand their services to their intended audience. As a result, their program provides transportation to the activity sites, meals, and a weekly stipend for youth participants. With these services, the program has been able to create educational and recreational opportunities and link youths to local community experiences and adult mentors. Youth participants gain confidence in their skills and a sense of agency as they demonstrate their knowledge of water testing and species identification. By using a cadre of caring adults and a creating a social network among the youths, the program also provides participants with a sense of belonging and a safe space in which they have a voice. Thus while the explicit goals of water monitoring and environmental literacy are accomplished, the implicit goals of access and equity are pursued.

Milwaukee, Wisconsin, United States

Creating inclusive environmental education opportunities often involves adjusting more than the curriculum and instructional practices. It may also encompass adjusting mission statements, marketing practices, budget priorities, and facilities to support effective programming (Anderson and Kress, 2003). An urban nature center in Milwaukee, Wisconsin, with a goal to become the most accessible and inclusive facility in the region, illustrates this approach to inclusion. The center recently changed its tagline from "a place for all seasons" to "a place for all seasons, a place for everyone." Their website and social media highlight ongoing physical accessibility efforts, whereas their capital campaign and grant-writing efforts are focused on renovating their bathrooms for wheelchair access, expanding their network of boardwalk trails, redesigning their amphitheater for increased accessibility, and building a deck to enable all visitors to study birds and other wildlife. Staff members have engaged in professional development related to inclusion, have conducted an accessibility survey of their site, and are planning a survey of other outdoor recreation opportunities for people in their area with disabilities. These efforts grew out of field trip requests from inclusive schools, an increase in senior living facilities near the nature center, and a desire to serve veterans and their families. By becoming a more accessible site, this nature center is laying the foundation for a more inclusive program.

United States, Cuba, and Spain

Particularly in urban contexts, cultural competence entails an appreciation of how important one's neighborhood is to identity, well-being, and personal safety, and of how green places can serve as safe spaces for all residents. Anguelovski's (2015) study of Dudley (Boston, Massachusetts), Cayo Hueso (Havana, Cuba), and Casc Antic (Barcelona, Spain) neighborhoods showed how green places were motivators for action and strengthening identities among vulnerable urban residents. In these neighborhoods, environmental projects, from organizing community gardens to establishing and managing playgrounds, served as avenues to defuse tensions, facilitate colearning, and promote sharing across different ethnic and cultural groups. Urban environmental educators have the opportunity to serve as bridge builders in such community work to revitalize neighborhoods, address environmental injustices, and work and learn alongside neighbors while remaking places in empowering ways.

Conclusion

We are witnessing a vast array of promising urban innovations in the realms of urban planning, education, health and wellness, design, and social engagement. Numerous cities are advancing livability principles through transportation, housing, and walkability initiatives. At the same time, evidence suggests that connecting with the natural world positively impacts emotional, physical, psychological, and communal well-being. A healthy built environment and strong social networks also impact quality of life and intersect with issues of social justice.

Inclusivity is not only necessary to create more effective environmental education. It also helps to address urban environmental and social issues, such as aging populations, access to education, youth development, and equity and justice. Much like ecological variability can improve the resilience of ecosystems, voices of diverse populations from different backgrounds can enhance cities in the face of ecological and social changes (Krasny and Tidball, 2009b). Accomplishing this, however, requires that we understand and value learners' life experiences and engage with them in meaningful ways. Environmental educators must recognize the historical roots of marginalization in our field (and beyond), realize the systemic nature of oppression, and make strides to change our practices to be more inclusive while mitigating social and environmental issues of local concern.

We need to work in solidarity with others, educate ourselves constantly, listen actively, and recognize the deep, humble work involved in building authentic relationships in community with others.

References

Aikenhead, G. S. (1996). Science education: Border crossing into the subculture of science. *Studies in Science Education, 27*(1), 1–52.

Anderson, L., and Kress, C. B. (2003). *Inclusion: Including people with disabilities in parks and recreation opportunities.* State College, Pa.: Venture Publishing.

Anguelovski, I. (2015). *Neighborhood as refuge: Community reconstruction, place remaking, and environmental justice in the city.* Cambridge, Mass.: MIT Press.

Bennett, J. M. (2014). Intercultural competence: Vital perspectives for diversity and inclusion. In B. Ferdman and B. R. Dean (Eds.), *Diversity at work: The practice of inclusion* (pp. 155–176). San Francisco: Jossey-Bass.

Devine, M. A. (2012). A nationwide look at inclusion: Gains and gaps. *Journal of Park and Recreation Administration, 30*(2), 1–18.

Haluza-DeLay, R. (2001). Nothing here to care about: Participant constructions of nature following a 12-day wilderness program. *Journal of Environmental Education, 32*(4), 43–48.

Haluza-DeLay, R. (2013). Educating for environmental justice. In R. B. Stevenson, M. Brody, J. Dillon, and A. E. J. Wals (Eds.), *International handbook of research on environmental education* (pp. 394–403). New York: Routledge/AERA.

Krasny, M. E., and Tidball, K. G. (2009a). Community gardens as context for science, stewardship and civic action learning. *Cities and the Environment, 2*(1), 1–18.

Krasny, M. E., and Tidball, K. G. (2009b). Applying a resilience systems framework to urban environmental education. *Environmental Education Research, 15*(4), 465–482.

Lewis, S., and James, K. (1995). Whose voice sets the agenda for environmental education? Misconceptions inhibiting racial and cultural diversity. *Journal of Environmental Education, 26*(3), 5–13.

Madfes, T. J. (2004). *What's fair got to do with it? Diversity cases from environmental educators.* San Francisco: WestEd.

Pillemer, K., Fuller-Rowell, T. E., Reid, C., and Wells, N. (2010). Environmental volunteering and health outcomes over a twenty-year period. *The Gerontologist, 50*(5), 594–602.

Russ, A., and Krasny, M. (2015). Urban environmental education trends. In A. Russ (Ed.), *Urban environmental education* (pp. 12–25). Ithaca, N.Y., and Washington, D.C.: Cornell University Civic Ecology Lab, NAAEE and EECapacity.

Sax, J. L. (1980). *Mountains without handrails: Reflections on the national parks.* Ann Arbor: University of Michigan Press.

Suzuki, D. (2003). *The David Suzuki reader: A lifetime of ideas from a leading activist and thinker.* Vancouver, B.C.: Greystone Books.

U.S. Access Board. (2014). *Accessibility standards for federal outdoor developed areas.* Washington, D.C.: United States Access Board.

21

EDUCATOR PROFESSIONAL DEVELOPMENT

Rebecca L. Franzen, Cynthia Thomashow,
Mary Leou, and Nonyameko Zintle Songqwaru

Highlights

- Professional development in urban environmental education addresses content and contexts including urban places and people, and it engages educators in investigating environmental issues, citizen science, service learning, and other hands-on experiences.
- Environmental education professional development takes advantage of multiple resources found in the city, including the built and natural environment and human capital.
- Professional learning communities that are educator-driven and allow for planning time are important components of professional development.
- A professional development model for urban environmental education encompasses six elements: interdisciplinary and integrated content, context, pedagogy, resources, field experiences, and professional learning communities.

Introduction

This chapter proposes a conceptual framework for professional development in urban environmental education, building on the work of Orr (1992), Leou (2005), Strauss (2013), and Russ (2015). Adding "urban" as a descriptor throws a new set of criteria into the mix of professional development, as urban environmental education brings in ethnic minority, immigrant, and other nontraditional participants and broadens our perspectives on environmental education per se. Breaking down what is required to understand urban complexity and its relationship to environmental education reveals new viewpoints and directions for professional development. Listening from the "inside-out" through immersion experiences with community-based service organizations, schools, and even "street life" broadens the notion of what work needs to be done in urban areas. We suggest professional development strategies for environmental educators working with urban audiences and in urban settings, in both schools and nonformal programs.

Urban environmental education includes using urban environments as a learning context that leads to collective action. Collective action refers to working with stakeholders within a community to establish a common agenda, learn about the forces that impact environmental conditions, and find venues to influence change from within the community. Learning about local resources through active participation and immersion in field experiences may help educators, as well as youths, see connections within their communities. Parks, streets, buildings, bridges and piers, community gardens, cemeteries, and industrial areas are all resources for studying cities and the local environment.

Through immersion experiences and related experiential learning, educators gain confidence and develop skills to use the urban environment as a context for teaching and learning. Knowing how and why urban communities work the way they do shapes the preparation of environmental educators. In short, an educator should understand the content and context, be aware of resources and teaching strategies, and gain field experiences.

Professional development opportunities are varied. For example, professional development for environmental educators includes credit and noncredit courses and degrees through universities, online courses, workshops hosted by organizations such as Project Learning Tree, meetings of professional associations, and face-to-face and online networking and sharing resources, including through the use of social media. Universities (e.g., Antioch University New England, Antioch University Seattle, and the University of Wisconsin–Stevens Point), national programs like that funded by the U.S. Environmental Protection Agency, nongovernmental organizations like The Nature Conservancy, smaller nonprofits like Common Ground in New Haven, Connecticut, and environmental education professional associations such as the North American Association for Environmental Education increasingly offer opportunities for urban environmental education professional development. The authors of this chapter represent several professional development programs in cities (Table 21.1), which offer guidance for university faculty, professional associations, and other groups that provide

TABLE 21.1   Overview of professional development programs conducted by chapter authors

PROGRAM	AUDIENCE	GOALS FOR PROFESSIONAL DEVELOPMENT
Fundisa for Change Programme, South Africa	Fundisa for Change partners, teachers, curriculum advisors	School subjects, pedagogical strategies, situated learning, and practical knowledge and experience
Master's degree in Urban Environmental Education at IslandWood and Antioch University Seattle, U.S.	Formal and informal educators, change agents	Urban ecology and complex systems, community engagement and youth leadership, change management
New York University Wallerstein Collaborative for Urban Environmental Education and Environmental Conservation Education master's program, New York City, U.S.	Formal and nonformal educators	Environmental literacy
University of Wisconsin–Stevens Point online course, Stevens Point, U.S.	Formal and nonformal educators from across the globe	Urban environmental literacy and leadership, comfort and sense of empowerment in natural and built urban settings

professional development opportunities. In addition to offering practical suggestions, we propose a conceptual framework that encompasses interdisciplinary and integrated content, context including place and audience, pedagogy, resources, field experiences, and professional learning communities.

Interdisciplinary and Integrated Content

Professional development for urban environmental educators should reflect the interdisciplinary nature and integrated content of urban environmental education. Focusing on sustainability issues and other topics that cross disciplinary boundaries enables educators to integrate curriculum into multiple subject areas. Including educators from different disciplines and sectors can "enliven workshops as teachers share different perspectives on content and pedagogy" (Vogel and Muth, 2005, p. 36), as well as aid in developing critical and systems thinking. For example, a summer program at New York University incorporated science, history, language arts, and mathematics for more than a hundred K-12 teachers from various disciplines, which enabled participants to think creatively in developing lessons that integrated science, social studies, and language arts. Teachers incorporated storytelling in studying the history of the Hudson River and used historical maps to examine changes in coastal habitats over time. Although not specifically focused on urban environmental education, Fundisa for Change (2013) in South Africa seeks to expose educators to environmental and sustainability concepts specified in the school curriculum. During the training sessions, educators engage with environmental subject content knowledge, change-oriented teaching methods, and assessment practices aimed at developing students' competencies in sustainability (Wiek, Withycombe, and Redman, 2011).

Professional development in urban environmental education addresses the urban environment and the organisms that live there. Urban ecosystems are a unique, complex integration of built infrastructure, ecological and social processes, and ecosystem services. The resilience and sustainability of the urban physical environment is closely connected to the physical, social, and mental well-being of residents. Therefore, professional development in urban environmental education should address environmental justice and environmental health. For example, in the master's degree program in Urban Environmental Education at IslandWood in Seattle and in the coursework at the University of Wisconsin–Stevens Point, students read environmental justice case studies and engage in online and face-to-face discussion of social and environmental equity.

Context: Place and Audience

Professional development often uses a place-based framework (Sobel, 2005) that focuses on experiential learning in parks, along rivers, in school and community gardens, and in other urban settings. For example, the University of Wisconsin–Stevens Point encourages educators to use urban environments through conducting a site inventory developed by the state forestry education program. The inventory helps educators see familiar places in new ways, such as site microclimates that include variations in wind, sun, and temperature. Additionally, the IslandWood Urban Environmental Education master's degree in Seattle prepares educators to address urban environmental issues through social, educational, economic, and cultural aspects of urban life. Graduate students are immersed in the inner-city community of the Central District, Seattle, where university coursework is complemented by experiences in schools and in community organizations focused on affordable housing, access to healthy food, health services, public utilities, and civic engagement. Students learn about community environmental education strategies including entrepreneurship, youth and community development, and environmental justice.

In addition to connecting educators with a local urban place, professional development can help educators connect to program participants. For example, students in an online course at the University of Wisconsin–Stevens Point learn about the needs of learners in urban environments and how to relate to these audiences. By including students from diverse backgrounds, the IslandWood Urban Environmental Education master's degree program trains future educators who can serve as leaders and role models for urban youths interested in environmental stewardship.

Pedagogy

Engaging students in citizen science, service learning, and in learning about and addressing environmental issues are common pedagogical practices in cities and are consistent with a focus on collective action. Hands-on experiences can foster educators' ability to guide students in addressing urban environmental issues. For example, participants in the University of Wisconsin–Stevens Point urban environmental education online course interview a community leader about local environmental issues, reflect on what they have learned, and describe how it will affect their current practice. One nonformal educator participating in the course interviewed a program director for environmentally endangered lands. As a result of the interview, the educator realized the influence of local politicians on conservation issues, and she intends to involve the local government in her environmental education programming. Another example comes from Seattle, where graduate students spend ten weeks identifying the economic, environmental, social, and political influences that shape the urban community. They capture this information in a case study of an environmental issue and create a community portrait from a research question generated from that case study. The portraits help students identify how and why urban communities work the way they do, and they identify local drivers, assets, and avenues for change.

New York University's Wallerstein Collaborative for Urban Environmental Education and master's degree program in environmental conservation education trains and provides opportunities for formal and nonformal educators to work together in citizen science and service-learning projects. Formal and nonformal educators collaborate to create pollinator gardens and bird sanctuaries in school courtyards, engage in street tree care, and monitor water quality. Working in partnership with the nongovernmental organization New York City Audubon, the master's degree students team up with classroom teachers to monitor horseshoe crabs and clean up litter in the

Gateway National Recreation Area. Workshops are conducted in collaboration with environmental nonprofit organizations and universities, including Frog Watch, Cornell University's Bird Sleuth, Hudson River Estuary Program, and Jane Goodall's Roots & Shoots.

Resources

Using a variety of nonformal settings gives educators access to organizations, professionals, and other resources not readily available in schools. Such resources widen an educator's network of professionals in the community, including park staff members, local artists, museum educators, and conservation experts (Cruse, Zvonar, and Russell, 2015), who can be drawn on when educators develop their urban environmental education programs. At the University of Wisconsin–Stevens Point, professional development participants research a setting different from their own (such as a nature center, if they are a schoolteacher) to learn about the program and engage in discussion with classmates about how they might utilize this local facility. Similarly, Fundisa for Change uses urban settings to teach environmental concepts; for example, participants visit a dam and water purification plant to see how water in a reservoir is purified before being used by urban residents.

Developing relationships with university-based experts and local organizations enables educators to access a range of human resources such as historians, urban planners, scientists, artists, and conservationists. The New York University Wallerstein Collaborative has developed a network of experts who assist educators with field trip planning, research projects, sustainability initiatives, career awareness, school garden development, citizen science, service learning, and learning related to science, technology, engineering, and math. The Wisconsin Center for Environmental Education has outreach staff members, who provide expertise for educators working in forestry and energy education and green schools. Staff members travel to a school multiple times in a year to support teachers, host one-day workshops, and answer phone calls and e-mails from educators. Not only can relationships assist with teaching, they can also lead to partnerships for working on environmental issues. These and other partnerships can lead to collective impact on urban sustainability when stakeholders from different sectors agree to address a specific problem using a common agenda, align their efforts, and use common measures of success.

Teacher planning time is an often overlooked, yet critical resource for teacher professional development (Shavelson, 1976). Professional development programs can build in time to allow for creativity and planning. For example, the University of Wisconsin–Stevens Point online urban environmental education course and Fundisa for Change allow students time to develop a lesson or program plan. Additionally, New York University's professional development programs encourage teachers to take an active role in planning environmental education projects and field trips. New York University staff members also meet with teachers at their school sites to plan activities and lessons and reflect on the goals and objectives of their environmental education activities.

Field Experiences

Through rich field experiences, professional development programs introduce educators to a variety of urban settings that can be utilized for teaching and learning. For example, students in the IslandWood Urban Environmental Education master's degree program spend three days per week in a community-based practicum, a reflective seminar, and a leadership forum. The practicum consists of hands-on mentored experiences in schools and community, designed to bring the theoretical elements of the academic coursework to life (Figure 21.1). Example practicums include a food justice program initiated by Seattle Parks and Recreation, storm water runoff education at King County Wastewater Treatment Center, and climate justice education through the nonprofit organization Puget Sound Sage. Mentored field experiences are also part of professional development at New York University; instructors serve as ongoing, long-term

FIGURE 21.1. Graduate students explore the social and ecological dynamics of urban communities by observing and analyzing trends in development, gentrification, diversity, and equity in Seattle, Washington, United States. Credit: Cynthia Thomashow.

FIGURE 21.2. Participants in a professional development program gain field experiences in New York City. Credit: Tania Goicoechea and Mary Leou.

coaches to provide the support educators need to implement new ideas into their environmental curriculum (Figure 21.2).

As another example, Fundisa for Change uses the spiral model, which views professional development as "a process that enables teachers to gain better understanding of their professional practice and reflect on it in light of policy over extended periods of time" (Squazzin and du Toit, 2002, p. 22). The spiral model enables educators to contextualize the teaching of environmental content knowledge in the settings where they teach, as environmental issues may have different relevance in different contexts. Field experiences include studies of ecosystems, water catchment, and water purification. Educators also reflect on current practice and implement new ideas in their classrooms, and then reflect on their implementation and get feedback from colleagues and facilitators.

Professional Learning Communities

Professional learning communities provide the support that enables educators to implement urban environmental education under challenging conditions. Allowing educators to determine their own professional development and support needs and resources to address these needs, as well as to learn from each other, empowers educators and enables them to personalize professional development. Professional learning communities also allow educators much-needed planning time and opportunities to co-create resources with other educators.

Learning communities can bring together educators representing diverse sectors including universities, K-12 schools, museums, nature centers, and community-based organizations. Through an online project-based learning community offered by Cornell University, forty educators representing diverse settings co-wrote an e-book titled "Urban Environmental Education," which became a resource for other educators (Russ, 2015). The "Urban Environmental Education Collective" Facebook group is another online professional learning community where educators share resources and seek input on their educational practices.

By working collaboratively, formal and nonformal institutions can establish long-term professional learning communities. In New York City, the Urban Advantage Program is a partnership between city government agencies and nonformal institutions such as the American Museum of Natural History and New York Botanic Garden, which provides long-term professional development for middle school teachers seeking to foster science, technology, engineering, and mathematics learning in nonformal settings. In South Africa, Fundisa for Change allows space during professional development sessions for curriculum advisors and teachers from different subjects to share and exchange expertise and experiences. Participants have reported that they share resources with colleagues after the experience, as well as run training for other teachers in their schools. Finally, in the IslandWood Urban Environmental Education master's degree program, students who enter the program as a cohort use reflective seminars to create professional learning communities with mentors and community partners.

Conclusion

Professional development in urban environmental education attempts to meet the needs of formal and nonformal educators working in diverse settings. Professional development may be offered by universities, professional associations and networks, or nongovernmental and nonprofit organizations. Creating and implementing professional development programs that address integrated and interdisciplinary content, the urban context, hands-on pedagogy, resources, field experiences, and professional learning communities has been shown to support diverse educators working in varied settings.

References

Cruse, M., Zvonar, A., and Russell, C. (2015). Partnerships between non-formal environmental education programs and school communities. In A. Russ (Ed.), *Urban environmental education*. Ithaca, N.Y., and Washington, D.C.: Cornell University Civic Ecology Lab, NAAEE and EECapacity.

Fundisa for Change Programme. (2013). *Introductory core text.* Grahamstown, South Africa: Environmental Learning Research Centre, Rhodes University.

Leou, M. J. (2005). *Readings in environmental education: An urban model.* Dubuque, Iowa: Kendall/Hunt Publishing Company.

Orr, D. W. (1992). *Ecological literacy: Education and the transition to a postmodern world.* Albany: State University of New York Press.

Russ, A. (Ed.) (2015). *Urban environmental education.* Ithaca, N.Y., and Washington, D.C.: Cornell University Civic Ecology Lab, NAAE and EECapacity.

Shavelson, R. (1976). Teacher's decision making. In N. L. Gage (Ed.), *The psychology of teaching methods: 75th Yearbook of the National Society for the Study of Education* (Part 1). Chicago: University of Chicago Press.

Sobel, D. (2005). *Place-based education: Connecting classrooms and communities.* Great Barrington, Mass.: The Orion Society.

Squazzin, T., and du Toit, D. (2000). *The spiral model: New options for supporting the professional development of implementers of outcomes-based education.* Johannesburg, South Africa: Learning for Sustainability Project.

Strauss, D. (Ed.). (2013). *The LEAF anthology of urban environmental education: Teaching resources for the urban environmental high school teacher.* Arlington, Va.: The Nature Conservancy.

Vogel, A., and Muth, C. (2005). Intellectual energy flow. In *NSTA WebNews Digest.* Accessible at http://www.nsta.org/publications/news/story.aspx?id=51194.

Wiek, A., Withycombe, L., and Redman, C. L. (2011). Key competencies in sustainability: A reference framework for academic program development. *Sustainability Science, 6,* 203–218.

Part V
EDUCATIONAL APPROACHES

22

CITIES AS CLASSROOMS

Mary Leou and Marianna Kalaitsidaki

Highlights

- Cities can be dynamic classrooms for promoting environmental literacy.
- Urban ecosystems can be used for learning about local biodiversity and ecology.
- Cities and their environmental problems create opportunities for developing interdisciplinary curricula.
- Place-based education provides a framework for urban environmental education.

Introduction

With more people living in urban areas, cities are becoming critical places for fostering environmental literacy and sustainability. Urban environmental education can take advantage of the fact that cities are complex ecosystems where social, physical, and biological processes intersect (Berkowitz, Nilon, and Hollweg, 2003). The term "social-ecological system" is often applied to cities to reflect their complex interactions, which include not only their geographic location, but also the people who inhabit them. As complex social-ecological systems, cities present social and environmental challenges that affect the quality of life of residents, but at the same time cities offer opportunities for sustainable living and education.

City as Classroom, one of five trends in urban environmental education (see chapter 30), encompasses nature study, citizen science, inquiry-based learning, and neighborhood inventories. It draws from place-based education, which Sobel (2005) defines as the process of using hands-on experiences in the local community and environment as a starting point to teach concepts across disciplines. Applied to urban environmental education, place-based education is a process whereby teachers use the varied resources of a city to engage students in authentic experiences and learning in the places where they live.

In this chapter, we use examples from Greece and the United States to illustrate how learning in cities can foster environmental literacy, raise awareness about local environmental problems, and engage students in discussions of sustainable choices. We use place-based education as a framework, but we also draw on education for sustainability. In so doing, we discuss ways in which place matters and shapes what we teach and how we teach. In short, this chapter identifies ways in which cities can be used as vibrant outdoor classrooms, with the goal to help teachers and other educators develop curriculum that is inquiry-based and fosters the development of problem-solving skills and an environmental stewardship ethic.

Cities as Places

Cities as social-ecological landscapes provide myriad resources for teaching about the environment. The character of a city is determined by geologic factors and location, as well as by natural, historic, social, economic, and cultural dimensions. Collectively these factors can open up doors that enable educators and students to consider how the past has determined the present and how we might envision the future. People shape places, but places also shape people (Gruenewald, 2003). Ultimately, where we live strongly influences our values and attitudes and how we think about the environment.

By examining cities closely, educators and students can discover how humans have shaped the city to build homes, shopping centers, sewers, parks, roads and highways, which interact with each other to form complex urban social-ecological systems. This complexity challenges us to consider how the needs of urban residents are met, while maintaining natural areas, critical habitats, and open spaces in order to foster urban sustainability. It also challenges us to consider how healthy environments and green spaces contribute to the individual and community well-being of city residents.

Cities as classrooms offer students and teachers opportunities to consider solutions to complex environmental problems that impact their local environment, such as waste, water and air quality, clean energy, health, and access to green space. They also allow program participants to explore community assets, such as large urban parks; smaller community gardens, rain gardens, and pocket parks; and their associated biodiversity and ecosystem services. A focus on cities and their problems and assets has implications for teaching and learning and the creation of curricula that address sustainability. These curricula are not found in textbooks or traditional classroom teaching, but rather in the city itself.

Urban Environmental Problems and Opportunities

Cities are places where major environmental problems affect residents' health and quality of life. Urban stresses such as air pollution, energy consumption, traffic congestion, noise, and waste are regarded as some of the most serious environmental problems in Europe (European Environment Agency, 2011), but these problems are global and not limited to any geographic area. A major challenge in cities is finding a balance between the need for economic development and conservation of natural areas.

Learning about the growth and development of cities challenges us to consider alternative ways of living and sustaining ourselves. How will our actions today help create the context for life in the future? For cities on the coast, physical modifications of the coastline have led to deterioration of habitats and a growing list of threatened species. Historical centers and monuments suffer from neglect and changes in land uses. Resilience—of individuals, communities, and social-ecological systems—is central to the new curricula as cities prepare for the inevitable impacts of sea level rise, increased frequency and magnitude of storms and droughts, and changing access to healthy food, energy, and water (see Krasny, Lundholm, and Plummer, 2010; Smith, DuBois, and Krasny, 2015; DuBois and Krasny, 2016).

Where we find problems we find opportunities for exploration and learning. Cities are places where problems can be identified, investigated, and understood through a variety of student-centered pedagogies like issue investigation (Hungerford et al., 1985), citizen science, monitoring, and mapping. The neighborhood, park, shoreline, and school, community, or municipal garden provide the laboratories for learning, and museums, zoos, aquaria, and community-based organizations can be enlisted to support the use of cities as classrooms. Learning often focuses on the interconnectedness between ourselves and urban ecosystems. The examples below illustrate how cities have been used as classrooms to help students learn about social and ecological concepts and environmental issues.

Studying Urban Biodiversity Loss
and Urban Environmental Problems
in Rethymno, Greece

Rethymno is a coastal city of forty thousand residents on the island of Crete in Greece; it consists of a complex system of green spaces, people, and infrastructure. Green spaces within Rethymno give students in the Department of Education at the University of Crete opportunities to study ecology using real-life examples. Moreover, the conceptualization of cities as social-ecological systems allows students to explore urban environmental problems in the framework of place-based education. The four examples below foster ecological literacy and decision making in public and private contexts.

In one project, students learned about the ecological and potential economic consequences of an invasive species in the city. Invasive species are a serious cause of biodiversity loss, and cities are the principal entry points from which invasive species spread (Müller and Werner, 2010). The red palm weevil (*Rhynchophorus ferrugineus*), an insect from Asia that feeds on palm trees, was accidentally introduced in Greece. Infested trees have an umbrella-like appearance and die if left untreated. Treatment involves the use of pesticides and costs money. Because exotic palm trees are used extensively for landscaping in public and private areas, the insect has been impossible to contain and is threatening the native palm tree. Students identified infested palm trees in Rethymno and recorded their condition using photographs taken on their smartphones. They discussed the economic implications of the red palm weevil for the city and the pros and cons of using exotic versus native plants for landscaping. This activity gave rise to many questions: Which trees are native to Crete? Why are exotic trees popular for landscaping? What are the ecological, social, and political pros and cons of native versus exotic trees for landscaping? Which choice is sustainable? The question arose of why Rethymno should look "exotic" to attract tourists, which students may investigate in a new project focused on sustainable tourism. This case shows how university classes can use the city for interdisciplinary learning that has relevance to students' lives, and in so doing begin to addresses questions related to sustainability. Because the red palm weevil has been declared a pest of global significance (European Commission, 2011), it can be studied in other parts of the world.

Cities can also be used as places to study conservation of threatened species. The loggerhead turtle (*Caretta caretta*), a sea turtle that nests on the sandy beaches of Rethymno during summer, is listed as a threatened species. ARCHELON, a Greek turtle-protection nongovernmental organization, monitors turtle nesting activity and promotes turtle conservation. Students conducting a study of loggerhead turtles learned about a species that depends on coastal and marine ecosystems for its survival. Students identified human activities that obstruct turtle reproduction, and they reflected on their own behavior on the beach and on the future of this species in the context of the tourist industry.

Consistent with place-based education, and regarding the city as a complex social-ecological system, another Rethymno program engages students in following walking itineraries in the city, with a goal to foster interdisciplinary learning and raise awareness of local urban environmental problems. Selected stops at points of ecological and historical interest focus on local history, urban biodiversity, biodiversity loss, natural resources management, waste production and management, transportation, building design, and sustainable alternatives (Figure 22.1a). Students connect what they learn with additional disciplines including art, citizenship, and human rights.

In yet another Greek program that uses the city as a classroom, botanical trails were developed within the university campus (Figure 22.1b) and the city's municipal garden. The emphasis on urban flora is used to address young people's plant blindness, that is, the inability to see or notice plants and to recognize their importance for humans and the biosphere (Wandersee and Schussler, 1998). Similar to the initiatives described above, the goal of the botanical trails is first to acquaint students with the city and its biodiversity, and then engage them with the broader community and foster environmental stewardship.

FIGURE 22.1.   (a) Students on an urban trail in Rethymno. Credit: Zaharenia Kefaloyanni. (b) Students study local flora on the university campus. Credit: Marianna Kalaitsidaki.

Hudson River Summer Program in New York City

In New York City, opportunities to use open spaces and natural resources in ways that enhance science education and teacher development abound. One example is the Hudson River Summer Program for Educators developed by the New York University Wallerstein Collaborative for Urban Environmental Education. This program trained one hundred New York City schoolteachers over a period of four years to use the Hudson River estuary as a context for teaching and learning. Each summer, teachers attended an intensive three-week, field-based program that provided interdisciplinary learning experiences.

The program integrated classroom sessions with field experiences in sites in and around the city. Teachers learned about the history, ecology, and development of the New York Harbor and in so doing forged connections with New York's Hudson River and its estuary. Piers, field stations, coastal areas, museums, water taxis, and schooners became part of the curriculum (Figure 22.2). The river became a textbook, a field lab, and a springboard for learning about history,

FIGURE 22.2.   Harbor Herons Tour, New York Water Taxi, New York City. Credit: George Leou.

geology, ecology, chemistry, and other content areas. Through this place-based process, familiar places took on new meaning and helped teachers develop an identity with place in ways they had not done so before. As one teacher summarized, "I have raised a sail! With my own eyes I've seen an isopod, a diving beetle, jelly fish, and exuvia, a red eft, an eyed-click beetle, and the elegant harbor herons." To her amazement she now had firsthand knowledge of biota within the estuarine ecosystem; she also deepened her understanding of the biota's interdependence with human systems.

These experiences awakened curiosity in the participants and motivated them to create similar experiences for their students. Teachers integrated the river into their curricula by developing field trips, lesson plans, and units of study about the Hudson River that integrated science, social studies, and language arts. One participant proposed that the Hudson River become a theme for all third graders in her school. Teachers came to the realization that providing a context for learning is essential to teaching science, and fostering environmental stewardship is part of the responsibility of teaching. As one teacher noted, "I believe the effectiveness of this program stems from the fact that it sells a concept—not a product. An effective concept that teaches us as humans, reminding us of a fragile environment that sustains us along with the notion that we have to sustain it right back! This reminds me of my responsibility, the one I accepted when I decided to become a teacher. . . . I have come to the realization that even though I teach science, I'm really not teaching science unless I do so in its natural setting. The Hudson River is not only home, but it's as natural as it gets, and my new responsibility is to make it accessible to my students."

These outcomes would not have been possible without using the city as a classroom. Today, twelve years after its inception, the Hudson River program has evolved into a citizen science program where teachers and students come to the Hudson River to collect water quality data in collaboration with New York University. Others have engaged in service-learning projects such as coastal cleanups to protect vital horseshoe crab breeding areas in Jamaica Bay, and some have developed related curricula that serve the needs of their urban students.

Conclusion

Cities are rich yet underused educational spaces that have a vital role to play in environmental education. They provide both content and context with which to engage students in a variety of learning activities in their own communities (Leou, 2005). These include scientific investigations, interdisciplinary projects, citizen science, and service learning, which can be used across grade levels and subjects. Additionally, cities provide access to history, ecology, and culture. Abandoned industrial sites, historic buildings, subway stations, cemeteries, and even shopping centers can become classrooms for study and investigation. Educators can develop "urban trails" to immerse students in developing an understanding of these sites and of the complexity of cities as social-ecological systems.

References

Berkowitz, A. R., Nilon, C. H., and Hollweg, K. S. (Eds.). (2003). *Understanding urban ecosystems: A new frontier for science and education.* New York: Springer.

DuBois, B., and Krasny, M. E. (2016). Educating with resilience in mind: Addressing climate change in post-Sandy New York City. *Journal of Environmental Education, 4*(47): 222–270.

European Commission. (2011). *The insect killing our palm trees: EU efforts to stop the red palm weevil.* Belgium: Directorate General for Health and Consumers.

European Environment Agency. (2011). *Europe's environment: An assessment of assessments.* Copenhagen, Denmark.

Gruenewald, D. A. (2003). Foundations of place: A multidisciplinary framework for place-conscious education. *American Research Journal, 40*(3), 619–654.

Hungerford, H., Litherland, R., Peyton, R., Ramsey, J., Tomera, A., and Volk, T. (1985). *Investigating and evaluating environmental issues and actions: Skill development modules.* Champaign, Ill.: Stipes Publishing.

Krasny, M. E., Lundholm, C., and Plummer, R. (Eds.). (2010). Resilience in social-ecological systems: The roles of learning and education. Special Issue of *Environmental Education Research, 15*(5–6), 463–674.

Leou, M. J. (2005). *Readings in environmental education: An urban model.* Dubuque, Iowa: Kendall/Hunt Publishing Company.

Müller, N., and Werner, P. (2010). *Urban biodiversity and the case for implementing the convention on biological diversity in towns and cities.* In N. Müller, P. Werner, and J. G. Kelcey (Eds.), *Urban biodiversity and design* (pp. 3–34). Oxford, UK: Blackwell Publishing.

Smith, J. G., DuBois, B., and Krasny, M. E. (2015). Framing for resilience through social learning: Impacts of environmental stewardship on youth in post-disturbance communities. *Sustainability Science, 11*(3), 441–453.

Sobel, D. (2005). *Place-based education: Connecting classrooms and communities.* Great Barrington, Mass.: Orion Society.

Wandersee, J. H., and Schussler, E. E. (1999). Preventing plant blindness. *American Biology Teacher, 61*(2), 82–86.

23

ENVIRONMENTAL ARTS

Hilary Inwood, Joe E. Heimlich,
Kumara S. Ward, and Jennifer D. Adams

Highlights

- Environmental arts catalyze environmental learning and action in cities worldwide.
- Environmental arts cultivate imagination and provoke reflection, helping citizens to think critically and creatively about environmental issues.
- Environmental arts help to bring about cultural shifts toward sustainability.

Introduction

Cities around the world are using the arts to enhance urban aesthetic experiences and motivate innovative environmental activism. Manifesting as flash mobs, immersive street theater, bike parades, pop-up installations, zero-carbon concerts, and participatory storytelling, artists are using their creativity and ingenuity to draw attention to and propose solutions for the environmental challenges of the twenty-first-century city. Often referred to as creative or artistic activism, environmental arts are becoming part of the curriculum in schools, universities, colleges, museums, and community centers, and they are being woven into the fabric of the city in unexpected spaces like parks, city streets, alleyways, and rooftops. This chapter provides an overview of some of the ways that the arts—visual arts, drama, dance, and music—are transforming environmental education in urban centers, and helping bring about cultural shifts toward sustainability.

Imagining a More Sustainable World Through the Arts

As part of the development of the environmental arts movement over the past several decades, artists, musicians, playwrights, dancers, and filmmakers have revealed critical insights about urban places and spaces. McKibben (2009) describes their cultural sway: "Artists, in a sense, are the antibodies of the cultural bloodstream. They sense trouble early, and rally to isolate and expose and defeat it, to bring to bear the human power for love and beauty and meaning against the worst results of carelessness and greed and stupidity."

As one of the founders of the 350.org campaign, McKibben draws on the power of the arts to catalyze action on climate change in cities around the world. Using media as diverse as comics, music videos, documentary photography, spoken word poetry, reverse graffiti, performance, puppetry, and aerial art, 350.org is harnessing the energy of artists in unique ways. In Istanbul, activists created a giant inflatable sculpture of lungs, inspired by the art of Artur von Balen, to highlight the effects of carbon dioxide emissions on human health. Working with artists in Lima, Peru, activists designed "Casa Activa," an arts and activism center that exemplifies what a sustainable future could look like. These and other projects are demonstrating that cities can be used for artistic activism in multiple ways: as inspiration, as material, and as exhibition site.

By cultivating imagination, engagement, connection, and reflection, artists help us to think critically and creatively about ecological degradation, resource extraction, climate change, and other environmental issues. They explore, analyze, and critique the complex materiality and social contexts of urban centers, often leading to innovative sustainability solutions. They demonstrate that the arts make for powerful and personal learning experiences that transcend age and life stage, inviting citizens to engage with their cities through emotional and creative lenses, and helping to shift attitudinal change into action about and for sustainability.

Greene (1995) referred to this power as "social imagination," that is, the capacity "to invent visions of what should be and what might be in our deficit society, on the streets where we live, [and] in our schools" (p. 5). Eisner (2002) recognized the similarity between the arts and sciences: "this is what the scientists and artists do; they perceive what is, but imagine what might be, and then use their knowledge, their technical skills, and their sensibilities to pursue what they have imagined" (p. 199). For many then, the arts are a form of research in their own right; they "provide a special way of coming to understand something and how it represents what we know about the world" (Sullivan, 2004, p. 61).

For urban dwellers, opportunities abound for becoming involved in arts-based creation, research, and activism. For example, student teachers at the University of Toronto regularly engage with its public eco-art collection; inspired by what they experience, many join the eco-art club looking to contribute to the next installation. For some, this is the start of engagement with the creative process or their own form of artistic activism; for others, it provides insights about how to do an environmental art project with their own students.

Engaging with Environmental Education through Art Making

Visual artists have been creatively addressing environmental issues in cities for decades, inspiring teaching and learning across multiple educational settings. Alan Sonfist recreated the history of nature in urban spaces ("Time Landscape," 1978); Agnes Denes planted a brownfield with wheat to raise questions about food security ("Wheatfield: A Confrontation," 1982); and Joseph Beuys invited citizens to collaboratively combat urban deforestation ("7000 Oaks Project," 1982). These early efforts led to aesthetic experiments that design and implement sustainability solutions. Mel Chin used hyper-accumulator plants to leach heavy metals from soil in an art installation intended to reclaim toxic land ("Revival Field," 1990). Noel Harding's "Elevated Wetlands" (1997) sculpture project showed that indigenous plant species could be grown to cleanse water from a polluted urban river. And JR's large-scale photographs ("Women are Heroes/Kenya," 2009) raised issues of eco-justice in a Kenyan shantytown.

These environmental art pioneers led the way for a new generation of artists, photographers, filmmakers, and architects to combine traditional and digital media to maximize the reach and power of their work. The "Beehive Design Collective" uses techniques drawn from popular education, storytelling, and advertising to collaboratively design large-scale narrative drawings that illustrate and mobilize support for citizens' social and eco-justice struggles. "No. 9," a community-based nonprofit that installs eco-art in urban parks and rivers to encourage citizens to explore their city and environmental issues simultaneously; artist Ian Baxter's ECOARTVAN was one such project that took learning to city streets. Additionally, artists and scientists of the "Cape Farewell" project bring their explorations of the Arctic, manifested in photography, sculptural installations, and light projections, to urban settings to draw attention to the effects of climate change. Finally, Maya Lin's "What Is Missing?" uses permanent sound and media sculptures, traveling exhibits, a Times Square video billboard, and an interactive website that displays videos and stories contributed by people around the globe to create awareness of the current sixth mass extinction and what we can do to reduce carbon emissions and protect habitats. These forms of artistic activism have opened up critical dialogue between curators, critics, and the public focused on instigating environmental learning through art (Spaid, 2002; Weintraub, 2012).

Introducing children to the works of environmental artists can inspire them to learn about the issues the artists raise as well as about the artistic processes itself. It can also spur children to experiment on their own, finding ways to address local environmental issues in their communities. Children at Runnymede Public School in Toronto created a series of imaginative art installations in their schoolyard to address local environmental problems including habitat destruction, air pollution from idling cars, and invasive species in their schoolyard. Their projects ranged from painted fence murals to large-scale stencils on the asphalt playground to a knitted sweater for a favorite oak tree. The art projects created opportunities for cross-curricular learning, raised awareness about environmental issues, and inspired other schools to create their own eco-artworks, all age-appropriate forms of eco-activism (Figure 23.1).

FIGURE 23.1.   (a) Fence paintings by grade six students aimed at bringing about positive environmental change in Toronto. Credit: Hilary Inwood. (b) A bird parade during the "Celebrate Urban Birds" event in Central Park, New York City, educates residents about local avifauna. Credit: Alex Russ.

Drama as a Tool for Environmental Learning

Theater has long been used as political commentary, social instruction, cultural normalization, and calls to action. In environmental education, theater is used to communicate educational messages, challenge political positions on environmental issues, and engage people in policy setting at the community level. Theater's role in urban environmental learning grew out of the Environmental Theatre movement, which broke down physical and psychological walls between performers and audience, engaged in full use of indoor and outdoor performance spaces, and forced audiences to consider themselves within the intention and meaning of the play (Schechner, 1971). Creating theater is a pedagogical approach (Reed and Loughran, 1984) that leads learners to challenge their assumptions about environmental issues and explore their local environments. In the town of Samadang, Turkey, theater performances were used with middle school students living near beaches where threatened sea turtles nest; a comparative study showed that students exposed to the theater performance had a significantly higher cognitive recall than did students in traditional classrooms (Okur-Berberoglu et al., 2014).

Theater provides fertile ground for engaging audiences in local environmental issues. The "Theatre of the Oppressed" was used to achieve transformative learning (including environmental) by allowing audiences to see the structure of oppression, and to inspire action by engaging them in finding solutions. Inspired by this work, the nongovernmental organization Ecologistas en Acción (Ecologists in Action) in Madrid uses social theater to address issues of water privatization and engages the audience in discussions with the characters following performances. Similarly in "Forum Theatre," the protagonist is oppressed, does not know how to fight, and fails. The audience is invited to replace the protagonist and act out on stage all possible solutions, ideas, and strategies. These uses of theater for social change led to its use as a tool for multiple environmental purposes: entertainment conveying messages to low literate communities around environmental justice issues; performances engaging residents in environmental design and policy making; and theater companies researching local issues, incorporating community members' words into presentations, and conducting talkbacks after the performance. Theater is also used for consciousness raising and as a tool for confrontation by environmental protesters and activists.

The use of theater as entertainment that conveys a message remains its most common use in schools and communities. In nonformal educational settings, environmental, heritage, and museum theater often uses educational entertainment around environmental issues, such as a sustainability theater performance in a science center or the conservation messages contained in a bird show at a zoo. In these settings, hundreds of thousands of individuals each year are exposed to environmental messages.

Embodying Urban Process and Experience through Dance

Dance has long been an expression of people's connections to their natural and built environments. It is an outward expression of humans' embodied knowledge, allowing us to both learn about and act on our relationship with the environment. In urban settings, Harvie noted that dance not only "*demonstrate[s]* urban processes" but is also a "*part of* urban processes, producing urban experiences and thereby producing the city itself" (as cited in Rogers, 2012, p. 68).

As with visual arts and theater, environmental dance refers to choreography that is informed by environmental issues. Stewart (2010) described environmental dance as an eco-phenomenological method that is "concerned with the human body's relationship to landscape and the environment, including the other-than-human world of animals and plants" (p. 32). Artists usually work in nontraditional dance spaces and use the natural and built environment to inform movement. As part of iMAP, choreographer Jennifer Monson used an interdisciplinary approach, drawing on history, geography, and hydrology, to study water resources and the urban environment, resulting in a site-based performance that highlighted the relationship between human intervention and natural processes in a neglected urban park in Brooklyn, New York City. In another effort, the Ananya Dance Theatre, a group of women artists of color in Minneapolis, created works that address environmental justice issues in marginalized communities around the world, highlighting grassroots advocacy work being done by women to address these issues. In Austin, Texas, choreographer Allison Orr engaged municipal garbage collectors in choreography that juxtaposed their own collection movements with those of their massive garbage trucks. A crowd gathered to watch the final production on an abandoned airport runway. The entire process, from the creation to the public performance, was captured in the documentary "Trash Dance." This project moved the largely unseen collectors to an aesthetic center, which allowed the audience to appreciate their vital roles in the environmental health and sanitation of the city.

The environmental dance movement is slowly filtering into urban schools. The Council of Ontario Drama and Dance Educators developed a unit plan where teachers and students "explore the environment through dance composition" (CODE, 2009) and address larger questions about using dance to address social issues and advocate for environmental change. In another example, the Interdisciplinary Laboratory for Art, Nature and Dance created BIRD BRAIN to engage urban elementary students in learning about bird migration through cityscapes. Dance connected to the environment is a dialogue between humans and nature that emphasizes the shared agency of humans, nonhumans, and their physical setting (Kramer, 2012). By integrating dance into environmental education, learners are encouraged to share and create their own kinesthetic and embodied understandings of their environment.

Place, Identity, and Sustainability through Music

Humans have used music as a means for environmental expression for thousands of years, to convey the beauty of the natural and built world, celebrate the features of local communities, or protest against the exploitation of people and places. From Vivaldi's "Four Seasons," where the beauty of seasonal environmental changes come to life, to Paul Kelly's "Sydney from a 747," where the sparkle of Sydney's city lights seen from an airplane are the focus, we have always sung about our places in a manner that imbues them with human connection and cultural significance. Indeed, it is this affective impact of music that makes it so powerful.

The protest song is not new, but highlights the ways in which human beings use music to engage with issues of exploitation and inequality. Songs such as "Simple Song of Freedom" by Bobby Darin and "The Day After Tomorrow" by Tom Waits protest against the futility of war, while eco-activist songs aim to raise awareness as well as call for change. In Australia, the band Midnight Oil sings about injustice for Indigenous people in "Beds Are Burning" and about corporate environmental vandalism in "Blue Sky Mine"; Gurrumul sings about the disappearing land in "Galupa"; and Christine Anu about "My Island Home" and the sense of belonging we have to our place of origin.

Similar trends are appearing in music education in schools. In an exploration of place, four participating preschools in "The Living Curriculum" project (Ward, 2010) researched the flora and fauna of local suburban environments, and reflected their habitats, interspecies relationships, and coexistence with humans through story, verse, and song. These songs became the students' "Sydney Songs," representing the intersection of the human and nonhuman in the places where the children lived. This musical mapping of place is akin to what Somerville (2013) called "a postmodern emergence" (p. 56), where a place becomes known through story, drawing, singing, and mapping. Knowing and caring about places that are meaningful to us are precursors to developing stewardship dispositions.

In 2012, teacher education mentors from Antofagasta, Chile, visited Western Sydney University and engaged in master classes on representing their local natural and built environment using visual arts and music. The songs written for this occasion focused on the *camanchaca*, a weather phenomenon in Antofagasta, and the *vischaca*, a chinchilla-type animal common in the Antofagasta community and surrounding mountains. This project highlighted the multiple uses of environmental or place-based music for understanding community and environmental relationships, for investigating human and other-than-human worlds, and for building interwoven musical bridges between them.

Conclusion

As demonstrated by the examples above, the arts play a crucial role in environmental learning in urban centers. They do this by raising awareness about environmental degradation, by introducing a new means to voice dissension, and by proposing imaginative sustainability solutions. The arts involve the public in creative forms of activism, helping them to bring about positive environmental change in unique and personal ways through visual arts, music, dance, drama, and other art forms. By engaging those in urban centers in memorable arts experiences that connect them to the places and spaces in which they live, artists in all media are demonstrating an inclusive and innovative approach to environmental education. The arts reach learners who may not be reached in other ways, and they ensure that a broad audience can be involved in making the cultural shifts needed to move urban communities toward sustainability.

References

CODE (2009). Dance and environmental education. Retrieved from http://code.on.ca/resource/dance-and-environmental-education.

Eisner, E. (2002). *The arts and the creation of mind*. New Haven, Conn.: Yale University Press.

Greene, M. (1995). *Releasing the imagination: Essay on education, the arts, and social change*. San Francisco: Jossey-Bass.

Kramer, P. (2012). Bodies, rivers, rocks and trees: Meeting agentic materiality in contemporary outdoor dance practices. *Performance Research, 17*(4), 83–91.

McKibben, B. (2009). Four years after my pleading essay, climate art is hot. Retrieved from: http://grist.org/article/2009-08-05-essay-climate-art-update-bill-mckibben.

Okur-Berberoglu, E., Yalcin-Ozdilek, S., Sonmez, B., and Olgun, O. S. (2014). Theatre and sea turtles: An intervention in biodiversity education. *International Journal of Biology Education, 3*(1).

Reed, H. B., and Loughran, E. L. (1984). *Beyond schools: Education for economic, social and personal development.* Amherst: University of Massachusetts Press.

Rogers, A. (2012). Geographies of the performing arts: Landscapes, places and cities. *Geography Compass, 6*(2), 60–75.

Schechner, R. (1971). On environmental design. *Educational Theatre Journal, 23*(4), 379–397.

Somerville, M. (2013). *Water in a dry land: Place learning through art and story.* New York: Taylor and Francis.

Spaid, S. (2002). *Ecovention: Current art to transform ecologies.* Cincinnati, Ohio: Contemporary Arts Center.

Stewart, N. (2010). Dancing the face of place: Environmental dance and ecophenomenology. *Performance Research, 15*(4), 32–39.

Sullivan, G. (2004). *Art practice as research: Inquiry in the visual arts.* Thousand Oaks, Calif.: Sage Publications.

Ward, K. (2010.) The living curriculum: A natural wonder: Enhancing the ways in which early childhood educators scaffold young children's learning about the environment by using self-generated creative arts experiences as a core component of the early childhood program. PhD thesis. University of Western Sydney, Milperra, Australia.

Weintraub, L. (2012). *To Life! Ecoart in pursuit of a sustainable planet.* Berkeley: University of California Press.

24

ADVENTURE EDUCATION

Denise Mitten, Lewis Ting On Cheung,
Wanglin Yan, and Robert Withrow-Clark

Highlights

- Urban adventure education acts as a catalyst for urban environmental learning.
- Urban adventure education contributes to urban sustainability through helping participants experience positive relationships with self, other people, places, and the natural world in cities.
- Urban natural spaces have underused potential for urban adventure education.
- Similar to environmental education, adventure education uses experiential methods to convey messages.
- By working together, urban adventure and environmental education can strengthen outcomes for both.

Introduction

In the purest sense, outdoor education has been practiced since humans first evolved and elders taught children how to gather food, secure shelter, and avoid dangers. We walked miles a day searching for food, constructed shelters, and formed social groups with other humans. Embedded in outdoor activities and entangled with the natural world, we continuously learned. Present-day humans, especially in developed countries and cities, are more sedentary across their lifespan. This lack of activity accounts for an estimated 6 to 10 percent of all deaths from major noncontagious diseases and 9 percent of premature deaths worldwide. This is as many deaths as those attributed to smoking, uniformly regarded as a major noncontagious disease risk factor. Bringing outdoor activities into urban environments through adventure education helps people improve their health by encouraging them to be physically active while spending time in nature. Time in nature leads to health benefits through contact with the natural elements, participation in physical activity including recreation and stewardship, and social interactions (Ewert, Mitten, and Overholt, 2014).

This chapter explores the benefits of adventure education and of pairing adventure and environmental education in urban environments. Through participation in outdoor activities, people learn about their surroundings and places they might not otherwise visit. These group experiences increase social ties and may increase pro-environmental behaviors, which contribute to ecosystem health and human well-being, as well as urban sustainability.

What Is Adventure Education?

Prior to the 1970s the term outdoor education included teaching about technical skills, such as camp craft, canoeing, and rock climbing, as well as teaching environmental knowledge. About that time people started differentiating between outdoor, adventure, and environmental education, creating the different fields we have today. The label adventure education came into wide usage in the 1980s and was shaped by indigenous people guiding explorations of western explorers, the North American camping movement, and the Outward Bound movement initiated by Kurt Hahn. Initially, the goal of Outward Bound was to strengthen the will of young men so they could prevail against adversity during World War II, where the United Kingdom was encountering staggering losses at sea. This goal was achieved, in part, by proving mastery over the environment, and mainstream adventure education began using nature as a backdrop for activities that enabled clients to conquer behavioral and physical challenges. In these early programs, the natural environment was not necessarily respected or protected.

But adventure education practitioners, drawing from the camping movement in the United States, specifically as it was developed for female participants, incorporated a deep and respectful connection to nature in their programs (Mitten and Woodruff, 2010). Miranda and Yerkes (1996) reported that girls' camps focused on relationships and community values and emphasized the aesthetic and spiritual kinship of humans to nature and to one another. The pedagogy called for campers to develop tools that would enable them to thrive in light of changes caused by urbanization. In this way, girls' camps became social incubators for the politically active citizen.

Today many adventure education practitioners understand that program goals need to include learning about and caring for the environment. Mitten and Clements (2007) claim that adventure education is about relationships, including creating a positive relationship with the natural world. Using experiential activities, participants learn life skills such as cooperation and self-efficacy, which help them become successful contributors to their community.

Adventure education today is a multidimensional and transdisciplinary field based on the philosophy of experiential education as well as underlying theories of experiential learning, human development, organizational behavior, social justice, and ecological consciousness. It is a process-oriented approach to learning that encourages and educates about systems thinking. The uniqueness of adventure education is that the participants' exploration or adventure includes some combination of novelty in activity or setting, immersion in place, and a sense of co-creating the experience. These endeavors usually involve problem solving, group work, decision making, resolving or managing conflicts, and reaching for new goals and opportunities, along with continuous refection. When adventure education includes activities that tie students' novel experiences to their everyday life, it can have profound impacts on values, attitudes, and behaviors and therefore on the choices, responses, and successes of participants in their relationships, practices, and general living. Adventure therapy, wilderness therapy, and related fields use adventure education for specific clinical outcomes. Similarly, urban environmental education can use adventure education to enhance environmental learning and sustainability outcomes.

Benefits of Adventure Education

Adventure education benefits are primarily measured through self-report surveys and interviews, which include self-growth, spiritual, and body image measures and qualitative data. Research has suggested that adventure education offers a variety of outcomes for participants including leadership development, empowerment, increased self-efficacy, improved confidence, development of a positive self-concept, increased psychological resilience, and exposure to and learning about environmental issues (Palmberg and Kuru, 2000; Sibthorp, Paisley, and Gookin, 2007). Participants experience greater appreciation of their physical body through physical activity and time in nature, feelings of well-being and spiritual renewal, and positive relationships (West-Smith, 1997). Ewert and colleagues (2014) reported that the benefits attributed to adventure education are likely due to a combination of immersion in the natural environment, engaging in novel activities with other people, an openness to learning and change, and reflecting about the experiences with a facilitator or individually. In short, researchers use recreational, cultural, ecological, psychological, and educational lenses when studying urban adventure education.

Adventure education and environmental education work together to create an atmosphere that encourages a sense of place and pro-environmental behaviors (Lee, 2011). Participating in outdoor activities allows people to feel and experience a place through physical activity and ultimately to feel connected to a place, making adventure education an excellent tool for urban, place-based environmental education. Martin (2004) claimed that outdoor adventure helped students gain a sense of connectedness to and caring for nature, which was a prominent factor in cultivating "conservationist" attitudes. This positive place and nature attachment may lead to a desire to learn about local natural areas, leading to environmental literacy and a positive environmental identity. Palmberg and Kuru (2000) suggested that activities in adventure education can stimulate environmental education and nature studies by helping students learn about and experience nature, as well as learn about action strategies to protect the environment.

Adventure education is often associated with challenging activities and the perception of risk. However, Bardwell (1992) found changes in behaviors and attitudes from programs that did not highlight the risk aspect of adventure. Daniel et al. (2010) reported that the contemplative time of the solo experience in many adventure education programs (where participants spend several hours or days alone) enhanced participants' feelings of self-understanding and self-worth, underscoring the need for both active and quiet adventure activities.

Adventure Education in Urban Areas

Adventure education brings to mind mountaineering, rock climbing, or kayaking in the wilderness, which results in criticisms that it is only accessible to people who have disposable income and often excludes people from diverse ethnic backgrounds. Locating adventure education programs in urban areas makes them accessible to urban residents, including those with lower incomes, who may not have access to wilderness adventure education (Warren et al., 2014).

Adventure programming in urban areas is not new. In 1874, the Philadelphia chapter of the YWCA organized a summer camp to provide social contact and restoration for female factory workers (Mitten and Woodruff, 2010). Today, adventure education activities (e.g., low and high ropes courses with zip lines, skateboard parks) increasingly take place in urban environments. For example, programs using rock climbing are found in urban areas from Wissahickon Park in Philadelphia to Topanga State Park just north of Los Angeles. The Timucuan Ecological and Historical Preserve, part of the U.S. National Park system, is a field trip destination for K-12 students less than ten miles away from Jacksonville, Florida, where students engage in outdoor activities while learning about ecological concepts. In 2015, the preserve received a federal field trip transportation grant for fourth graders, increasing accessibility for students who had never visited this area. Outward Bound offers the Yosemite Backpacking to San Francisco Urban Service Program, which includes a week in the wilderness followed by a week in a bustling urban environment where students learn about economic and social issues facing cities and engage in a service project.

Urban or municipal parks often have open space, hiking trails, and lakes and are well-positioned to integrate adventure and environmental education. The U.S. Fish and Wildlife Service has many preserves located in and near cities including New Haven, Baltimore, New Orleans, and Santa Barbara, and it could combine adventure activities such as hiking, canoeing, cycling, and camping with environmental education. Adventure activities such as canoeing, compass use, fishing, and a public ropes course at Alley Pond Park in New York City pair well with learning about the park's natural features, including its glacial moraine, fresh and saltwater wetlands, tidal flats, and forests.

Urban adventure education programs can help parents and children learn about and feel secure engaging in unstructured outdoor playtime (D'Amore, 2015). A group in Columbia, Maryland, offers Sunday afternoon outings for families at least twice a month, which include hiking, river play, boulder scrambling, and tree climbing. Since launching in March 2014, this program has sponsored eighty urban outings that have engaged more than 250 families, equating to more than 6,500 hours in nature for families, many of them new to adventuring in the outdoors. Below we describe the use of urban adventure education in Hong Kong, the United States, and Japan.

Metropolitan Hong Kong

Many cities around the world contain surprisingly large undeveloped territory. In the compact city of Hong Kong, more than 40 percent of the territory has been designated as protected area and open space in urban parks and podium (elevated) gardens, including in the city center. The Hong Kong government has organized and funded activities that integrate adventure and environmental

FIGURE 24.1. University students joining the guided visitor tour in Mai Po Nature Reserve, Hong Kong. Credit: Lewis Ting On Cheung.

education by allowing residents to explore the natural and cultural aspects of their place (Figure 24.1) (Cheung, 2013). Recent educational reform in Hong Kong encourages schools to offer students learning experiences outside of the classroom, which has promoted adventure education (e.g., ropes course, rock climbing) in primary, secondary, and tertiary schools. Geography, biology, and liberal studies teachers in particular use urban adventure education for students to experience and learn about their community and surrounding natural environments, as well as to build students' leadership, confidence, and interpersonal skills. These educational opportunities aim to help Hong Kong's citizens understand their surrounding environment, increase their sense of place and sense of belonging, and raise their conservation awareness, thus contributing to the city's sustainable development.

Minneapolis, Minnesota, United States

The organization Woodswomen launched the Women and Children Bonding in the Outdoors Program in the 1980s for residents of the Minneapolis and St. Paul metropolitan area. A grant from the Emma B. Howe Foundation enabled

Woodswomen to target socially and economically disadvantaged women and children. The popular adventure education programs filled almost immediately.

Program goals included helping participants gain knowledge about where to engage in outdoor activities in the metropolitan area and to develop the skills to do so. In order to provide ongoing benefits, the women and children needed to be able to replicate their activities outdoors after attending the program. To that end, the gear was simple and serviceable, and the program emphasized activities such as fishing, canoeing, hiking, and camping in city and county parks. For example, women and children learned about fishing at the docks on Lake Calhoun with a child-friendly local expert. The program helped women and children expand their outdoor skills, increase their sense of place, and develop appreciation and care for the natural world. It also gave them a safe place to bond as a family, with other participants, and with the natural environment (Mitten and Woodruff, 2010). They learned about local parks within walking distance or accessible via bus and gained knowledge and skills about using time outdoors for stress management and restoration for themselves and their family.

Japan: Onigokko Game

Onigokko is a traditional Japanese playground game involving two or more people. The directive is: run away from the person nominated as "Oni" (evil), who is trying to tag everyone. As players are tagged, they put their hand on the place on their bodies that was tagged and become another Oni. The game ends when one person remains untagged. Today Yan Lab at Keio University has converted this traditional game into an urban adventure education activity using city streets or country villages as playgrounds (Yan et al., 2011). Team members collect points by visiting checkpoints and touching (e.g., photographing) rival teams. Camera-embedded GPS mobile phones are used as a tool for positioning, tagging, and communicating, and a web server is used for planning games, monitoring the movements of teams, and sharing information among players. Real-time communication by mobile phones enables players to think spatially and move strategically (Figure 24.2). Players perceive the game as thrilling and demonstrate improvements in spatial thinking. Advantages of this game for urban adventure education are that it is playable in the real world using mobile devices, it enables participants to become familiar with areas using checkpoints, and it engages participants in a rich bonding experience facilitated by "touching and tagging" rules.

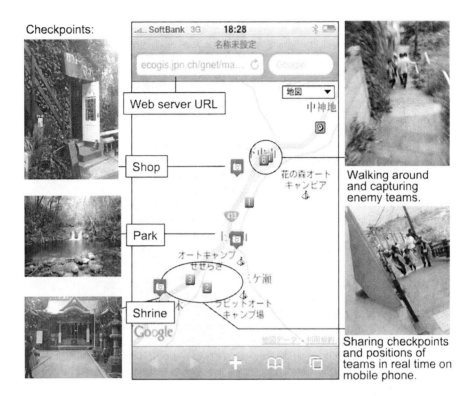

FIGURE 24.2. Onigokko system for urban adventure education. The middle image is from a smartphone, the left side photos are checkpoints, and the right side photos show teams playing. Credit: Wanglin Yan.

Conclusion

Educators can use urban adventure education as a catalyst for urban environmental education. Offering adventure education opportunities in urban environments helps people to experience its benefits, including positive relationships with self, other people, places, and the natural world. Participants can rediscover themselves and create a positive identity in an urban environment. Engaging in urban adventure education at venues such as in the streets, at abandoned industrial sites or parks, or on a river or island offers opportunities for participants to learn about their living environments. Experiencing and gaining knowledge about living places can contribute to sense of place and environmental awareness, which may lead participants to engage in activities to improve environmental and community well-being. Coupling urban adventure education with environmental education, and in particular connecting adventure experiences with actions, can help participants enhance their environment and community and contribute to urban sustainability.

References

Bardwell, L. (1992). A bigger piece of the puzzle: The restorative experience and outdoor education. In K. A. Henderson (Ed.), *Coalition for education in the outdoors: Research symposium proceeding* (pp. 15–20). Bradford Woods, Ind.: Coalition for Education in the Outdoors.

Daniel, B., Bobilya, A. J., Kalisch, K. R., and Lindley, B. (2010). Lessons from the Outward Bound solo: Intended transfer of learning. *Journal of Outdoor Recreation, Education, and Leadership, 2*(1), 37–58.

Cheung, L. T. O. (2013). Improving visitor management approaches for the changing preferences and behaviours of country park visitors in Hong Kong. *Natural Resources Forum, 37*(4), 231–241.

D'Amore, C. (2015). Family nature clubs: Creating the conditions for social and environmental connection and care. PhD dissertation, Prescott College, Prescott, Arizona.

Ewert, A. W., Mitten, D. S., and Overholt, J. R. (2014). *Natural environments and human health.* Oxfordshire, UK: CABI Publishing.

Lee, T. H. (2011). How recreation involvement, place attachment and conservation commitment affect environmentally responsible behavior. *Journal of Sustainable Tourism, 19*(7), 895–915.

Martin, P. (2004). Outdoor adventure in promoting relationships with nature. *Australian Journal of Outdoor Education, 8*(1), 20–28.

Miranda, W., and Yerkes, R. (1996). *The history of camping women in the professionalization of experiential education.* In K. Warren (Ed.), *Women's voices in experiential education* (pp. 24–32). Dubuque, Iowa: Kendall/Hunt Publishing Company.

Mitten, D., and Clement, K. (2007). Responsibilities of adventure education leaders. In D. Prouty, J. Panicucci, and R. Collinson (Eds.), *Adventure education: Theory and applications* (pp. 79–99). Champaign, Ill.: Human Kinetics.

Mitten, D., and Woodruff, S. (2010). Women's adventure history and education programming in the United States favors friluftsliv. *Norwegian Journal of Friluftsliv.* Prepared for: Henrik Ibsen: The Birth of "Friluftsliv": A 150 Year International Dialogue Conference. Available at http://norwegianjournaloffriluftsliv.com/doc/212010.pdf.

Palmberg, I. E., and Kuru, J. (2000). Outdoor activities as a basis for environmental responsibility. *Journal of Environmental Education, 31*(4), 32–36.

Sibthorp, J., Paisley, K., and Gookin, J. (2007). Exploring participant development through adventure-based programming: A model from the National Outdoor Leadership School. *Leisure Sciences, 29*(1), 1–18.

Warren, K., Roberts, N. S., Breunig, M., and Alvarez, M. G. (2014). Social justice in outdoor experiential education: A state of knowledge review. *Journal of Experiential Education, 37*(1), 89–103.

West-Smith, L. (1997). Body image perception of active outdoorswomen: Toward a new definition of physical attractiveness. PhD dissertation, University of Michigan.

Yan, W., Maeda, T., Oba, A., and Ueda, C. (2011). Onigokko: A pervasive tag game for spatial thinking. In Proceedings of the 2nd International Conference on Computing for Geospatial Research & Applications—COM.Geo 2011. New York: ACM Press.

25

URBAN AGRICULTURE

Illène Pevec, Soul Shava, John Nzira,
and Michael Barnett

Highlights

- Urban agriculture includes rooftop and community gardens, greenhouses, hydroponic systems, plant nurseries, small livestock husbandry, and vertical farms, located indoors, on vacant lots, on roofs, on postindustrial landscapes, and on other sites.
- Urban environmental education taking place in urban agriculture sites can integrate intergenerational and multicultural learning and contribute to environmental and science knowledge, positive youth development, job skills, and improved diets, and it can enhance social capital, environmental quality, and economic development.
- Urban agriculture provides opportunities to learn about systems: local crops feed local people; plants create habitat for other life forms; and organic waste nurtures soil and plant growth.

Introduction

Urban agriculture refers to the cultivation of urban spaces to improve food and nutrition security for urban households. Its practices encompass community, allotment, rooftop, vertical, school and home vegetable gardens alongside urban farms, farmers' markets, working forests, indoor hydroponics, plant nurseries, fish farming, and urban poultry and small livestock husbandry. Urban agriculture's contribution to urban food security, food supply systems, and agrobiodiversity is significant against a background of increasing rural-to-urban migration, particularly in developing countries (Mougeot, 2005). Urban agriculture practice and related learning vary depending on economic, sociocultural, and educational needs.

In addition to a focus on food security, urban gardening has emerged in response to urban degraded spaces that pose a threat to health and human security (Shava and Mentoor, 2014). Helping to transform such spaces offers diverse environmental education opportunities to educators and their students (Pevec, 2016). Urban school food gardens can serve as sites for environmental education and enhancing nutrition for children and youth and can provide food and social resources for communities in crisis.

Urban agriculture also provides green landscapes that have aesthetic and cultural value and provide stress relief and health benefits (Pevec, 2016). Light (2003, p. 51) coined the term "ecological citizenship" to describe "the fulfillment of ecological aims in a city concerned with both caring for ecosystems and building better civic communities." Urban agriculture can be a learning ground for nurturing ecological citizenship (Travaline and Hunold, 2010). The international Transition Towns movement educates people of all ages in more than seven hundred communities about urban agriculture, permaculture, beekeeping, and localizing economies, with the goal to create sustainable communities.

Growing food in cities is not a recent occurrence. Urban agriculture has existed as long as people have lived in cities. The Aztecs grew at least half the food consumed by Tenochtitlan's 200,000 residents on *chinampas* (artificial islands in shallow lake beds). Van Gogh's 1887 painting "Vegetable Gardens in Montmartre: La Butte Montmartre" portrays gardens providing fresh vegetables to nineteenth-century Parisian markets and restaurants. Allotment gardens in northern Europe and community gardens in many other countries have long provided a place for gardeners to plant food, train youth, create micro-enterprises, share information and harvests, and develop environmental awareness through observation and engagement. In this chapter, we first describe school gardens in North America and urban agriculture in southern Africa as sites for urban environmental education, after which we provide a brief overview of urban agriculture policies in several countries.

School Gardens as Sites for Urban Environmental Education in North America

Many school gardens in North America arise from the need to provide healthy food to hungry children as an alternative to nutrient-poor foods that result in childhood obesity. Schools also provide fertile environments for coupling urban agriculture with environmental education to foster ecological citizenship among students. The American educator and philosopher John Dewey, who used gardens in his University of Chicago laboratory school to enable children to understand life's interconnectedness, greatly influenced environmental education. A hands-on approach to education permeates the urban agriculture movement and the renaissance in school gardens, where knowledge emerges from practice.

Government education policy in the United States historically has included a focus on school gardens. The U.S. Department of Education and the U.S. Army collaborated to create the United States School Garden Army during World War I to ensure that all children would learn to grow food at school and help feed their families while farmers' crops were shipped to American troops. The resultant agricultural curriculum, the first national curriculum in the United States, enabled youth to become food producers rather than just consumers. It imparted practical gardening skills while promoting self-reliance and citizenship (Hayden-Smith, 2006). World War II inspired a renaissance in home gardening in England and the United States with backyard victory gardens, and families consumed more vegetables than before or after the war. While the United States as a whole no longer mandates school gardens, the state of California passed legislation that provides funding and curriculum support to school gardens, and some universities train teachers to use gardens for environmental education and nutrition.

Many urban youths have little knowledge of where or how their food is grown. School gardens provide opportunities to learn how to grow produce and to gain skills that can lead to a career in agriculture, nutrition, or another science, technology, engineering, or mathematics field. They help urban youth understand that agriculture is significantly broader than farming in remote fields (Tsui, 2007). School and after-school gardening programs also provide living laboratories for urban youth to connect with nature and each other with guidance from teachers and knowledgeable mentors (Figure 25.1). The diverse populations in cities offer rich human resources that school gardening can draw on, including retired farmers, grandparent gardeners, eager youths, and teachers wanting to engage students in experiential learning.

In the United States and Canada, the Master Gardener program of the U.S. Department of Agriculture Cooperative Extension Service trains experienced gardeners in horticulture science, who then become volunteer garden educators. The 4-H Junior Master Gardener Teacher/Leader Guide is a comprehensive agriculture curriculum for elementary schools. Agriculture in the Classroom, another Cooperative Extension Service initiative, works with state universities

FIGURE 25.1.   East Harlem High School rooftop garden. Credit: Illène Pevec.

to provide agricultural resources to K-12 students nationwide. In addition, non-profit organizations such as Evergreen in Canada, the National Gardening Association, the American Community Gardening Association, and the American Horticultural Society in the United States, and city botanical gardens offer gardening education resources to schools. The resources help students demonstrate healthy environmental practices via gardening, provide nutrition education and practical farming skills, and spell out the organizational steps involved in starting and maintaining community and school gardens and farms (Travaline and Hunold, 2010).

After-school programs in U.S. cities also seek to improve children's environments and food access through urban food growing. Oakland, California's "Love Cultivating Schoolyards" program teaches youth to transform barren grounds into gardens; those youths then mentor younger children in growing food. The youths operate a farmers' market stand after school to sell affordable produce to parents. West Oakland Woods Farm uses game theory to teach youths how to create a business by growing food for restaurants. Another Oakland program, Green Pioneers, runs year-round gardening programs in which youths learn about aquaponics (a system comprising fish and plants in which the plants use fish feces as nutrients), permaculture, and organic agriculture. Green Pioneers participants share their knowledge with younger children and adults.

In New York City, the award winning Bronx Green Machine teaches "green technology" skills to inner-city youth. Students of all ages plant food, flowers, and trees, feed the urban hens, and care for the environment while developing life skills such as teamwork and accountability. The youths distribute vegetables to seniors and sell them at farmers' markets in the South Bronx, the poorest congressional district in the United States. The program founder, Stephen Ritz, teaches "science through growing vegetables" and has created a model hydroponic indoor classroom and kitchen, which has made his and his students' diets healthier (Pevec, 2016).

Mike Barnett at Boston College in the United States has developed an award-winning hydroponics program that has been implemented at more than five hundred U.S. schools as well as schools in China, with a long-term goal of interesting K-12 students in studying and working in science (Figure 25.2). Hydroponics allows food to be grown in urban areas with minimal space, and it bypasses barriers to urban agriculture posed by soil contamination.

FIGURE 25.2. Hydroponic food growing. Credit: Mike Barnett.

Whereas school vacation during summer's peak growing season limits student engagement in outdoor gardening in colder climates, hydroponic growing indoors makes year-round environmental studies and food production possible. Students learn about science, social issues in food distribution, and marketing challenges as they grow food from seed and sell the produce at farmers' markets. Not only does the program help reduce the carbon footprint of shipping food, it also provides opportunities for youths to foster social justice by improving equitable food access.

The Boston College program has found that hydroponics is ideal for integration into multiple subject areas because it utilizes principles and concepts from a range of disciplines (Patchen, Zhang, and Barnett, in review). For example, variables that impact plant growth in hydroponics systems include light (LED, high intensity, sunlight), electrical conductivity of the nutrient solution, and the amount and rate of flow of water (physics topics); nutrient solution pH and nutrient composition and concentration (chemistry topics); and the light and nutrient needs of different plants and the impacts changes in these variables have on plant health (biology topics).

Research across four U.S. states has shown that school gardening programs help youths develop environmental commitment, healthier food choices, connections with the larger community, and pride and confidence in their food-growing and decision-making skills (Pevec, 2016). Studies with more than three hundred third grade children engaged in science learning in gardens found that caring, responsibility, and positive attitudes toward the environment increased (Skelly and Bradley, 2007). As youth learn to tend bees, chickens, and other small animals and create green cityscapes through food gardens, they gain knowledge, skills, and environmental awareness (Travaline and Hunold, 2010; Pevec, 2016).

Urban Agriculture in Southern Africa

Urban agriculture in southern Africa emerges largely from the need for food security and livelihood sustenance in poor urban households. Backyard and community gardens provide food and minimize expenses. As people of diverse indigenous and rural backgrounds come together in cities, they maintain their cultures through the food crops they plant in their gardens and traditional dishes they prepare in their homes. Because indigenous people bring their agrobiodiversity and ethnobotanical knowledge to cities, urban gardens preserve crop and cultural diversity and provide opportunities for informal knowledge sharing and learning (Galuzzi, Eyzaguirre, and Negri, 2010; Shava et al., 2010).

In Johannesburg, South Africa, the Soweto Mountain of Hope exemplifies self-organized community members reclaiming and reusing land for gardening aimed at eradicating injustice and the environmental and social problems of degraded land (Shava and Mentoor 2014). School food programs use gardens to provide food for vulnerable children and become sites for environmental education. Ukuvuna Farm, located in the municipality of Midrand in Gauteng (the most urbanized province in South Africa with 96 percent urban population), demonstrates sustainable solutions through urban agriculture using permaculture principles. Permaculture is "the conscious design and maintenance of agriculturally productive ecosystems which have the diversity, stability, and resilience of natural ecosystems" (Mollison, 1990, p. ix). A permaculture approach to agriculture weaves people with the landscape. At Ukuvuna, cultural biodiversity is encouraged through intergenerational knowledge transfer between elders and children. The relationship between food, culture, and biodiversity becomes evident as gardeners identify traditional seed varieties and conserve them by sharing and replanting (Figure 25.3). Seed saving also fosters collaboration among food growers. During school holidays, students visit Ukuvuna and learn using all their senses.

FIGURE 25.3. Bapong Primary School in Brits, the North West province, South Africa. Credit: John Nzira.

Urban Agriculture Policy

Urban agriculture is now a permanent feature of the urban landscape and is being included in urban planning processes. Urban land-use policy can support urban agriculture, which contributes significant food resources to burgeoning urban populations (Bryld, 2003). Cape Town, South Africa, adopted an urban agriculture plan in 2007 to contribute to human well-being and environmental health. Cape Town's Philippi Horticultural Area is a six-thousand-acre urban farm that provides 50 percent of the fresh food consumed in the city (Lim, 2014). Belo Horizonte, Brazil, pioneered a comprehensive policy framework for food security with a goal to eliminate hunger. The city received the 2009 Future Policy Award by the World Future Council for its success in embracing urban community farms, school gardens, and periurban farms. The Belo Horizonte plan provides city contracts to supply low-cost food to farmers' markets and to restaurants serving affordable meals in underserved communities. In addition to land-use policy, human rights, and social justice, environmental education in schools is incorporated into this urban agriculture plan. Seattle, Washington; Portland, Oregon; and Vancouver, British Columbia, also have food and land-use policies, which has resulted in widespread urban agriculture with environmental education embedded in community and school gardens. Additionally, the American Planning Association has adopted urban food planning as a policy priority in the United States. These examples offer a small sampling of recent policies and practices strengthening urban agriculture and environmental education.

Conclusion

Urban agricultural practices play a significant role in supporting urban biodiversity, environmental education, and household food security. Agricultural environmental education activities include learning about the importance of agrobiodiversity and the role of urban gardens in ecosystem health in cities. Multicropped gardens attract pollinators and other wildlife, thus providing ecosystem services. Community and school gardens create safety zones for recreation and social interaction, thus fostering social capital (Pevec, 2016).

Even though urban agriculture offers people the opportunity to collectively engage in improving their local environment and fostering social cohesion, many planners in developed and developing countries have yet to see this as a desirable land use (Harris, 2009). Policy makers are starting to recognize the collaboration, responsibility, health, and generosity of spirit that occur when gardeners from multiple generations work together in cities. A policy shift legalizing and supporting agriculture in urban open spaces would contribute to community sustainability (Bryld, 2003) and resilience, while providing opportunities for urban environmental education.

References

Bryld, E. (2003). Potentials, problems, and policy implications for urban agriculture in developing countries. *Agriculture and Human Values 20*(1), 79–86.

Galluzzi, G., Eyzaguirre, P., and Negri, V. (2010). Home gardens: Neglected hotspots of agro-biodiversity and cultural diversity. *Biodiversity and Conservation, 19*(13), 3635–3654.

Harris, E. (2009). The role of community gardens in creating healthy communities. *Australian Planner, 46*(2), 24–27.

Hayden-Smith, R. (2006). Soldiers of the soil: A historical review of the United States School Garden Army. Monograph, Winter 2016. University of California–Davis.

Light, A. (2003). Urban ecological citizenship. *Journal of Social Philosophy 34*(1), 44–63.

Lim, C. J. (2014). *Food city*. Routledge: New York.

Mollison, B. (1990). *Permaculture: A practical guide for a sustainable future*. Island Press: Washington, D.C.

Mougeot, L. J. A. (Ed). (2005). *Agropolis: The social, political, and environmental dimensions of urban agriculture*. New York: Earthscan.

Patchen, A., Zhang, L., and Barnett, M. (in review). Growing plants and scientists: Fostering positive attitudes toward science among all students in an afterschool hydroponics program. Manuscript submitted for publication.

Pevec, I. (2016). *Growing a life: Teen gardeners harvest food, health and joy*. New York: New Village Press.

Shava, S., and Mentoor, M. (2014). Turning a degraded open space into a community asset – the Soweto Mountain of Hope greening case. In K. G. Tidball and M. E. Krasny (Eds.), *Greening in the red zone: Disaster, resilience and community greening* (pp. 91–94). Dordrecht: Springer.

Shava, S., Krasny, M. E., Tidball, K. G., and Zazu, C. (2010). Agricultural knowledge in urban and resettled communities: Applications to socio-ecological resilience and environmental education. *Environmental Education Research, 16*(5–6), 575–589.

Skelly, S. M., and Bradley, J. C. (2007). The growing phenomenon of school gardens: Measuring their variation and their affect on students' sense of responsibility and attitudes toward science and the environment. *Applied Environmental Education & Communication, 6*(1), 97–104.

Travaline, K., and Hunold, C. (2010). Urban agriculture and ecological citizenship in Philadelphia. *Local Environment: The International Journal of Justice and Sustainability, 15*(6), 581–590.

Tsui, L. (2007). Effective strategies to increase diversity in STEM fields: A review of the research literature. *The Journal of Negro Education, 76*(4), 555–581.

26

ECOLOGICAL RESTORATION

Elizabeth P. McCann and Tania M. Schusler

Highlights

- Ecological restoration involves revitalizing neglected, degraded, damaged, or destroyed habitats.
- Restoration-based education involves learners in ecological restoration with an intentional educational purpose.
- Urban restoration-based education can enhance personal and community well-being while improving ecosystem services in degraded environments.
- Restoration-based education can benefit from consciously forming partnerships, integrating local values alongside socioeconomic and ecological considerations, and being sensitive to issues of power and diverse cultures.

Introduction

Urbanization has destroyed and fragmented native habitat, leading to biodiversity loss. Yet many urban areas remain home to pockets of ecological diversity. And postindustrial, degraded urban sites have tremendous potential for both biological and cultural revitalization. Recognizing this potential, people in cities around the globe are engaging in ecological restoration, which in addition to revitalizing degraded sites, can develop leadership, teamwork, job readiness skills, and interest in conservation careers among participants (Figures 26.1–26.3).

FIGURE 26.1. Members of the Friends of the Forest Preserve's Conservation Corps remove invasive species to restore native prairie and savanna surrounding Powderhorn Lake in Chicago. Credit: Alex Russ.

FIGURE 26.2. Students at Rocking the Boat help restore oyster reefs in New York Harbor, New York City. Credit: Alex Russ.

FIGURE 26.3. Volunteers at the Bang Pu Nature Education Centre learn about the local environment and restore mangrove forest in Bangkok's suburbs. Credit: Alex Russ.

In ecological restoration, humans renew or restore degraded, damaged, or destroyed habitats and ecosystems. This can involve activities like cutting invasive brush to restore ecosystem structure of an oak savanna, planting native seedlings to encourage the regeneration of a forest, or enabling periodic flooding to restore hydrological processes in a wetland. While biologists and ecologists focus on restoration as a strategy to conserve biodiversity, ecological restoration also can enable meaningful human interaction with the natural world in urban areas where most of the world's population resides. By promoting both human-nature and human-human interactions, restoration initiatives are well-suited to enhance the resilience of individuals, communities, and ecosystems.

Krasny et al. (2013) describe that learning through ecological stewardship and restoration projects in Asia, Africa, and North America occurs along a continuum from informal educational opportunities to those intentionally planned and designed. Wherever along this continuum learners engage collectively in activities to restore ecosystems, both learning and transformation of degraded social-ecological systems are possible. This chapter focuses on those ecological restoration efforts intentionally designed to include an educational purpose, otherwise known as "restoration-based education." Like ecological restoration itself, restoration-based education is a process occurring over time that includes social and ecological components. Restoration-based education has the potential to create learning landscapes that enhance biodiversity and ecosystem services while offering learners—including children, adults, and families—opportunities to reverse negative environmental trends through their collective hands-on/minds-on efforts.

Restoration often focuses on revitalizing natural habitats, but Standish, Hobbs, and Miller (2013) suggest that restorationists also consider novel ecosystems and gardening with iconic species, given the altered biophysical realities and constraints within cities. All these options hold the potential to bolster learners' knowledge, attitudes, and motivation to act as stewards in their community. Participating in restoration also offers learners opportunities to explore and connect with the natural world in urban contexts. Exposure to natural elements like water, trees, flowers, grasses, animals, and other diverse life forms fosters human creativity and imagination. This chapter describes some of the contexts where restoration-based education occurs, highlights educational and ecological impacts, and discusses the importance of partnerships, inclusivity, cultural relevance, and social justice in the restoration education process.

Restoration-Based Education: Contexts and Impacts

Restoration-based education occurs in formal and nonformal educational settings. For example, it may take place in a schoolyard, through service learning at a university, within a summer youth program, as part of a green jobs training program, or as residents in a neighborhood or region join volunteer stewardship networks. Learners engage in direct, hands-on activities such as removing invasive species or collecting and planting native seeds, and in research, planning, monitoring, and evaluating outcomes of their restoration efforts. Restoration goals can focus on education and other human outcomes, such as science learning, youth development, or job skills, or education can be embedded within projects whose primary goal is restoring native species and ecological processes. Regardless of the main goal, restoration-based education can simultaneously benefit individuals, communities, and ecosystems as it engages people in collective actions to improve their local place.

Restoration projects in schoolyards invite students to explore the wonders of nature just outside their classrooms. Teachers can use a small plot of ground to teach natural history, science, math, art, geography, and other subjects. Research indicates that through active involvement in schoolyard restoration projects, students become "attuned to the living world in ways that the lawn-and-asphalt landscaping more typical of schoolyards simply will not allow" (Bell, 2001, pp. 152–153). For example, a year-long project involving invasive species removal in degraded urban ecosystems—on school grounds and in public green spaces— increased middle school students' environmental awareness and motivation to serve as stewards (Dresner and Fischer, 2013).

Earth Partnership provides a model for restoration-based education, which emphasizes a ten-step cyclical process that encompasses planning and hands-on restoration efforts in school and community contexts. Examples of planning activities include studying local species and habitats, investigating site history and landscape patterns, and analyzing site design considerations like soils, shade, and aesthetics. Hands-on activities include site preparation, planting, and invasive species removal (Hall and Armstrong, 2011; McCann, 2011). Another important component is community outreach, which has facilitated learning and environmental outcomes in urban contexts like Chicago, Detroit, Cleveland, Sacramento, southeast Florida, and Puerto Rico. Earth Partnership recently launched three initiatives—Latino Earth Partnership, Indigenous Arts and Sciences, and Global Earth Partnership—to expand their educational efforts based on this cyclical restoration education model (Cheryl Bauer-Armstrong, personal communication, 2016). The multiple phases of restoration processes provide diverse opportunities for learning through action. Such action can vary from one-time events to long-term investment in a particular urban restoration project; longer-term learner engagement, however, is likely to have greater educational impact.

Involvement in designing or planning restoration projects can lead to learning for both students and adults. In Seattle, sixth graders who actively engaged in charrettes for the design of a park-based, outdoor learning laboratory increased their understanding, caring, and competence regarding habitat creation and restoration (Rottle and Johnson, 2007). In the Cape Flats Nature initiative in Cape Town, South Africa, local organizations and schools helped identify ways that natural areas and associated restoration efforts provide ecosystem services in oppressed, impoverished contexts (Ernstson et al., 2010). In Ames, Iowa, public participation in designing and implementing a restored urban riparian buffer resulted in collaborative learning about water quality, familiarity with storm water management, and changed perceptions of stream ecosystem functions. These outcomes relied on opportunities for dialogue, ongoing interaction among researchers and participants, flexibility, and hands-on engagement of urban residents (Herringshaw, Thompson, and Stewart, 2010).

In addition to environmental learning, restoration can be a means toward other youth outcomes, such as green jobs training or positive youth development.

For instance, MillionTreesNYC demonstrated potential for engaging low-income eighteen- to twenty-four-year olds in restoration through green-collar employment training. While challenges exist, this case showed promise for catalyzing intellectual engagement, social and emotional benefits, and a sense of accomplishment among participating youths (Falxa-Raymond, Svendsen, and Campbell, 2013). Kudryavtsev, Krasny, and Stedman (2012) documented how action-oriented, direct experiences like restoration projects in youth programs facilitate ecological place meaning and enhance teens' lives in the Bronx in New York City.

Studies indicate that restoration-based education can benefit ecosystem services, biodiversity, and ecosystem health alongside student and teacher learning outcomes (McCann, 2011; Hall and Bauer-Armstrong, 2011). For instance, a 2005 study of four Wisconsin school restorations determined that while the restored school grounds lacked ecological integrity, they had more animal and plant life—and teacher and student engagement—than the previously monotonous landscapes (Anthonisen, 2005). Similarly, New York City schools and their partner organizations' oyster restoration efforts (Figure 26.2) seek to filter pollutants from harbor water.

Inclusive urban ecological restoration reflecting diverse values and perceptions of nature can strengthen connections to local nature, enhance neighbors' sense of community, and lead to other community development projects. For example, in Toronto, local perspectives realigned a restoration beyond its initial rewilding purposes toward other local interests like food production, health, and employment (Newman, 2011). Palamar (2010) argues that environmental justice principles can be employed to improve the design and implementation of restorations, particularly in urban contexts where social and ecological considerations are key. Her case study of New York City's Green Guerillas illustrates the potential for communities to recognize their own needs and cultivate the expertise required for some types of ecological restoration projects.

Restoration-based education can be considered a civic ecology practice, which is a community-based environmental stewardship action that enhances green infrastructure and well-being, particularly in urban contexts (Krasny and Tidball, 2015). Community-based restoration projects fall within this framework, including watershed restoration and similar initiatives such as community forestry and community gardens. Attributes of cultural diversity, ecosystem services, diverse knowledge and experience, adaptive learning, social learning, self-organization, and social capital all contribute to resilient social-ecological systems. In urban contexts, Krasny and Tidball (2015) contend that civic ecology practices may cultivate resilience by enhancing biological diversity and ecosystem services, integrating various forms of knowledge and emphasizing participatory approaches to natural resource management.

Restoration for All: Partnerships, Inclusion, and Justice

The remainder of this chapter focuses on key considerations for successful restoration education efforts. First, effective restoration-based education involves partnerships among multiple organizations, such as schools, universities, natural resource agencies, local governments, nonprofit organizations, grassroots citizens groups, museums, and science centers. Krasny et al. (2013) emphasize the essential role of partnerships in restoration projects ranging from dragonfly habitat in Japan and indigenous species restoration in Cape Flats, South Africa, to the large-scale Cheonggye-cheon River restoration in Seoul, South Korea, each of which resulted in varying educational, ecological, communal, and cultural benefits. The multidecade Bronx River restoration project in New York City is a partnership of schools, community groups, nonprofit organizations, government agencies, and businesses located within the Bronx River watershed (Krasny and Tidball, 2015).

Like other ecosystems, urban ecosystems are cultural constructs, reflecting the values, beliefs, and behaviors that shape them. In the process of forming partnerships, educators and ecologists run the risk of prioritizing scientific knowledge and goals over local knowledge and community-based values. Even the term "restoration" can be interpreted metaphorically and holds underlying assumptions of rationality and human capacity to improve upon a natural resource. Describing extensive restoration efforts in Chicago, Illinois, and San Francisco, California, Gobster (2012) outlines social, ecological, and managerial considerations when undertaking restorations in urban contexts to meet diverse goals. His case study of park lands along Chicago's lakefront reminds us that nature means different things to different people, which must be accounted for in restoration processes. Gobster's (2012) long-term research about these large metropolitan regions informs his suggestion that urban park restorations consider a wider array of values and uses for youths and adults. Attention paid to inclusivity and authentic participation, particularly in dense urban contexts, can avoid favoring one type of nature over another and inadvertently privileging some groups while excluding others.

Along with balancing social and ecological considerations, urban restoration-based education should be culturally responsive. Culturally competent educators acknowledge the interconnectedness of place and culture, demonstrate an acute sensitivity to learners' personal experiences in their total environment, and realize that such experiences often entail oppression across race, class, gender, and other cultural dimensions (Newman 2011; Gruenewald, 2008, cited in McCann, 2011; see also chapter 6). To be inclusive, scientists, planners, educators, and community members make space in the process of designing and implementing a restoration project for cultural perspectives that reflect ways of knowing beyond the dominant Western, positivistic tradition of individualism, linear progression, and rationality. Doing so embraces a wider array of voices, ideas, and possibilities. Authentic, culturally inclusive engagement of youths and adults, attention to human development and learning, interdisciplinary curricular integration, and evaluation are key considerations for effective restoration-based education (McCann, 2011).

Respecting local cultural values and knowledge helps to counter the risk that restoration, and education embedded within it, alienates disadvantaged people and neglects social justice. Inherent tensions exist within the desire to enhance ecosystem services provided through urban green space restorations. As cities realize the potential for remnant urban lands and other underutilized spaces to boost ecosystem services and improve city dwellers' health and well-being, urban greening may also increase housing and property costs, resulting in gentrification, displacement of low-income residents, and continued disparities in access to green space. Communities of color and low-income neighborhoods rife with public health challenges oftentimes have limited access to safe, well-managed parks and other open space. Tomblin (2009) outlines intersections between the ecological restoration movement and the environmental justice movement and points out commonalities across them. Indigenous Peoples' Restoration and Environmental Justice Restoration illustrate how justice and restoration efforts can intersect to consider the ecological, cultural, and justice elements of restoring degraded ecosystems.

In short, consciously forming partnerships; integrating local values, traditions, and socioeconomic alongside ecological considerations; and being sensitive to diverse cultures and issues of power are critical to restoration-based education. Doing otherwise can lead to misinterpretations, failure, and even environmental injustices. By applying these principles, restoration-based education can become an important tool in urban environmental education.

Conclusion

Restoration-based education, that is, ecological restoration efforts intentionally designed to include an educational purpose, offers a way to restore urban habitats and ecosystem services while increasing learners' ecological understanding and enhancing individual, community, and ecosystem resilience. Involvement through various phases of a restoration project—whether in a vacant lot, schoolyard, or larger ecosystem—can allow youths and adults to feel a sense of ownership, competence, and connection to their place and community. Learners across the lifespan begin to understand ecological concepts and investigate the natural and cultural history of a place that is (or may become through restoration action) important and relevant to them. This engagement, in turn, can result in participants viewing themselves as part of a larger system, rather than removed from the natural world or thinking that they live in a world without solutions.

When done well, urban restoration-based education can bridge the gap between the natural and built environment through hands-on community engagement. In this era of globalization and transformation of cities and their landscapes, inspirational restoration initiatives have been launched across the globe. Environmental educators have the opportunity to further facilitate change through inclusive, just restoration education practices, which in turn positively impact urban sustainability.

References

Anthonisen, E. C. (2005). Use and status of ecological restoration in schoolyards in Dane County, Wisconsin. Master's thesis. University of Wisconsin–Madison.

Bell, A. C. (2001). Engaging spaces: On school-based habitat restoration. *Canadian Journal of Environmental Education, 6*(1), 139–154.

Dresner, M., and Fischer, K. A. (2013). Environmental stewardship outcomes from year-long invasive species restoration project in middle school. *Invasive Plant Science & Management, 6*(3), 444–448.

Ernstson, H., van der Leeuw, S. E., Redman, C. L., et al. (2010). Urban transitions: On urban resilience and human-dominated ecosystems. *Ambio, 39*(8), 531–545.

Falxa-Raymond, N., Svendsen, E., and Campbell, L. K. (2013). From job training to green jobs: A case study of a young adult employment program centered on environmental restoration in New York City, USA. *Urban Forestry & Urban Greening 12*(3), 287–295.

Gobster, P. H. (2012). Alternative approaches to urban natural areas restoration: Integrating social and ecological goals. In J. Stanturf, D. Lamb, and P. Madsen (Eds.), *Forest landscape restoration: Integrating natural and social sciences* (pp. 155–176). New York: Springer.

Hall, R., and Bauer-Armstrong, C. (2011). Educating teachers and increasing environmental literacy. In D. Egan, E. Hjerpe, and J. Abrams (Eds.), *Human dimensions of ecological restoration: Integrating science, nature and culture* (pp. 363–373). Washington, D.C.: Island Press.

Herringshaw, C., Thompson, J., and Stewart, T. (2010). Learning about restoration of urban ecosystems: A case study integrating public participation, stormwater management, and ecological restoration. *Urban Ecosystems 13*(4), 535–562.

Krasny, M. E., Lundholm, C., Shava, S., Lee, E., and Kobori, H. (2013). Urban landscapes as learning arenas for sustainable management of biodiversity and ecosystem services. In T. Elmqvist, M. Fragkias, J. Goodness, B. Güneralp, B., et al. (Eds.), *Urbanization, biodiversity and ecosystem services: Challenges and opportunities: A global assessment* (629–664). Dordrecht: Springer.

Krasny, M. E., and Tidball, K. G. (2015). *Civic ecology: Adaptation and transformation from the ground up*. Cambridge, Mass.: MIT Press.

Kudryavtsev, A., Krasny, M. E., and Stedman, R. C. (2012). The impact of environmental education on sense of place among urban youth. *Ecosphere, 3*(4), 29.

McCann, E. (2011). Teach the children well. In D. Egan, E. Hjerpe, and J. Abrams (Eds.), *Human dimensions of ecological restoration: Integrating science, nature and culture* (pp. 315–334). Washington, D.C.: Island Press.

Newman, A. (2011). Inclusive urban ecological restoration in Toronto, Canada. In D. Egan, E. Hjerpe, and J. Abrams (Eds.), *Human dimensions of ecological restoration: Integrating science, nature and culture* (pp. 63–75). Washington, D.C.: Island Press.

Palamar, C. (2010). From the ground up: Why urban ecological restoration needs environmental justice. *Nature and Culture, 5*(3): 277–298.

Rottle, N. D., and Johnson, J. M. (2007). Youth design participation to support ecological literacy: Reflections on charrettes for an outdoor learning laboratory. *Children, Youth and Environments 17*(2): 484–502.

Standish, R. J., Hobbs, R. J., and Miller, J. R. (2013). Improving city life: Options for ecological restoration in urban landscapes and how these might influence interactions between people and nature. *Landscape Ecology, 28*(6), 1213–1221.

Tomblin, D. C. (2009). The ecological restoration movement: Diverse cultures of practice and place. *Organization Environment, 22*(2), 185–207.

27

GREEN INFRASTRUCTURE

Laura B. Cole, Timon McPhearson,
Cecilia P. Herzog, and Alex Russ

Highlights

- Green infrastructure, such as urban parks, community gardens, green buildings, and green roofs, represents a network of human-managed and natural ecosystems that together enhance ecosystem health and climate change resilience, contribute to biodiversity, and benefit human populations through the maintenance and enhancement of ecosystem services.
- Environmental education *in*, *about*, and *for* green infrastructure provides significant opportunities for improving human-nature connections in the city.
- Environmental education *in* green infrastructure entails formal and informal place-based learning in built and natural green infrastructure settings.
- Environmental education *about* green infrastructure offers a framework for teaching about the benefits of urban green infrastructure, such as ecosystem services.
- Environmental education *for* green infrastructure provides opportunities for promoting urban environmental stewardship by engaging residents in the planning, maintenance, and use of green infrastructure projects.

Introduction

The term "sustainable city" evokes images of green roofs, energy-efficient buildings, bioswales, bike lanes, urban forests, and other types of green infrastructure. These urban features clearly have value for ecosystem and human health, but they also have great educational potential. Green infrastructure can help urban residents improve their understanding of complex sustainability issues, provide opportunities for residents to interact with urban nature, and potentially encourage citizens to take actions to enhance the environment in cities.

Green infrastructure can be defined as a network of human-managed and natural ecosystems that together enhance ecosystem health and resilience, contribute to biodiversity, and benefit human populations through the maintenance and enhancement of ecosystem services (Gómez-Baggethun et al., 2013; McPhearson et al., 2016; Novotny, Ahern, and Brown, 2010). Green infrastructure projects provide a broad array of human and ecosystem services in areas such as food, energy, security, climate regulation, water management, education, and aesthetics. The field of urban ecology has advanced a conceptual framework that considers the ecology *in*, *of*, and *for* cities (McPhearson et al., 2016). This framing reflects ecological research taking place *in* cities; a systems approach to study the ecology *of* cities that considers the complexity and dynamic interactions of social, ecological, economic, and built components; and how the field can be positioned *for* advancing urban sustainability and resilience (Childers et al., 2015; Grimm et al., 2008; Pickett et al., 2001). These ideas resonate with the work of Lucas (1972), who proposed an education *in*, *about*, and *for* the environment. By synthesizing these ideas, we propose a framework of urban environmental education *in*, *about*, and *for* green infrastructure (Figure 27.1),

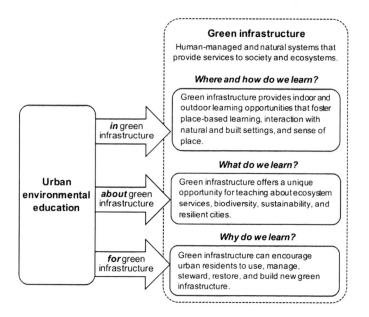

FIGURE 27.1. Urban environmental education *in*, *about*, and *for* green infrastructure.

and we bring these themes to life by sharing several case examples. Put another way, we address three questions related to green infrastructure education: Where and how do we learn? What do we learn? Why do we learn?

Education *in* green infrastructure refers to the rich opportunities for place-based education in cities. Here we discuss opportunities for using green infrastructure in classroom and after-school activities and deepening student contact with and attachment to their local environment. Education *about* green infrastructure refers to the vast learning opportunities provided by infrastructure projects in cities, where ecosystem services are entangled with human development and can teach fundamental lessons about systems thinking, sustainability, and resilience. Finally, education *for* green infrastructure focuses on the need for increased public education regarding the benefits of green infrastructure, which could increase public support, management, and stewardship of present and future green infrastructure projects.

Environmental Education *In* Green Infrastructure

Environmental education *in* green infrastructure is concerned with rooting education in place. If green infrastructure in cities can be used for environmental education, then the lessons learned are necessarily about the local environment where learning occurs. In the words of Geertz, "[N]o one lives in the world in general" (1996, p. 259). Place-based education in green infrastructure can make abstract ecological principles concrete.

Demonstration projects can illuminate the potential for environmental education *in* green infrastructure. For example, the Center for Sustainable Building Research at the University of Minnesota in the United States initiated a demonstration project titled "Art, Story, and Infrastructure: A Model for Experiential Interconnection in Environmental Education." This project takes kindergarten students on a tour of the urban water cycle using water infrastructure from the Minnesota landscape, from treatment facilities to the school building sink, all the while incorporating place-based environmental education and participatory art. Another example is the Urban Ecology Center at Riverside Park in Milwaukee, Wisconsin (Figure 27.2). This center showcases a green building, solar power station, public art, urban wasteland being transformed into a park, riparian habitats, classrooms, and a climbing wall, all of which are intended to improve visitors' environmental experiences and knowledge. Educational efforts such as these are rich in their ability to string together disciplines like civil engineering, landscape architecture, and building design to trace both ecological and human processes, all grounded in the learners' lived environment.

FIGURE 27.2.   The Riverside Park branch of the Urban Ecology Center, Milwaukee, Wisconsin, United States. Credit: Urban Ecology Center.

Despite the potential to use place-conscious education and systems thinking to advance sustainability education, current public educational models face challenges in using these approaches. Such strategies may require additional financial resources and time from school districts and teachers. Moreover, some green infrastructure projects lack access and educational interpretation, making them difficult destinations for classroom field trips. Further, the place-based nature of education in green infrastructure may not align with more abstract, place-neutral methods of educational assessment that emphasize measurement and accountability. Challenges notwithstanding, examples around the world illustrate the potential of environmental education *in* green infrastructure. Cities, schools, and community organizations may need to collaborate and invest additional resources to unleash this potential.

Environmental Education *About* Green Infrastructure

Urban environmental education provides opportunities to teach *about* the benefits of green infrastructure and therefore improve urban residents' understanding of the impact that green infrastructure has on their own health and well-being. This approach includes lessons about planning and designing multi-functional and inclusive urban green infrastructure. Teaching *about* green infrastructure can borrow ideas from urban ecology to increase public understanding of high-performing social, ecological, and biophilic landscapes (Beatley, 2011; Novotny, Ahern, and Brown, 2010). In particular, the concept of ecosystem services, a widely used term in urban ecology (Elmqvist et al., 2013), can be used to frame the benefits of green infrastructure and ecosystems for human health and well-being. For example, in San Francisco, the California Academy of Sciences provides tours of its Leadership in Energy and Environmental Design (LEED)–certified green building to teach visitors about using green infrastructure to reduce waste, save energy, reuse materials, provide healthy indoor environments, create rooftop habitats for birds and insects, and other ecosystem services (Figure 27.3).

In general, ecosystem services refer to those ecosystem functions of green infrastructure that are used, enjoyed, or consumed by humans. Ecosystem services can be categorized into four types: provisioning services (e.g., drinking water, raw materials, and medicinal plants); regulating services (e.g., pollination, water purification, carbon sequestration, flood control, climate

FIGURE 27.3. At the California Academy of Sciences in San Francisco, California, United States, a docent educates visitors about ecosystem services provided by the green roof, including insulation, storm water control, and fresh air, which help the academy and surrounding parkland thrive. Credit: Alex Russ.

regulation); habitat and supporting services (e.g., nutrient cycling, soil formation, photosynthesis, habitat for species); and cultural services (e.g., recreational, educational, and spiritual experiences) (Gómez-Baggethun et al., 2013; Millennium Ecosystem Assessment, 2005; TEEB, 2011). Urban residents, whether they recognize it or not, rely on ecosystem services produced by green infrastructure both within and outside the city. Urban green infrastructure is especially important in providing services with direct impact on human health and security such as air purification, noise reduction, urban cooling, and storm water runoff mitigation, but it also provides places for social cohesion and connection, recreation, and development of sense of place. Further, green infrastructure is being increasingly used as a nature-based solution for climate change adaptation and mitigation in cities (McPhearson et al., 2016). For example, cities are investing in green infrastructure as a specific management tool for combining engineered and ecological systems (e.g., bioswales) in place of engineered systems lacking ecological or green features (e.g., concrete sewer drains) to provide ecosystem services such as cooling, storm water management, urban heat island reduction, carbon storage, flood protection, and recreation (Novotny, Ahern, and Brown, 2010).

Environmental education *about* green infrastructure reflects the ways cities provide opportunities for complex and interdisciplinary sustainability lessons. Green infrastructure offers lessons in science, mathematics, art, design, history, social studies, and beyond. From storm water pathways to pocket parks with bird habitat to plazas with permeable surfaces, green infrastructure in cities provides endless venues for lessons about how human settlements interact with ecosystems. In urban environmental education, green infrastructure gives visibility to processes such as water flowing through cities, sunlight converted to heat and electricity, food being grown, species migration using greenway trails, and urban forests that support biodiversity and recreation.

Cities are complex and best studied as an entanglement of systems that are social, cultural, technical, and ecological in nature (e.g., Grimm et al., 2008; McPhearson et al., 2016; Pickett et al., 2001). By focusing on the multiple functions of green infrastructure, urban environmental education teaches about systems thinking. For example, urban community gardens provide food, absorb excess storm water, mitigate microclimate fluctuations, support urban biodiversity, and provide aesthetic benefits. These gardens become places for recreation, reflection, social bonding, and cohesion. Similarly, green roofs and vegetated areas can increase rainwater infiltration and reduce peak flood discharge and associated water pollution while also delivering mental and physical health benefits such as providing spaces for recreation, relaxation, and reducing stress.

These kinds of green infrastructure projects are critical for building community resilience, and they simultaneously offer rich contexts for urban environmental education.

Environmental Education *For* Green Infrastructure

Environmental education can amplify public support *for* green infrastructure. Urban environmental educators can play a critical role in fostering support for current and future green infrastructure projects, helping cities push toward a community-based form of urban land management that has been described as urban ecological or civic ecology stewardship (Krasny and Tidball, 2015; Svendsen and Campbell, 2008). Environmental education can help to promote, create, and maintain green infrastructure in multiple ways.

First, educators can involve adults and children in the planning and maintenance of green infrastructure. Such projects may require deep and sustained partnerships between local governments, grassroots groups, nonprofit organizations, businesses, and schools. For example, in the Bronx, New York City, community-based organizations such as the Bronx River Alliance, Youth Ministries for Peace and Justice, and The POINT Community Development Corporation involved high school students and other urban residents in designing a concept plan for greenways along an urban river and streets. As another example, the 1.2-hectare Grands-Moulins–Abbé-Pierre garden in Paris offers an inspiring case of how residents actively manage green spaces and rediscover nature in the city. These examples show that diverse members of urban communities can play a role in decision making about green infrastructure development.

Second, urban environmental education can involve people in using green infrastructure. With bike lanes, gardens ready for growing vegetables, and green buildings open for tours, cities are providing green infrastructure projects that become dynamic examples of sustainability woven into the daily life of citizens. In this way, green infrastructure acts as a stage for informal environmental education as people spontaneously engage "hands-on" with green infrastructure projects. For example, many community-based education/restoration organizations in the United States offer free canoeing in restored urban waterways for residents to rediscover local recreational opportunities, potentially raising public support for urban open space.

Third, education related to green infrastructure may inspire interest and future action to expand green infrastructure in cities. Berlin offers an example of how

FIGURE 27.4. Natur-Park Südgelände in Berlin resulted from the efforts of civically engaged residents. Credit: Cecilia Herzog.

citizens knowledgeable about the benefits of open and multifunctional spaces supported the revitalization of an urban green space. In the 1980s, local residents formed a nonprofit organization to protect an eighteen-hectare railyard. The railyard had been abandoned for five decades during Berlin's separation of East and West, a circumstance that allowed the landscape to regenerate while untouched by development. Despite the area's proximity to a densely populated neighborhood, civic activists and professional planners influenced policy makers to protect it. Their efforts, along with ecological research, helped transform the area into the Natur-Park Südgelände, opened in 2000 (Kowarik and Langer, 2005) (Figure 27.4). The park offers a model for green infrastructure that fosters a strong sense of place for residents by nurturing cultural values related to art, education, and sport. In this way, it also provides opportunities for education *in* and *of* green infrastructure.

Conclusion

Urban environmental education *in, about,* and *for* green infrastructure offers a unique voice as cities design, build, and promote ecologically and socially conscious infrastructure. In particular, we suggest that environmental education *in* green infrastructure can offer nature-based opportunities for place-based environmental education, help to build sense of place, and use spaces that otherwise may not be perceived as educational (e.g., waste-management facilities, mechanical rooms of green buildings, and bioswales). Advancing environmental education *about* green infrastructure can showcase the social and ecological benefits of urban green infrastructure to residents' everyday lives, thus increasing awareness of the value of urban nature. Finally, we suggest that environmental education can be employed *for* encouraging hands-on stewardship or restoration of green infrastructure and for programs that encourage cities to build new green infrastructure and better manage existing infrastructure.

References

Beatley, T. (2011). *Biophilic cities: Integrating nature into urban design and planning.* Washington, D.C.: Island Press.

Childers, D. L., Cadenasso, M. L., Grove, J. M., Marshall, V., McGrath, B., and Pickett, S. T. (2015). An ecology for cities: A transformational nexus of design and ecology to advance climate change resilience and urban sustainability. *Sustainability, 7*(4), 3774–3791.

Elmqvist, T., Fragkias, M., Goodness, J., Güneralp, B., et al. (Eds.). (2013). *Urbanization, biodiversity and ecosystem services: Challenges and opportunities: A global assessment.* Dordrecht: Springer.

Geertz, C. (1996). Afterword. In S. Feld and K. Basso (Eds.), *Senses of place* (pp. 259–262). Sante Fe, N.M.: School of American Research Press.

Gómez-Baggethun, E., Gren, Å., Barton, D. N., Langemeyer, J., et al. (2013). Urban ecosystem services. In T. Elmqvist, M. Fragkias, J. Goodness, B. Güneralp, et al. (Eds.), *Urbanization, biodiversity and ecosystem services: Challenges and opportunities: A global assessment* (pp. 175–251). Dordrecht: Springer.

Grimm, N. B., Faeth, S. H., Golubiewski, N. E., Redman, C. L., et al. (2008). Global change and the ecology of cities. *Science, 319*(5864), 756–760.

Kowarik, I., and Langer, A. (2005). Natur-Park Südgelände: Linking conservation and recreation in an abandoned railyard in Berlin. In I. Kowarik and S. Körner (Eds.), *Wild urban woodlands* (pp. 287–299). Berlin: Springer-Verlag.

Krasny, M. E., and Tidball, K. G. (2015). *Civic ecology: Adaptation and transformation from the ground up.* Cambridge, Mass.: MIT Press.

Lucas, A. M. (1972). Environment and environmental education: Conceptual issues and curriculum implications. PhD dissertation, Ohio State University.

McPhearson, T., Pickett, S. T. A., Grimm, N., Niemelä, J., et al. (2016). Advancing urban ecology toward a science of cities. *BioScience, 66*(3), 198–212.

Millennium Ecosystem Assessment. (2005). *Ecosystems and human well-being: Synthesis.* Washington, D.C.: Island Press.

Novotny, V., Ahern, J., and Brown, P. (2010). *Water centric sustainable communities: Planning, retrofitting and building the next urban environment.* Hoboken, N.J.: John Wiley & Sons.

Pickett, S. T. A., Cadenasso, M. L., Grove, J. M., Nilon, C. H., Pouyat, R. V., Zipperer, W. C., and Costanza, R. (2001). Urban ecological systems: Linking terrestrial ecological, physical, and socioeconomic components of metropolitan areas. *Annual Review of Ecology and Systematics 32*: 127–157.

Svendsen, E., and Campbell, L. K. (2008). Urban ecological stewardship: Understanding the structure, function and network of community-based urban land management. *Cities and the Environment (CATE), 1*(1), 4.

TEEB (2011). The economics of ecosystem and biodiversity: TEEB manual for cities: ecosystem services in urban management. Ecosystem Services in Urban Management. UNEP, the European Union.

28

URBAN DIGITAL STORYTELLING

Maria Daskolia, Giuliana Dettori,
and Raul P. Lejano

Highlights

- Stories play a fundamental role in facilitating human communication, meaning making, and contextualization of ideas and emotions through concrete examples, as well as by supporting the understanding of cause-effect and temporal relations.
- Stories can mediate the understanding of complex concepts and issues related to our environments and sustainability, the formation of our personal and collective identity with regards to our habitats, the transmission of cultural heritage, and the articulation of shared visions of the world.
- Digital storytelling, the practice of crafting and sharing stories with the use of digital media, adds to the expressive, communicative, collaborative, and learning potential of traditional storytelling.
- In urban environmental education, digital storytelling can help address and define our relationships to city environments and related complex problems by providing opportunities to generate new meanings and perspectives, reflect on our role and identity, and examine the interplay between human-made and natural components in cities.

Introduction

Throughout human existence and history, storytelling has played an essential role (Bruner, 1990). In traditional cultures it was central to transmitting values and practices and was inextricably related to people's lands. Stories of all kinds have helped people survive, fortified their connection to nature, and deepened their understanding of and engagement with the world (Marmon Silko, 1996). Throughout time, contexts, and cultures, people have consistently used stories to express themselves, convey practical information, share personal experiences with others, add to collective memory, and interpret the world. Our personal and cultural identities are tightly bound to the stories that have been passed to us from our ancestors and the ones we are creating and will leave to generations to come.

Stories carry and stir our emotions, wisdom, and imagination, and they enable us to connect to our inner self, to others, and to the world. Crafting stories is an intrinsically social activity, because stories are created to be shared and are usually the products of collaboration among several persons (Dettori, 2012). Either as an individual or a group practice, storytelling provides people with opportunities to capture, represent, share, and preserve their experiences, knowledge, and emotions. In these ways storytelling helps people to express themselves, develop new perspectives, and build their personal and collective identities (Bruner, 1990).

Digital storytelling is the practice of making and telling stories through the use of digital media. It shares with traditional storytelling the creation of a plot, but it facilitates the story's deployment and presentation by the combined use of digital material and tools, such as photographs and videos, sound, music, graphics and animations, hypertexts embedded in blogs, and podcasts. In most cases, digital stories take the form of short movie-like or cartoon-like videos realized by means of low-cost digital cameras and readily available editing software. In this respect, digital storytelling has become part of a greater social movement started in the mid-1990s, adhering to the democratization of the use of media by "ordinary people" without technical or other expertise in producing videos. In fact, the wide range of readily available and easy-to-use digital tools gave rise to new possibilities of making and communicating stories, where computer-based representations replace or constructively encapsulate and extend traditional forms of narration. As a result of the interaction facilities provided by digital media, digital storytelling has enabled people to combine their experiences and memories with their interpretations and visions of the world, and it has given them "voice" to articulate and stand for their views.

This chapter focuses on the untapped potential for using digital storytelling as a tool for teaching and learning about the environment and sustainability in formal and nonformal urban education contexts (Daskolia, Kynigos, and Makri, 2015). We first analyze and discuss the learning opportunities digital storytelling opens up for urban environmental education. We next illustrate these opportunities using three examples of storytelling-based learning activities that were implemented in different contexts, with different means, and for different audiences. We conclude with reflections on these examples and on the ease and versatility of employing digital storytelling in urban environmental education contexts.

Digital Storytelling in Urban Environmental Education

Storytelling as a pedagogical strategy is not new. In almost all traditional cultures, making and telling stories is a core part of the educational process and a "tool" for teaching values and practices (Bruner, 1990). In Western societies and more conventional school settings, recognition of the potential of storytelling for teaching and learning is growing (Dettori and Paiva, 2009). Research has shown that storytelling can support students in expressing and sharing ideas, interpreting disciplinary knowledge, and deepening their understanding of various topics (Bruner, 1990).

In the last two decades, digital storytelling has gained considerable ground in K-12 schools and universities and in nonformal settings, including school clubs, youth organizations, community centers, and nongovernmental organizations. Digital storytelling has extended and enriched traditional storytelling modalities. It also has created new and dynamic learning contexts defined by the storyteller(s), the digital media, and the stories themselves.

In environmental education, stories have been used to spur conversations and reflections about one's relationships with nature (Sauvé, 1996). But the use of traditional or digital storytelling for environmental learning offers many more possibilities, including in urban education settings. For example, a core dimension of storytelling practice is forming a plot, that is, a consistent sequence (as opposed to an otherwise disparate set) of actions and events. This allows learners to instinctively perceive and then understand cause-effect and temporal relationships among concepts and facts. As configurations of actions, agents, relations, places, and events (Dettori, 2012), digital stories about urban sustainability, urban space management, or civic participation become contextualized and real, thus helping learners overcome the inherent complexity and abstraction of social-environmental issues (Daskolia, Kynigos, and Makri, 2015). Moreover, the construction of a story plot entails a concise synthesis of disparate components of the topic at stake and necessitates a clear standpoint on the part of the storyteller. In short, storytelling can serve as a way for learners to explore and make sense of complex urban environmental and sustainability concepts and issues (Daskolia and Kynigos, 2012).

Extending the idea of plot to that of a network, Lejano, Ingram, and Ingram (2013) approach both the city and digital storytelling in an urban context, as including not just actions and events but heterogeneous factors such as places, goals, means, interactions, circumstances, and unexpected results, all interwoven with each other. Thus, by constructing a digital story about a park, a waterfront, a garden, or other urban place, storytellers build connections among themselves, the city, and nature (Lejano et al., forthcoming). Such stories become autobiographical or part of one's self-identity and constitute one route toward overcoming alienation from the city's environments and nature. Moreover, through making and sharing digital stories about urban milieus, learners build "occasions" (formal or otherwise), in which they highlight what they love and do in particular places of their city. Digital storytelling thus becomes a means to bridge the private and public spheres of living in the city (Lejano et al., forthcoming) and to express one's visions of sustainable and resilient societies. With Internet-enabled chat, blogging, and other digital media, digital storytelling in an urban context not only becomes democratized but turns narration-based environmental education into an everyday aspect of urban life.

Authoring a digital story on an urban environmental or sustainability issue shapes the authors' representations of the issue and affects their experience of narrating and acting in the world. By immersing themselves in realistic scenarios and connecting disciplinary contents with personal and collective experience, storytellers engage in understanding current reality and their role in it, while defining and addressing everyday issues related to their living context (Daskolia, Kynigos, and Makri, 2015). Moreover, compared to traditional oral stories, digital stories necessitate a more intense involvement of the author in production but once complete, they become "objects" in themselves, open to interpretation and reflection by others. When carried out as a collaborative process, with several individual stories plotted and constructed in parallel, digital storytelling gives rise to "meta-stories" (Freidus and Hlubinka, 2002), that is, stories carried across different media and community members, combining "voices" and interweaving perspectives into a shared and concerted view.

Digital storytelling about urban environmental and sustainability issues can thus become a significant learning experience for both authors and audiences. This occurs by inviting authors and audiences to integrate stories into their worldview (Smith, 2015), by fostering place-related consciousness (cf. Russ et al., 2015), and by boosting participation and empowerment to foster social-ecological systems resilience, responsible citizenship, and individual well-being (cf. Krasny and Tidball, 2009).

Three Case Studies

Digital storytelling is increasingly employed in a broad range of urban educational contexts and with diverse audiences. In this section we present three examples of employing learner-generated storytelling to address aspects of urban life. All three examples involve people collaboratively producing stories, sometimes bringing individuals together across age and ethnic divides.

"C My City!" Involving Children and Youth as Tourist Guides in Their Home City

By identifying children and young people as stakeholders and decision makers in their city, Ohashi et al. (2012) designed and realized a project called "C my city!" The project was conceived as an after-school activity by a Finnish school and integrated architectural and environmental education. It involved forty students from Helsinki, aged seven to twenty, as volunteer tourist guides who introduced their city through digital storytelling (Figure 28.1). Students participated in

FIGURE 28.1. A digital story on the C my city! web-based map of Helsinki. Reprinted with permission from http://cmycity.net.

neighborhood fieldwork and classroom training in digital media and produced thirty-eight stories, which they embedded in a web-based map. The underlying aim of this digital storytelling project was to build community awareness and the capacity to participate in urban planning among nonexpert urban residents by harnessing their expressive means as well as their familiarity, sense of place, and responsibility toward their local environment.

Fairfield Stories: Digital Storytelling by Refugees and Immigrants in Western Sydney

The Fairfield Stories project (Salazar, 2010) was designed and conducted through a collaboration among the University of Western Sydney, Information and Cultural Exchange (a nonprofit community cultural arts organization), and Fairfield City Council in Western Sydney. Recently arrived African refugees and second-generation Cambodian youth participated in the project and collaboratively produced short digital stories during workshops. The project viewed digital story creation as a means for participants to value personal life experiences and collective memories and to trigger an intercultural dialogue about what "citizenship" means. It also aimed to develop self-determination, civic empowerment, and inclusion in a marginalized urban community and to position participants "as agents of their own change, and as protagonists or active social subjects in contemporary processes of global transformation" (Salazar, 2010, p. 57).

CoCreSt: Collaborative Creativity in Storytelling about Urban Sustainability among Greek University Students

This project was designed and realized within an introductory university foundation course in environmental education at the University of Athens, Greece, to foster sustainability literacy in students through new modes of creative expression (Daskolia, Kynigos, and Makri, 2015). Undergraduate students training to become secondary education teachers collaboratively produced digital stories on the theme of urban sustainability (Figure 28.2). During a three-month period, the students worked in groups to progressively identify, share, and compare their interpretations of local urban sustainability. They then integrated their ideas and suggestions in short, photo, or animated stories, depicting their shared experience of living in Athens and their visions of sustainability in this city.

FIGURE 28.2.   Selected frames from a digital story produced by Greek undergraduate students in CoCreSt. Reprinted with permission from *Constructivist Foundations* (http://constructivist.info/10/3/388).

Conclusion

We have presented just a few of the many possible ways of employing digital storytelling in an urban environmental education context. All three examples highlight how digital storytelling can be a means of expression and a meaning-making resource for learning about urban environmental topics. In the Finnish example, the request to narrate city-related stories to visitors incited students to notice places and aspects of their nearby urban environments that they may have taken for granted. The participants' wide age range necessitated negotiations to integrate their points of view. In the Australian example, differences among refugee and immigrant participants were even more marked, which again gave rise to a meaning-making process through identification and communication of shared experiences and perspectives. In this case digital storytelling was used as a tool for fostering social empowerment and participation of marginalized communities in the city. Finally, in the example from Athens, the emphasis was on understanding the difficult concept of urban sustainability through collaborative identification of local problems and solutions. All three projects involved inquiry about the issue at stake, identification of individual interpretations, comparison of perspectives, and negotiation of shared meanings to create consistent stories that were meaningful to all group members.

The three cases of learning through digital storytelling differ in terms of the topics addressed, the age and cultural identity of the participants, the digital media used, and the overall learning design of the activities. This variety of aims, actors, tools, and contexts illustrates the versatile potential of digital storytelling in urban environmental education. Yet all three examples also illustrate the ease with which digital storytelling can be employed as a pedagogical approach, involving people with no particular technical skills, and without expensive equipment. This feature, together with the learning entailed in making and sharing digital stories, suggests opportunities for urban environmental educators to integrate digital storytelling in multiple urban environmental education contexts.

References

Bruner, J. (1990). *Acts of meaning*. Cambridge, Mass.: Harvard University Press.

Daskolia, M., and Kynigos, C. (2012). Applying a constructionist frame to learning about sustainability. *Creative Education, 3*(6), 818–823.

Daskolia, M., Kynigos, C., and Makri, K. (2015). Learning about urban sustainability with digital stories: Promoting collaborative creativity from a constructionist perspective. *Constructivist Foundations, 10*(3), 388–396.

Dettori, G. (2012). Supporting learners' interaction by means of narrative activities. In J. Jia (Ed.), *Educational stages and interactive learning: From kindergarten to workplace training* (pp. 107–120). Hershey, Pa.: IGI Global.

Dettori, G., and Paiva, A. (2009). Narrative learning in technology-enhanced environments. In S. Ludvigsen, N. Balacheff, T. de Jong, A. Lazonder, and S. Barnes (Eds.), *Technology-enhanced learning: Principles and products* (pp. 55–69). Berlin: Springer.

Freidus, N., and Hlubinka, M. (2002). Digital story-telling for reflective practice in communities of learners. *Newsletter ACM SIGGROUP Bulletin 23*(2), 24–26.

Krasny, M. E., and Tidball, K. G. (2009). Applying a resilience systems framework to urban environmental education. *Environmental Education Research, 15*(4), 465–482.

Lejano, R., Ingram, M., and Ingram, H. (2013). *The power of narrative in environmental networks*. Cambridge, Mass.: MIT Press.

Lejano, R., Lejano, A., Constantino, R., and Almadro, A. (forthcoming). *Narrative, self, and the city*. Amsterdam: Benjamins Press.

Marmon Silko, L. (1996). *Yellow woman and a beauty of the spirit: Essays on Native American life today*. New York: Touchstone.

Ohashi, Y., Ohashi, K., Meskanen, P., Hummelin, N., Kato, F., and Kynäslahti, H. (2012). What children and youth told about their home city in digital stories in 'C my city!' *Digital Creativity, 23*(2), 126–135.

Russ, A., Peters, S. J., Krasny, M. E., and Stedman, R. C. (2015). Development of ecological place meaning in New York City. *Journal of Environmental Education, 46*(2), 73–93.

Salazar, J. F. (2010). Digital stories and emerging citizens' media practices by migrant youth in Western Sydney. *Migration, 3*, 55.

Sauvé, L. (1996). Environmental education and sustainable development: A further appraisal. *Canadian Journal of Environmental Education, 1*(1), 7–34.

Smith, J. (2015). Self-discovery through digital storytelling: A timeless approach to environmental education. In A. Russ (Ed.), *Urban environmental education* (pp. 60–64). Ithaca, N.Y., and Washington, D.C.: Cornell University Civic Ecology Lab, NAAEE and EECapacity.

29

PARTICIPATORY URBAN PLANNING

Andrew Rudd, Karen Malone, and M'Lis Bartlett

Highlights

- Engaging youth and underrepresented groups in urban planning addresses concerns about equity and provides opportunities for engaging multiple innovative perspectives.
- Urban environmental education provides a framework to understand difficult trade-offs inherent in urban planning.
- Urban planning brings a spatial perspective to urban environmental education pedagogy.
- Together the tools of participatory urban planning and environmental education may help create more sustainable cities for all.

Introduction

Cities worldwide face increasing challenges in their pursuit to become just and sustainable social-ecological systems. None will be harder hit than the fastest-growing cities of the developing world, which are set to absorb nearly three billion additional people in the next thirty to forty years. Among the many challenges are sociospatial ones, such as urban sprawl, segregation, and congestion, as well as ecological ones, such as habitat degradation, urban heat island effect, and water pollution. Addressing these challenges in an integrated manner can strengthen the underlying disciplines of urban planning and environmental education, in process and outcome. Urban planning brings a holistic spatial approach to sectoral environmental efforts such as isolated initiatives to improve air quality. Further, when the process engages local residents from underrepresented groups, urban planning can set the stage for exploring solutions before inequitable and unsustainable patterns are locked in. Urban environmental pedagogy can build capacity for engagement in planning processes generally dominated by adults and professionals. Drawing on recent efforts to articulate a global urban sustainability agenda, this chapter describes how integrated, participatory design and urban environmental education can enhance learning, ownership, agency, and long-term sustainability of place.

In recognition of the important role urbanization plays in the health and welfare of people and our planet, the United Nations 2030 Agenda for Sustainable Development offers seventeen Sustainable Development Goals (UNGA, 2015). These include Sustainable Development Goal 11: to "[m]ake cities and human settlements inclusive, safe, resilient and sustainable." Though policy makers in the intergovernmental sphere have been relatively reactive in addressing cities, this new agenda represents a decisive shift to proactively approach sustainable urbanization. Sustainable Development Goal 11 goes further, focusing explicitly on urban planning at three scales. At the national-subnational scale, one target within this goal is to "[s]upport positive economic, social and environmental links between urban, peri-urban and rural areas by strengthening national and regional development planning." At the scale of the city, a target is to "enhance inclusive and sustainable urbanization and capacity for participatory, integrated and sustainable human settlement planning and management in all countries." And at the scale of the neighborhood, the goal seeks to "provide universal access to safe, inclusive and accessible, green and public spaces, in particular for women and children, older persons and persons with disabilities."

As inspiring as the Sustainable Development Goals' urban-planning-related targets may be, they still raise the question of how to integrate urban planning and environmental education in practice and what the civic engagement initiatives underpinning them might look like. Part of the answer may be found in the engagement of underrepresented groups—such as children, youth, and low-income and minority residents—in urban development, particularly early on in the planning process, when the most consequential spatial decisions are made. Urban environmental education is one tool that can help integrate the participation of these groups in urban planning while also improving urban planning outcomes.

Integrating Urban Environmental Education and Urban Planning

In concert with the Sustainable Development Goals, UNESCO has proposed that "sustainable development for all countries is only truly possible through comprehensive cross-sector efforts that begin with education" (UNESCO, 2014, p. 2). Urban environmental education integrates the study of natural systems with the study of our built environment; understanding how natural and built systems interact and impact human well-being is key to planning more sustainable communities. Including environmental education practices in urban planning processes can enhance our ability to make difficult decisions about complex environmental problems and social inequity. These in turn equip urban stakeholders to engage in authentically participatory urban planning.

Participatory urban planning has its roots in the efforts of international development to include poor and oppressed peoples as we seek to eliminate poverty and other social concerns. Influenced by the social justice movements, U.S. planners and designers of the 1960s and 1970s supported the democratic engagement of local people in making decisions about their own communities; in particular, they sought to support the agency of low-income communities of color to improve the environments in which they lived (Hester, 1987). Now a part of the planning and design lexicon, participatory planning still has its detractors. Some have criticized the participatory process as reformist, a tool of those with power to build consensus for top-down decisions (Juarez and Brown, 2008). Others suggest that participation in public planning may be a new form of NIMBY-ism ("not in my back yard") (Hester, 1987). Further criticisms may be leveled at processes that engage youths in cursory ways rather than truly engage them in decision making (Hart, 1997). Despite these concerns, participatory efforts—from regional planning for sustainable transit systems, to community greenway planning, to the creation of safe places for children to play—perform vital roles in engaging people in the shared process of place making.

The environmental implications of urban configuration are enormous. Once configuring spatial elements are in place, they are difficult and expensive to change, whether at the scale of the metropolitan region, city, or neighborhood. As the initial programmatic phase of planning and design tends to lock in a city-region's transport infrastructure, participation at this stage would give residents more choice in determining the form that their commutes take. Urban environmental education practices can help engage youths and adults alike in learning about and debating plans and eventual outcomes inherent in urban planning. Likewise, integrated urban environmental education and planning practices can clarify how spatial relationships influence people's behavior and can help participants make informed choices about urban land use and transport systems. For example, the distance between cities and related core functions, such as housing, jobs, and services, dictates how far one must travel; the density of dwellings determines whether there will be critical mass to support a public transit system; and the mix of land uses largely predetermines walkability. Though many people may wish for a private car, this generally comes at the expense of decreased densities, distanced jobs, lengthened commutes, and increased per capita energy use and emissions, 70 percent of which come from transport and buildings. Engaging underrepresented groups in sociospatial decision making can yield sustained stewardship efforts and sustainable cities for decades to come (Corburn, 2003).

With the rapid urbanization of our planet, never has there been a more important time to support the participation of local residents, particularly young people. Many cities are growing spatially significantly faster than their populations. As they use land increasingly inefficiently, they forfeit the advantages of agglomeration and their environmental impact worsens (UN-Habitat, 2012). Though some urban citizens may be aware that this is happening, fewer are aware of its consequences. It is in this space that environmental education may play a key role as a means and end in achieving the Sustainable Development Goals (Malone, 2015). Fully 60 percent of the area expected to be urban in 2030 remains to be built (Fragkias et al., 2013). This presents the world with an extremely limited window of opportunity to influence the growth of its fastest growing cities so that their spatial patterns preconfigure behavior that is both equitable and sustainable.

Involving citizens—particularly children and youths—early in the urban planning process can make their participation more authentic (Hart, 1997). Participatory planning—when it engages young people in information sharing, learning, and caring about one's environment—supports the environmental education tenet that caring and knowledge are necessary (if not sufficient) to support future environmental stewardship (Hollweg et al., 2011). The participatory planning process entails knowledge acquisition, knowledge sharing, skill building, and action that are deeply embedded in place. It thus parallels environmental education scholarship that calls for the engagement of students in culturally sensitive, local, placed-based explorations of environmental issues (Sobel, 2005), and it shows that such projects can provide students with the opportunity to practice skills for future engagement in environmental advocacy and stewardship (Schusler and Krasny, 2008). UNESCO's Growing Up in Cities project has provided a model of participatory action research that integrates environmental education and planning practices by involving young people in collaborating with adults to evaluate the quality of life in their low- and mixed-income urban environments. Over the past twenty years in a number of cities across the globe, young people have shared issues of concern, researched their own communities, and suggested changes that have resulted in improved urban design for residents (Chawla and Driskell, 2006). Wherever possible, the youths' findings have underpinned policy and design actions for more inclusive urban environments.

Children's involvement in the planning process builds critical environmental awareness and offers new insights on designing an inclusive cityscape. A recent example is the Child Friendly Bolivia project, which engaged children from three communities in La Paz in an urban planning process (see http://child-friendlycities.org). This participatory urban planning model used the Child-Friendly Community Self-Assessment Tool for Children to provide opportunities for children in formal and nonformal settings to share their experiences with other children, the community, and the city mayor's office. The findings also contribute to a global movement of understandings about children growing up in today's world and being active global citizens. This is particularly timely when engaging with young people and communities is being viewed as central to achieving the Sustainable Development Goals both as the means and the end (Malone, 2015). The Child-Friendly Community Self-Assessment Tool for Children case study that follows illustrates outcomes of engaging young people in urban planning.

Case Study: La Paz, Bolivia

In September 2012, Karen Malone, staff member from University of Western Sydney, conducted a project with eighty young children living in the slum communities on the upper reaches of the valley of La Paz, Bolivia (Malone, 2013). Malone was one of the original researchers with Chawla who conducted an eighty-country study for UNESCO Growing Up in Cities and has since continued to build the methodology from those early iterations into her research and work with children (Chawla and Malone, 2002). The project in Bolivia used a place-based participatory research methodology that drew on key aspects of Growing Up in Cities and the Child-Friendly Community Self-Assessment Tool for Children. Choosing from a number of visual, oral, and mobile place-based research tools, including surveys, interviews, drawings, photography, roaming range maps, and guided tours, children collected rich descriptive and visual data of their experience of their place and their visions and plans for improving its child friendliness and sustainability (Figure 29.1).

FIGURE 29.1.   Engaging in Child Friendly Research workshops, La Paz, Bolivia. Credit: Karen Malone.

The purpose of the research in La Paz was to support the city council and UNICEF in devising an urban strategy that included the needs of children, in particular those who are most disadvantaged or hard to reach. The study focused on three neighborhoods on the very high reaches of the valley, close to the city of El Alto. The location of these neighborhoods magnified the challenges for both community members and those seeking to support them. In addition to transport and infrastructure concerns, residents in these communities contend with land steepness and instability (landslides and flooding are common occurrences), poor housing (often makeshift and shabbily constructed), pollution (council trash pickups are infrequent and difficult to organize, and the remaining trash traps pollution), and security risks (including child abduction, crime, and street violence). This short case study focuses on two key research outcomes: children's participation and urban planning actions.

Participation

Engaging with children and communities in an authentic and active way is fundamental to good participatory planning. This research engaged children and their families in vulnerable communities in a participatory process based on principles of nondiscrimination and equity. The use of the Children Friendliness tools, along with thoughtful reflection on the children's capacity to be involved in the study, enabled researchers to plan activities and use methods to gather student input that ensured that poor, marginalized children, those often forgotten or ignored in city planning processes, were represented. Researchers were conscious of creating a safe and secure environment for participation. For instance, they did not expect children to travel to the researchers nor did they use research activities that might be foreign or intimidating. Cameras and drawings provided entry points for discussions in focus groups, and all activities were conducted in local community spaces, facilities, and sports grounds in order to help create a safe environment for the children.

Urban Planning Action

Turning ideas into action is central to a participatory research model and was critical to the project in Bolivia. A good example related to transport. At the time of this study, city planning and design professionals had begun to discuss different transport possibilities that could open up opportunities for residents living in high-density urban slums to access the central city areas. Erecting a cable car from downtown to the top ridge of the valley was one such proposal. Part of the challenge was that such a system needed to be cheap and accessible to be viable. Children participating in the study spoke of their "dream" for this cable car to be built because it would enable quick, effective, and safe transport down to the valley. The children conveyed their support for the cable car idea through presentations to city officials. The construction of the Teleferico transport system two years later was evidence of a large infrastructure building project that yielded long-lasting results for children, their families, and their societies (Malone, 2015). It is now the world's largest mass-transit cable car system, with three lines and a total distance of more than 10 km, 11 stations, 427 cabins, and a capacity of 18,000 passengers an hour. Traveling on the Teleferico with children from the study and speaking to them about the difference this has made to their lives provides evidence of the impact urban planning that responds to community needs can have on community and environmental well-being in a city.

Conclusion

Organized and facilitated in disparate circles of practice, urban environmental education and participatory design share a common goal to engage people in the creation and care of sustainable urban communities. As critical as participation is, it is important to understand it as a means to an end rather than an end in itself. If the desired end is a more sustainable form (and more sustainable behavior that results from it), then a city's residents need to be involved early in the urban planning process. Moreover, understanding trade-offs inherent in sustainable urban planning can help residents make informed choices about the patterns their cities will take and how those patterns will balance amenity and sustainability over the short and long term. Taken together, urban planning and urban environmental education may be able to simultaneously increase residents' agency in decision making about their neighborhoods and cities, and improve the social-environmental impacts of the decisions that are made.

References

Chawla, L., and Malone, K. (2002). Neighborhood quality from children's eyes. In P. Christensen and M. O'Brien (Eds.), *Children in the city: Home neighbourhood and community* (pp. 118–141). London: Routledge.

Chawla, L., and Driskell, D. (2006). The Growing Up in Cities project: Global perspectives on children and youth as catalysts for community change. *Journal of Community Practice, 14*(1–2), 183–200.

Corburn, J. (2003). Bringing local knowledge into environmental decision making improving urban planning for communities at risk. *Journal of Planning Education and Research, 22*(4), 420–433.

Fragkias, M., Güneralp, B., Seto, K. C., and Goodness, J. (2013). A synthesis of global urbanization projections. In T. Elmqvist, M. Fragkias, J. Goodness, B. Güneralp, et al. (Eds.), *Urbanization, biodiversity and ecosystem services: Challenges and opportunities: A global assessment* (pp. 409–435): Dordrecht: Springer.

Hart, R. A. (1997). *Children's participation: The theory and practice of involving young citizens in community development and environmental care.* London: Earthscan.

Hester, R. T., Jr. (1987). Participatory design and environmental justice: Pas de deux or time to change partners? *Journal of Architectural and Planning Research 4*(4), 289–300.

Hollweg, K. S., Taylor, J. R., Bybee, R. W., Marcinkowski, T. J., et al. (2011). *Developing a framework for assessing environmental literacy.* Washington, D.C.: North American Association for Environmental Education.

Juarez, J. A., and Brown, K. D. (2008). Extracting or empowering?: A critique of participatory methods for marginalized populations. *Landscape Journal, 27*(2), 190–204.

Malone, K. (2013). *Child friendly Bolivia: Researching with children in La Paz, Bolivia.* Penrith, Australia: University of Western Sydney.

Malone, K. (2015). Children's rights and the crisis of rapid urbanization: Exploring the United Nations post 2015 Sustainable Development Agenda and the potential role for UNICEF's Child Friendly Cities Initiative. *The International Journal of Children's Rights, 23*(2), 405–424.

Schusler, T. M., and Krasny, M. E. (2008). Youth participation in local environmental action: An avenue for science and civic learning? In A. Reid, B. B. Jensen, J. Nikel, and V. Simovska (Eds.), *Participation and learning* (pp. 268–284). Dordrecht: Springer.

Sobel, D. (2005). *Place-based education: Connecting classrooms and communities.* Great Barrington, Mass.: Orion Society.

UN-Habitat. (2012). *Urban patterns for a green economy: Leveraging density.* Nairobi: UN-Habitat.

UNESCO. (2014). *Sustainable development begins with education: How education can contribute to the proposed post-2015 goals.* Paris: UNESCO.

UNGA (United Nations General Assembly). (2015). *Transforming our world: The 2030 Agenda for Sustainable Development.* UN Doc A/RES/70/1.

30

EDUCATIONAL TRENDS

Alex Russ and Marianne E. Krasny

Highlights

- Urban environmental education practices fall into five broad trends: City as Classroom, Problem Solving, Environmental Stewardship, Individual and Community Development, and City as Social-Ecological System.
- Urban environmental education is driven by concerns about the well-being of communities and ecosystems, and its goals reflect an increasingly human-dominated world.
- Urban environmental education contributes to urban sustainability by addressing social and environmental issues.

Introduction

How to make sense of the myriad of urban environmental education programs? Urban environmental education aims to achieve multiple goals, uses various educational approaches, engages diverse participants, works in a variety of built and natural urban settings, addresses a range of environmental and social issues, and is conducted by schools, community organizations, nongovernmental organizations, government agencies, and private businesses. While each of these elements of urban environmental education is important, in this chapter we focus on goals because of their influence on program planning, evaluation, and research. We provide descriptions of five urban environmental education trends, which we previously distilled from a literature review (Russ and Krasny, 2015) and from our own experiences. While recognizing that we did not conduct a systematic literature review that would have identified and synthesized all the scholarly research on urban environmental education, we offer these five trends as preliminary categorizations to help readers make sense of the wide range of practices in this book. We suggest that urban environmental education is driven by concerns about the well-being of communities and ecosystems and that its goals and approaches are applicable to any environmental education programs in human-dominated settings.

Five Trends

One approach to understanding urban environmental education is to review its goals as described in the literature. In 2013, we analyzed one hundred articles, chapters, and books found by searching the phrase "urban environmental education" in Google Scholar and ERIC databases, and fifteen additional publications that were cited in the publications that came up from our original search but that used other terms such as "urban ecosystem education" or that were foundational to urban environmental education (see references in Russ and Krasny, 2015). Based on these publications, we identified underlying goals of urban environmental education and grouped them into five trends. Whereas our review was limited to publications in English, we discussed these trends with international colleagues during site visits to urban environmental education programs in Europe, South America, Asia, Australia, Africa, and North America and during professional meetings. Based on these visits and discussions, we revised the trends to make them more universally applicable (Table 30.1). We recognize, however, that practices vary widely depending on context and that practices are constantly evolving in response to social and environmental change.

The trends reflect how urban environmental education has expanded its approaches over its one-hundred-year-plus history. Although the term "urban environmental education" was first mentioned in the literature in the late 1960s (Shomon, 1969), related ideas date back to the first half of the twentieth century (e.g., Bailey, 1911; Philpott, 1946). Initially, educators in urban areas borrowed ideas from nature study, science education, and conservation education. Later they expanded their focus to encompass environmental and related social issues. From the 1970s onward, educators began integrating environmental education with community-based and other urban environmental stewardship programs. More recently, a growing number of educators have used environmental education as a

TABLE 30.1   Trends in urban environmental education

TRENDS	URBAN ENVIRONMENTAL EDUCATION GOALS	EXAMPLE EDUCATIONAL APPROACHES
City as Classroom	Facilitate learning about urban and other environments, ecology, science, geography, history, and other subjects using urban outdoor and indoor settings	Nature study, citizen science, environmental monitoring, inquiry-based programs, community mapping, neighborhood inventories, exhibits, storytelling, nature interpretation
Problem Solving	Solve or mitigate environmental problems and related social problems	Environmental activism, conservation education, action research, environmental justice education, climate change education
Environmental Stewardship	Foster community-based management of urban ecosystems, involve community members in decision making and action to improve urban natural resources	Grassroots stewardship and education, civic ecology education, restoration-based education, green jobs training, youth employment programs, public-private environmental partnerships, green infrastructure education, restoration-based education
Individual and Community Development	Foster positive youth development, community well-being, asset-based community development, positive social norms, and social capital	Youth development programs, intergenerational learning, outdoor adventure education, community development programs, programs advancing human health and equality
City as Social-Ecological System	Develop an understanding of cities as social-ecological systems, and reimagine how to manage cities to achieve desired environmental and social outcomes	Participatory urban planning, urban green design, adaptive and collaborative management, programs emphasizing cities as social-ecological systems and social-ecological systems resilience

tool for individual and community development in cities, while others have borrowed ideas from urban planning and related social sciences and environmental disciplines to engage participants in reimagining possibilities for sustainable development. Below we present each trend separately to help the reader understand the trends' goals and educational approaches. Since any one educational program likely pursues multiple goals, readers may want to avoid trying to place programs within a single trend, but rather envision how programs they are familiar with draw from several trends and integrate multiple goals.

Trend 1: City as Classroom

The goal of the City as Classroom trend is environmental and science learning. Educators help participants acquire environmental literacy, knowledge of the local environment, and proficiency in urban geography, ecology, biology, history, and other subjects through urban outdoor and indoor environmental education activities. Initially, programs within this trend were designed to teach science and nurture positive attitudes toward nature and were driven by the recognition that hands-on learning in local ecosystems can enhance understanding of the environment (Bailey, 1911). By the mid-twentieth century, educators were advised to teach about biology, natural sciences, and resource conservation specifically by using urban spaces, including schoolyards, water supply and sewage disposal facilities, transportation and green corridors, urban nature trails, vacant lots, greenhouses, parks, and urban rivers. Programs within this trend have expanded to use street trees, parks and other open spaces, green infrastructure, industrial sites, and museums to help people learn about biodiversity, environmental quality, and local and global ecosystem processes (see references in Russ and Krasny, 2015).

To learn about ecosystems and biodiversity, students engage in urban field studies, outdoor investigation, community garden inventories, ecosystem services measurement, citizen science, and inquiry-based activities. Educators and environmental leaders further strengthen cities' ability to serve as classrooms by establishing urban ecology centers, green infrastructure demonstration sites, interpretation trails, restored ecosystems, urban agriculture sites, and environmental classrooms in industrial facilities. In sum, City as Classroom is an established trend in urban environmental education the goal of which is to facilitate learning about science and the participants' local environment through exploration of history, communities, and natural and built elements in cities.

Trend 2: Problem Solving

The goal of the Problem Solving trend is to mitigate environmental and related social problems by engaging participants in decision making and local policy processes and by changing individual pro-environmental behaviors. Initially, this trend emerged in response to urban environmental issues such as air pollution, lack of green space, and environmental injustice and was an effort to expand on environmental education practices that focused on ecological knowledge and conservation outside cities, with little relevance to the everyday experiences of urban residents. In the 1940s and 1950s, professionals noted that cities provide opportunities to learn about environmental issues, such as treating rivers as sewers, and to contribute to decision making and mitigating these problems (e.g., Renner and Hartley, 1940). Environmental educators realized that while urban residents may have little interest in learning about ecology and wildlife in distant places, they may be concerned and motivated to learn about pollution, waste disposal, environmental risks, human health, traffic congestion, and lack of open space (see references in Russ and Krasny, 2015).

In addition to biophysical problems such as pollution and climate change, some publications proposed that urban environmental education should address social concerns such as poverty, unemployment, racism, marginalization, drugs, violence, access to recreation sites and environmental activities, food justice, and human health (Frank et al., 1994). Knowledge about and skills to address these social problems can be learned through environmental activism, field trips, meetings with professionals, urban farming, environmental art, taking photos of attractive and negative urban features, monitoring noise pollution, and other activities through which local residents improve their communities. Within this trend, programs often take place in collaboration with neighborhood councils, faith-based organizations, community centers, housing agencies, and grassroots initiatives. As a response to environmental degradation, climate change, and social issues, programs following this trend educate about the causes of these problems and often call for individual, community, corporate, and governmental action to mitigate them. In sum, the goal of the Problem Solving trend in urban environmental education is to address environmental and related social problems.

Trend 3: Environmental Stewardship

The goal of the Environmental Stewardship trend is to enhance urban ecosystems and ecosystem services, create and maintain green infrastructure, support biodiversity, and produce food by involving urban residents and their government, nonprofit organization, and private partners in hands-on environmental stewardship and management of urban natural resources. The assumption is that citizens and communities are able to design, restore, improve, and maintain local urban ecosystems, often in collaboration with government agencies, nonprofit organizations, and businesses, and at the same time learn about these ecosystems. For example, education can be integrated in such activities as tree planting, park beautification, landscaping in schoolyards, eradicating invasive species for native urban wildlife, restoring urban shellfisheries, replanting mangrove forests, creating and maintaining urban agriculture sites, and cleaning up litter in public spaces such as parks, vacant lots, shorelines, and cemeteries (see references in Russ and Krasny, 2015).

Recent work in civic ecology has expanded on this trend by suggesting that environmental education in cities can be situated in civic ecology practices—including community forestry, community gardening, and community-based habitat restoration—thereby contributing to biodiversity, ecosystem services, and social capital while providing opportunities for environmental learning (Krasny and Tidball, 2015). Programs within this trend may integrate community-based service learning; summer youth employment programs; urban gardening and farmers markets; installing and supporting green roofs, rain gardens, and other green infrastructure; cleanup of brownfield sites; and management of urban forests and wetlands. In sum, urban environmental education that fits this trend promotes learning through engaging in hands-on urban stewardship and restoration of degraded lands and waters in cities.

Trend 4: Individual and Community Development

The goal of this trend is to contribute to individual and community development. Urban environmental education programs within this trend promote citizenship and life skills, foster self-esteem, build social capital and community cohesion, strengthen mutual respect and feelings of belonging to a community, and empower communities to take collective action. Programs inspired by this trend often use the urban environment to foster positive youth development and community well-being (Schusler and Krasny, 2010). Starting in the 1980s, publications showed how urban environmental education may nurture students' creativity and reaffirm positive aspects of their cultures, develop youths' work ethic and teamwork skills, create positive attitudes toward learning, improve critical thinking, reduce dropout rates and gang and drug activity, and promote active citizenship (e.g., Verrett et al., 1990). Other publications called for building on and promoting positive youth attributes, such as resilience, social competence, autonomy, ability to solve problems, and a sense of hope for the future (Frank et al., 1994).

In this trend, individual and community development are linked because people who are empowered and informed about environmental and social issues can make positive changes in their communities. For example, educational programs may help city residents to articulate their goals for community well-being and participate in collective advocacy and urban planning to bring about those goals. Other programs may bring together children, educators, architects, environmental professionals, and artists to work on community design, art, and similar projects to serve community interests. Such programs often take place as part of corporate social responsibility initiatives, as well as in intergenerational, after-school, and youth employment programs conducted by community development, faith-based, youth development, and other community-based organizations. Some programs in this trend may use nature-related and outdoor experiences to improve participants' health and well-being and pay little attention to environmental outcomes. In sum, this trend considers individual development and community development as important outcomes of urban environmental education.

Trend 5: City as Social-Ecological System

City as Social-Ecological System helps people view cities as valuable systems, where social and ecological processes are equally important and where environmental management approaches are constantly invented and improved. This trend promotes the idea that cities are social-ecological systems (Krasny et al., 2013) that encompass nature and provide ecosystem services (Beatley, 2011) and that urban residents can influence and are influenced by social-ecological processes. Publications emphasize that natural or ecological elements exist in cities along with built, social, political, economic, and cultural elements, and that urban residents are able to connect to and appreciate urban nature. In line with this reasoning, urban environmental education can contribute to the development of an ecological place meaning among youth and can help them see cities not only as human habitat but also as wildlife habitat and ecologically valuable places (Kudryavtsev, Krasny, and Stedman, 2012; Russ et al., 2015).

In addition to portraying cities as social-ecological systems, this trend emphasizes that the social and ecological dimensions of cities coevolve and depend on each other. It suggests that social and ecological processes reinforce and counter each other in positive and negative feedback loops. This trend also incorporates ideas about how networks of government, civil society, and private partners enable environmental governance approaches that adapt to social-ecological changes (Krasny and Tidball, 2015). Programs following this trend acknowledge that we have only a partial understanding of how cities should be managed and that any urban resident or organization can participate in constructing new ways of designing and governing the urban environment. These ideas are consistent with the literature on social-ecological systems resilience, which focuses on the need for cities to adapt to ongoing change, such as shifting demographics, or to transform in light of disastrous events, such as hurricanes. Further, scholars suggest that urban environmental education may foster social-ecological resilience through strengthening social capital and restoring ecosystem services and that organizations that conduct urban environmental education are actors in polycentric governance systems (Krasny, Lundholm, and Plummer, 2011; see also chapter 11). In sum, this trend builds on social-ecological resilience and related systems thinking and green urbanism, and it helps people understand cities as integrated social-ecological systems, often through participation in collective decision making, adaptive and collaborative management, and stewardship action.

Conclusion

Urban environmental education programs usually integrate multiple goals related to each of the five trends. For example, in New York City, students attending the New York Harbor School (http://youtu.be/CcxaZm2NkCI) and Satellite Academy High School (http://youtu.be/7d5mQlLH3jo) learn about the environment and science in the classroom and through monitoring populations of oysters, and they engage in environmental stewardship through community gardening and oyster reef restoration. Educators leading these programs also describe how they contribute to positive youth and community development. Similarly, programs engaging youth in reconstructing dunes and trails after catastrophic flooding integrate the Environmental Stewardship, Individual and Community Development, and City as Social-Ecological System trends (Smith, DuBois, and Krasny, 2015).

Urban environmental education goals are dynamic and continue to evolve in response to urban challenges and opportunities. For example, a movement to allow children to engage in free play through creating more natural playgrounds in cities has recently taken hold, with the goal to foster children's physical, cognitive, and emotional health. As people experience greater environmental and social risks and uncertainty related to climate change and conflict, and as city residents develop various innovations to address environmental and social problems, we will undoubtedly see urban environmental education trends develop further. In this way, urban environmental education will continue to work alongside other disciplines and sectors, such as urban resource management, disaster preparedness planning, and human and community development, to address constantly changing social-ecological problems and contribute to urban sustainability.

References

Bailey, L. H. (1911). *The nature-study idea: An interpretation of the new school-movement to put the young into relation and sympathy with nature*, 4th ed. New York: MacMillan Company.

Beatley, T. (2011). *Biophilic cities: Integrating nature into urban design and planning.* Washington, D.C.: Island Press.

Frank, J., Zamm, M., Benenson, G., Fialkowski, C., and Hollweg, K. (1994). *Urban environmental education: EE toolbox—workshop resource manual*. Ann Arbor: School of Natural Resources and Environment, University of Michigan.

Krasny, M. E., Lundholm, C., Shava, S., Lee, E., and Kobori, H. (2013). Urban landscapes as learning arenas for biodiversity and ecosystem services management. In T. Elmqvist, M. Fragkias, J. Goodness, et al. (Eds.), *Urbanization, biodiversity and ecosystem services: Challenges and opportunities: A global assessment* (pp. 629–664). Dordrecht: Springer.

Krasny, M. E., Lundholm, C., and Plummer, R. (Eds.). (2011). *Resilience in social-ecological systems: The role of learning and education*. New York: Routledge.

Krasny, M. E., and Tidball, K. G. (2015). *Civic ecology: Adaptation and transformation from the ground up*. Cambridge, Mass.: MIT Press.

Kudryavtsev, A., Krasny, M. E., and Stedman, R. C. (2012). The impact of environmental education on sense of place among urban youth. *Ecosphere, 3*(4). doi: 10.1890/ES11–00318.1.

Philpott, C. H. (1946). How a city plans for conservation education. *School Science and Mathematics, 46*(8), 691–695.

Renner, G. T., and Hartley, W. H. (1940). *Conservation and citizenship*. Boston: D.C. Heath and Company.

Russ, A., and Krasny, M. (2015). Urban environmental education trends. In A. Russ (Ed.), *Urban environmental education* (pp. 12–25). Ithaca, N.Y., and Washington, D.C.: Cornell University Civic Ecology Lab, NAAEE and EECapacity.

Russ, A., Peters, S. J., Krasny, M. E., and Stedman, R. C. (2015). Development of ecological place meaning in New York City. *Journal of Environmental Education, 46*(2), 73–93.

Shomon, J. (1969). Nature centers: One approach to urban environmental education. *Journal of Environmental Education, 1*(2), 56–60.

Schusler, T. M., and Krasny, M. E. (2010). Environmental action as context for youth development. *Journal of Environmental Education, 41*(4), 208–223.

Smith, J. G., DuBois, B., and Krasny, M. E. (2015). Framing for resilience through social learning: Impacts of environmental stewardship on youth in post-disturbance communities. *Sustainability Science, 22*(3), 441–454.

Verrett, R. E., Gaboriau, C., Roesing, D., and Small, D. (1990). *The urban environmental education report*. Washington, D.C.: United States Environmental Protection Agency.

Afterword

Drawing on perspectives of eighty-two authors from around the world, this volume reflects on academic debates and practices in urban environmental education. The thirty chapters highlight challenges and opportunities facing not only educators working in urban areas, but also the field of environmental education more broadly. Readers are encouraged to reflect on how the unique features of cities—as places facing major environmental and justice issues yet also as hubs of innovation—influence environmental education goals and implementation.

Urban planning, social justice, climate change, and social-ecological systems resilience are areas environmental education has addressed in the past, but which are becoming increasingly salient for environmental education in cities. These wicked sustainability issues lend themselves to local or place-based approaches to environmental education, including those that take advantage of rich urban environments. As the chapters of this book demonstrate, transdisciplinary approaches that entail environmental educators working across disciplines and sectors are one way to address urban sustainability issues.

We also see in this book diverse ways of engaging in urban environmental education, such as participating in progressive local transitions, using new technologies, and seeding community collaborations. These educational approaches are laudable in that they encourage novel sustainability practices and systems, like cohesive and sustainable neighborhoods and community gardens. Some chapters acknowledge the importance of recognizing contradictions and conflict, although few reflect a process of ongoing engagement of environmental education in enforced cultures of struggle.

And here is where we see opportunities for the field: to become involved in places where environmental education has at times been less comfortable but where urban scholarship provides space for expansion. Urban environments are deeply entwined with struggles for dignity, survival, and basic livelihoods; challenges around health and sanitation; and questions related to equity and participation. These issues particularly impact the world's poor, many of whom live in informal urban settlements. How might those lenses shift our views on urban environmental education?

With such considerations, we offer two provocations, calling environmental educators to:

Disrupt the urban/rural binary. Recognizing that no universal definition of "urban" or "city"—historically, geographically, culturally, economically, or ideologically—exists, we encourage readers to critically consider what is meant by these terms. Recognizing and critiquing processes such as urban decay, suburban sprawl, migration, and gentrification will help challenge the urban/rural binary and make it more provocative, productive, and reflective of people's lived experiences.

Take to the field—or the streets? To understand urban settings in a deeper, more embodied way, spending time in the field—or, more accurately, in the streets—is essential. Here we may come to understand relationships between individual and collective forms of agency, the structures that constrain them, and, for example, how hard-won gains arise from grassroots action and protest politics. Such understandings, critical for the future of urban environmental education, must be developed *in situ*, as a form of expansive learning. At the same time, spending time in the streets helps re-envision the urban commons. We support this volume's authors in their place-based commitments, calling for collaborations among educators and other professionals working in urban settings.

We close by applauding the authors for providing thoughtful perspectives on urban environmental education. This volume offers tremendous opportunities for not only reflecting on readers' own areas of interest, but also sparking ideas for further—and perhaps unusual—collaborations, integrating research and practice, and encouraging questions that derive from the social and ecological realities in cities. We are hopeful that the aspiring and inspiring visions in this volume will be influential for both the theory and practice of urban environmental education.

Nicole M. Ardoin
Associate Professor, Stanford University, USA

Alan Reid
Associate Professor, Monash University, Australia

Heila Lotz-Sisitka
Professor, Rhodes University, South Africa

Édgar J. González Gaudiano
Senior Researcher, Universidad Veracruzana, Mexico

Contributors

Jennifer D. Adams
Department of Earth and Environmental Sciences; and
Department of Secondary Education
Brooklyn College, City University of New York
New York, New York, USA

Olivia M. Aguilar
McPhail Center for Environmental Studies
Denison University
Granville, Ohio, USA

Shorna B. Allred
Department of Natural Resources
Cornell University
Ithaca, New York, USA

Daniel Fonseca de Andrade
Department of Environmental Sciences
Federal University of the State of Rio de Janeiro
Rio de Janeiro, Brazil

Scott Ashmann
Professional Program in Education
University of Wisconsin–Green Bay
Green Bay, Wisconsin, USA

Dave Barbier
Office of Sustainability
University of Wisconsin–Stevens Point
Stevens Point, Wisconsin, USA

M'Lis Bartlett
School of Natural Resources
University of Michigan
Ann Arbor, Michigan, USA

Michael Barnett
Department of Teacher Education, Special Education, Curriculum and Instruction
Boston College
Chestnut Hill, Massachusetts, USA

Simon Beames
The Moray House School of Education
The University of Edinburgh
Edinburgh, Midlothian, UK

Chew-Hung Chang
Office of Graduate Studies and Professional Learning
National Institute of Education; and
Humanities and Social Studies Education Academic Group
Nanyang Technological University
Singapore

Tzuchau Chang
Graduate Institute of Environmental Education
Taiwan Normal University
Taipei, Taiwan

Louise Chawla
Program in Environmental Design
University of Colorado–Boulder
Boulder, Colorado, USA

Lewis Ting On Cheung
Department of Social Sciences
Hong Kong Institute of Education
Hong Kong, China

Belinda Chin
Sustainable Operations, Good Food Program
City of Seattle Parks and Recreation
Seattle, Washington, USA

Laura B. Cole
Department of Architectural Studies
University of Missouri
Columbia, Missouri, USA

Jason Corwin
Seneca Media and Communications Center
Seneca Nation
Salamanca, New York, USA

Amy Cutter-Mackenzie
School of Education
Southern Cross University
Gold Coast, Queensland, Australia

Maria Daskolia
Department of Philosophy, Pedagogy and Psychology
National and Kapodistrian University of Athens
Athens, Greece

Jacqueline Davis-Manigaulte
Family and Youth Development Program Area
Cornell University Cooperative Extension
New York, New York, USA

Victoria Derr
Environmental Studies
California State University, Monterey Bay
Seaside, California, USA

Giuliana Dettori
Institute for Educational Technology
National Research Council of Italy
Genoa, Italy

Bryce B. DuBois
Department of Natural Resources
Cornell University
Ithaca, New York, USA

Janet E. Dyment
Faculty of Education
University of Tasmania
Hobart, Tasmania, Australia

Johanna Ekne
Ekne Ecology
Malmö, Sweden

Thomas Elmqvist
Stockholm Resilience Centre
Stockholm University
Stockholm, Sweden

Johan Enqvist
Stockholm Resilience Centre
Stockholm University
Stockholm, Sweden

Mariona Espinet
Science and Mathematics Education Department
Autonomous University of Barcelona
Cerdanyola del Vallès, Catalonia, Spain

Ellen Field
College of Arts, Society and Education
James Cook University
Cairns, Queensland, Australia

Rebecca L. Franzen
Wisconsin Center for Environmental Education
University of Wisconsin–Stevens Point
Stevens Point, Wisconsin, USA

David A. Greenwood
Faculty of Education
Lakehead University
Thunder Bay, Ontario, Canada

Randolph Haluza-DeLay
Department of Sociology
The King's University
Edmonton, Alberta, Canada

Marna Hauk
Department of Sustainability Education
Prescott College
Prescott, Arizona, USA; and
Institute for Earth Regenerative Studies
Portland, Oregon, USA

Joe E. Heimlich
Center for Research and Evaluation
COSI; and
The Ohio State University
Columbus, Ohio, USA

Alexander Hellquist
Swedish International Centre of Education for Sustainable Development
Uppsala University
Uppsala, Sweden

Cecilia P. Herzog
Department of Architecture and Urbanism
Pontifical Catholic University of Rio de Janeiro
Rio de Janeiro, Brazil

Yu Huang
Institute of International and Comparative Education
Beijing Normal University
Beijing, China

Hilary Inwood
Ontario Institute for Studies in Education
University of Toronto
Toronto, Ontario, Canada

Marianna Kalaitsidaki
Department of Primary Education
University of Crete
Rethymno, Crete, Greece

Matthew S. Kaplan
Agricultural Economics, Sociology and Education
Pennsylvania State University
University Park, Pennsylvania, USA

Chankook Kim
Department of Environmental Education
Korea National University of Education
Cheongju, Chungbuk, Korea

Polly L. Knowlton Cockett
Werklund School of Education, University of Calgary
Grassroutes Ethnoecological Association
Calgary, Alberta, Canada

Hiromi Kobori
Tokyo City University
Tokyo, Japan

Cecil Konijnendijk van den Bosch
Department of Forest Resources Management
University of British Columbia
Vancouver, British Columbia, Canada

Jada Renee Koushik
School of Environment and Sustainability
University of Saskatchewan
Saskatoon, Saskatchewan, Canada

Marianne E. Krasny
Department of Natural Resources
Cornell University
Ithaca, New York, USA

Shelby Gull Laird
Arthur Temple College of Forestry and Agriculture
Stephen F. Austin State University
Nacogdoches, Texas, USA

John Chi-Kin Lee
Department of Curriculum and Instruction
Hong Kong Institute of Education
Hong Kong, China

Raul P. Lejano
Department of Teaching and Learning
New York University
New York, New York, USA

Mary Leou
Department of Teaching and Learning
New York University
New York, New York, USA

Kendra Liddicoat
Wisconsin Center for Environmental Education
University of Wisconsin–Stevens Point
Stevens Point, Wisconsin, USA

Shih-Tsen Nike Liu
Master Program of Environmental Education and Resources
University of Taipei
Taipei, Taiwan

David Maddox
The Nature of Cities
New York, New York, USA

Karen Malone
Centre for Educational Research
Western Sydney University
Sydney, New South Wales, Australia

Mapula Priscilla Masilela
Education Department
Rhodes University
Grahamstown, Eastern Cape, South Africa

Elizabeth P. McCann
Department of Environmental Studies
Antioch University New England
Keene, New Hampshire, USA

Marcia McKenzie
Educational Foundations
University of Saskatchewan
Saskatoon, Saskatchewan, Canada

Timon McPhearson
Urban Ecology Lab
The New School
New York, New York, USA

Sanskriti Menon
Urban Programmes
Centre for Environment Education
Pune, Maharashtra, India

Denise Mitten
Adventure Education
Prescott College
Prescott, Arizona, USA

Martha C. Monroe
School of Forest Resources and Conservation
University of Florida
Gainesville, Florida, USA

Mutizwa Mukute
Environmental Learning Research Centre
Rhodes University
Grahamstown, Eastern Cape, South Africa

Harini Nagendra
School of Development
Azim Premji University
Bangalore, Karnataka, India

John Nzira
Ukuvuna-Urban Farming Projects
Johannesburg, South Africa

Lausanne Olvitt
Environmental Learning Research Centre
Rhodes University
Grahamstown, Eastern Cape, South Africa

Illène Pevec
Fat City Farmers
Basalt, Colorado, USA

Felix Pohl
Independent Sustainability Consultancy
Wiesbaden, Germany

Andrew Rudd
Urban Planning and Design Branch
UN-Habitat
New York, New York, USA

Alex Russ (Alexey Kudryavtsev)
Department of Natural Resources
Cornell University
Ithaca, New York, USA

Tania M. Schusler
Institute of Environmental Sustainability
Loyola University Chicago
Chicago, Illinois, USA

Soul Shava
Department of Science and Technology Education
University of South Africa
Pretoria, South Africa

Philip Silva
Department of Natural Resources
Cornell University
Ithaca, New York, USA

Erika S. Svendsen
Northern Research Station
USDA Forest Service
New York, New York, USA

Nonyameko Zintle Songqwaru
Education Department
Rhodes University
Grahamstown, Eastern Cape, South Africa

Marc J. Stern
Department of Forest Resources and Environmental Conservation
Virginia Polytechnic Institute and State University
Blacksburg, Virginia, USA

Robert B. Stevenson
The Cairns Institute
James Cook University
Cairns, Queensland, Australia

Geok Chin Ivy Tan
Office of Teacher Education
National Institute of Education
Nanyang Technological University
Singapore

Cynthia Thomashow
Urban Environmental Education Graduate Program
IslandWood and Antioch University Seattle
Seattle, Washington, USA

Mitchell Thomashow
Philanthropy Northwest
Seattle, Washington, USA

Arjen E. J. Wals
Education and Competence Studies Group
Wageningen University
Wageningen, the Netherlands; and
Department of Pedagogical, Curricular and Professional Studies
University of Gothenburg
Gothenburg, Sweden

Kumara S. Ward
School of Education, Centre for Educational Research
Western Sydney University
Sydney, New South Wales, Australia

Robert Withrow-Clark
Butte College
Oroville, California, USA

Wanglin Yan
Faculty of Environment and Information Studies; and
Graduate School of Media and Governance
Keio University
Fujisawa, Japan

Index

Page numbers followed by letters *f* and *t* refer to figures and tables, respectively.